D0615944

"Finally, the definitive book on the pr[...] in our lives."
Andy Andrews, author of the *New York Times* best seller *The Traveler's Gift*

"Wow! This book could change the way you look at the Bible, at life, and at your faith. It did that for me. I've always been wary of my feelings and those of others. I thought it was the godly thing to do. I now know better and rejoice in the gift that this book will be to the Body of Christ. Finally, we can 'get out of the box' and dance. Read it and you'll thank me for recommending it."
Steve Brown, talk-show host of *Key Life*; professor of preaching, Reformed Theological Seminary

"Feel is an engaging book that's potentially liberating. God made emotions and Jesus expressed them; they need to be reclaimed and redeemed, not ignored or abandoned. Matthew Elliott does a service to the church through this thoughtful work.
Randy Alcorn, author of *Heaven* and *Deception*

"Many books today on the Christian life are baloney. Others just repackage what is widely known, or dress up tired platitudes with a new set of stories. This book is different. Based on solid research, it has truly fresh insights into our feelings and how God views them. I have been greatly helped personally by reading it, and I can't wait to pass it on to a bunch of other people who will eagerly receive its wisdom too. Best of all, in chapter after chapter, this book calls forth the godly feelings that, the author argues, God wants us to nurture and enjoy. Readers will discover here a path to enjoy God that they may never have glimpsed before."
Robert Yarbrough, PhD, New Testament department chairman, Trinity Evangelical Divinity School

"As Christians, it is easy for us to elevate reason at the expense of authentic emotion—and in the process lose our passion for the God who created both. Matthew Elliott helps us recapture what we've lost and discover what it truly means to feel. A timely message for our generation."
Alex and Brett Harris, authors of *Do Hard Things*

"I have always felt that as Christians we do not have enough balanced teaching about the subject of Emotion. I was so happy to see that Dr. Matthew Elliott, my close friend and former traveling assistant, has written a book on this subject. I want to urge you to read and think through what he has written. I pray that you will have a greater walk in truth and reality as a result of reading this very unique book."
George Verwer, founder, Operation Mobilization

"Matthew Elliott introduces us to a refreshing view of emotion that is based solidly on the teachings of the Bible. This book challenges us to respect our feelings, to learn from our emotional reactions, to view emotion as a friend, and to grow emotionally as we mature in Christ. This book will surely change the way we feel about emotion."
James R. Beck, PhD, senior professor of counseling, Denver Seminary

"Rarely do we start reading a book and exclaim, 'This is new!' But this is true for Matthew Elliott's excursion through the land of emotion. He makes us more conscious of our emotional makeup, emotional needs, and how God will use our emotion. He causes us to explore how we can teach ourselves and our children to live in emotional freedom. He encourages us to explore our emotions truthfully, honestly, and accurately. These are roads each of us must travel along. The journey is well worth the effort."
Major General Jerry Curry, Ret., U.S. Army

TESTIMONIES FROM *FEEL*: THE BLOG

"I have found my whole attitude has changed, as if I've done an about-face. I was really touched and my eyes were opened to attitudes I needed to change in my life."
Jan

"I have, like most Christians, battled with the place of emotions in church and in my Christian walk, and especially with the contradictions I see in the way I think and live and feel. The thoughts contained in this book have helped to put structure and meat to the bones of my own thinking. My thinking has changed over the course of reading this book as I have come to realize that emotions are not unspiritual but are actually traits of God himself. Also, to see that God's will is not some mechanistic oppressive thing, but is rather a father's emotional appeal for the heart of his people, is something that is incredibly encouraging and reminds me of what first attracted me to the person of Christ."
Stephen

"*Feel* is a fascinating foray into the seemingly untouched reaches of emotion in our everyday lives. Matthew Elliott walks us through the necessity of experiencing life as an emotional opportunity with the care of a loving father. *Feel* is a pivotal work for any wary soul who is searching for clarity to the muddied mix of a stoic spirituality and a frenetic culture."
Jared

"I enjoyed this book immensely. The author was so personal, honest, and vulnerable to his readers, using real life stories to illustrate his points. It was

challenging and convicting, but also uplifting. What I've been doing for such a long time is repressing my feelings. I've stuffed them in a box for a very long time and have lived most of the time by duty and very little passion (and then wondering why I don't know Jesus more intimately). I so long to live a passionate and vibrant life for Christ: to do the things He has for me and to grow more emotionally mature. I long to go from a type A, "to do" list person to a person listening, loving, and following hard after Christ. Thanks for giving me resources on how I can be the child of God that He longs for me to be."
Julie

"Although Matthew Elliott does not specifically refer to Isaiah 61, he writes of the ministry of Jesus, who came to bind up the brokenhearted, proclaim freedom for the captives, and release from darkness for the prisoners. Jesus promised abundant life, yet we are being robbed of that fullness of life by repressing and containing our emotions. This is an easy read that will warm your heart, excite your emotions, and challenge your thinking."
Marian

"This book is bold and insightful. (It could also incite a riot.) The more I read, the more I liked it. I am challenged to honestly love God more than anything else I would cherish. The book speaks to me, a person who spends a lot of time trying to get his ducks in a row with flawed tools under his own power."
Todd

feel
the power of listening to your heart

MATTHEW ELLIOTT

TYNDALE HOUSE PUBLISHERS, INC., CAROL STREAM, ILLINOIS

Visit Tyndale's exciting Web site at www.tyndale.com

Join the discussion at www.faithfulfeelings.com

TYNDALE and Tyndale's quill logo are registered trademarks of Tyndale House Publishers, Inc.

Feel: The Power of Listening to Your Heart

Designed by Luke Daab

Edited by Dave Lindstedt

Library of Congress Cataloging-in-Publication Data

Elliott, Matthew, Ph. D.
  Feel : the power of listening to your heart / Matthew Elliott.
    p. cm.
  Includes bibliographical references.
  ISBN-13: 978-1-4143-1664-2 (sc)
  ISBN-10: 1-4143-1664-X (sc)
  1. Emotions--Religious aspects--Christianity. 2. Christian life. I. Title.
  BV4597.3.E45 2008
  248.4—dc22   2007042730

Printed in the United States of America

14   13   12   11   10   09   08
7   6   5   4   3   2

TO LAURA: Best friend, lover, coworker. Your print is on every page, and I would not have it any other way.

Table of Contents

Acknowledgments

I was not very far into this project before I understood that there was no way I could go it alone. I was watching the "extra features" part of the *Hoodwinked* DVD with my family when I realized the kind of joint effort a truly good book involves. The makers of *Hoodwinked* made a great first movie by building a team of experts and advisors who knew a lot more than they did about making a film. I realized, in a much stronger way than I had before, that the task of writing this book must be a joint effort. That proved to be true, and it would take much more space than I have available here to give proper thanks to my partners. Nevertheless . . .

To Pieter, thanks for having eyes to see what this book might be and believing in me. To all those in my work world—publishing—who lent your advice and expertise, thanks for taking time out to review my work, encourage me, and push me to do better—most notably Les, Phillip, Stan, and Kathy. Thanks especially to Stan, who said, "Throw your PhD in a safe, lock it, and write the thing out of your head." That word of advice set me on a new path that I have been on ever since.

To my Tyndale family: You and the Taylor family have been a part of my life since I was five or so years old. Your generosity and example have affected me at very key points in my life—from Dr. Taylor's participation in my ordination, to your great encouragement of our ministry in Africa. It is a great privilege for me that you are publishing this book—it just feels right. Thanks.

Part of the credit for this work goes to the publishers who believed enough in this topic to publish my first book, *Faithful Feelings*. Thanks to IVP in the UK and Kregel in the USA.

After a coffee with part of the Tyndale family, Rev. Wendell Hawley, I understood that I needed some men to pray faithfully for me and this project. Thanks to all of you; there were points at which I could literally feel your encouragement and support. To Dave, Jim, Kent, Andrew, Bob and Dianne, and all my encouragers at church—I needed you. Thanks so much. A special thanks to the ones who did a theological review of my manuscript; thanks for holding me accountable for all I wrote. To Dr. Robert Yarbrough: It has meant much to have somebody who cared and supported me from the inception of my theological pursuits to now. You read and encouraged the genesis of this book in our little paper "Listen Up." Little could we have known that God would have those core ideas about emotion survive and flourish through a PhD and almost twenty years. I am proud to have you as a friend and mentor.

I am thankful for the work of the Tyndale team to make this book what it should be. Thank you, Jon Farrar, for guiding the project with enthusiasm. And my sincere thanks to Dave Lindstedt, for your grace and careful attention to detail. You have made everything stronger. May God bless your work.

Thanks to all who read advance copies of the book and participated in my crazy "blog" idea. You have added more insight and relevance than I could have imagined. Your thoughts have become a strong and exciting part of the book—I am thrilled.

A special thanks goes to all who supported and encouraged me. To my parents: What can I say? I could not ask for more. To Rebecca: You have done far more than you realize in making this book a reality. Your work, your passion for the vision, and your dedication are all greatly appreciated.

My last and heartfelt thanks must go to Ken Petersen. I could go on for several pages about all you have done. You have been God's great gift to me. Several months before we met, I felt that I should stop praying for a publisher for the book and start praying that God would bring someone to believe in the message and teach me how to write it. I could not have imagined that God would answer that prayer so far beyond what I hoped for. You have taken my offerings and made them sing so they are free to touch hearts and change lives. Your walking beside me and desiring to know it for yourself has made all the difference.

Thanks be to God for giving us these wonderfully complex emotions. Your strong hand has never let us down from the start of the journey; forgive my doubt! I want to dedicate this sacrifice of hours and days and weeks and years to your glory. May you use it as you see fit, and may it be a fragrant offering to you.

01 Feel

I sat with Ben over coffee.

A family friend for many years, Ben was talking with me about my favorite subject these days—how so many of us have been disconnected from our feelings and emotions. Then Ben told me one of the saddest stories I've heard in a long time.

A man from his church had asked to have breakfast with him. This friend of Ben's was spiritually strong, a pillar in the church. Anyone would say he was doing all the right things in pursuing the model spiritual life.

Over plates of eggs and bacon, the two of them talked about family news, their church, and books they'd read recently. In time, they finished their food and conversation. Ben thought their breakfast was about done.

But as Ben was getting ready to stand and leave, his friend blurted out, "I have to tell you something."

Ben realized then that his friend had invited him to breakfast for a different reason—that it was something hard for him to say, and he'd taken the entire meal to muster the nerve to say it.

"I am living out all the things I should be doing for God," he finally said. "I'm doing what I'm supposed to, like I've been taught. But I'm not happy. I'm not passionate about anything. To be perfectly honest, I'm not even passionate about God. I feel *nothing*."

He was overcome with emotion as he confessed what he had kept secret for so long. "Ben, I'm dead inside."

As Ben told me this story, his face displayed the anguish he felt for his friend. Then he asked me this penetrating question: "How might your understanding of feelings and emotions help this man?"

The sad thing is this man is only one of many who suffer in the same way. I've been there. I suspect you have as well. We've faithfully pursued a spiritual and godly life, yet somehow we find ourselves numb, without passion or pleasure, emotionally dead.

For years we've been taught by our culture and in our churches that emotions are not to be trusted; that reason and knowledge and logic are the firm foundation on which to build our faith and our spiritual lives; that it's our *attitudes* and *actions* that matter, not how we *feel* about things.

This disconnect between our faith and our feelings has been the focus of my heart ever since I was a teenager. I've been intrigued by what it means to truly *love* God and *hate* evil.

Trying to figure it all out, I studied philosophy, culture, and the Bible, and I've come to believe that we have fallen victim to two things that are terribly wrong.

First, we have made our relationship with God more about fulfilling our *duty* than expressing our *passion*. We make our spiritual lives into a list of dos and don'ts. We pursue this list more than we actually pursue Jesus. And this leads us to a life that eventually becomes tired and numb, devoid of feeling, dead.

Recently, I was talking to a friend whose small group was studying holiness—that is, being pure and pleasing in God's sight. Around the circle, each person commented about what it meant to be holy. Most of them mentioned something they could have done to be better or more perfect—something they thought they needed to *achieve* in order to be more holy. Some spoke of how hard it was to do everything they were "supposed to do" as Christians. (My friend commented that everyone seemed so tired.)

One woman shared her experience of serving a shift at a homeless shelter between two and four in the morning. My friend was in awe of that kind of commitment, but the woman went on to berate herself for failing to say a helpful thing to a fellow volunteer that morning. It was something "on her list" that she had failed to do. And in her mind, it was one more thing that kept her from being more holy.

My point here is not so much about whether doing this one thing would have made this woman more holy. It's that this sort of thing, multiplied many times in a single life, robs a person of the exuberance and passion and excitement of life with God. In time, you would expect her to wind up like Ben's friend: numb and dead inside but always looking for the next item to check off on the list, the one more *thing to do* to become more holy. In the meantime, she's losing her ability to feel.

The second thing that has gone terribly wrong is that we have become indoctrinated in the belief that emotions are unreliable, dangerous, and bad. Philosophy, psychology, our scientific culture, and the church have taught us that logic and reason must reign supreme, while feelings are trivialized and seen as something to be suppressed or ignored. Many successful contemporary writers have brainwashed us into believing that we must stifle what we *feel* in favor of what we *think.*

The messages I have read recently in popular inspirational books include the ideas that emotions leave us in a fog and cloud our thinking; the notion that in order to live a godly life, we must control our emotions; and the belief that following our emotions often leads us to sin.

I've heard nationally known speakers assert that anger, sorrow, and jealousy are signs of spiritual weakness; that our feelings cannot be trusted; and that God cares about what we believe, not what we feel.

These are all myths. None of them are true; none of them hold up to good science; and none of them are from the Bible.

And yet, by buying into these myths, many of us live distorted lives. We repress the very emotions that would give us life. Some of us have abandoned looking for God altogether or have left the church because we felt we couldn't find the new *heart* we were looking for.

But many spiritual leaders through the centuries got it right. We need to recapture some of the truths they taught. In the words of A.W. Tozer, "A state of emotion always comes between the knowledge and the act. . . . God intended that truth should move us to moral action. The mind receives ideas, mental pictures of things as they are. These excite the feelings and these in turn move the will to act in accordance with the truth. . . . But be sure that human feelings can never be completely stifled. If they are forbidden their normal course, like a river they will cut another channel through the life and flow out to curse and ruin and destroy."[1]

I have come to believe that our emotions were given to us by God to drive us to our best.

I have come to believe that emotions are among the most logical and dependable things in our lives.

I have come to believe that emotions give us a window to see truth like nothing else.

I have come to believe that the true health of our spiritual lives is measured by how we feel.

That is the great power in listening to your heart.

BLOG 01: FEEL

ANDREW]·····[I don't remember the day I decided to buy into those ideas, but you're right. I did. But I wasn't the victim. I chose them, and in some ways I like them. Feelings and emotions are dangerous. But the more I dwell on the teaching of Scripture, the more I realize how dangerous "controlling" my emotions has become. Sadly, I bought into the teaching—teaching that I believe is false teaching. How many facets of my life has it affected? Yet in all this discussion of feelings versus duty, is there still a place for duty (in the sense of loyalty)?

REBECCA]·····[As I read this first chapter, I realized that I have often felt like Ben's friend. Life oftentimes just feels like a routine, going through all the motions and doing all the "shoulds" in life, but never being satisfied with where I am going or who I am becoming. Sometimes I even lack a passion for life; my life feels empty, hollow, and like nothing else matters anymore. But, I often think to myself, good Christians shouldn't feel this way. However, it is only when we begin to acknowledge what we struggle with, and recognize how to best help others understand that these feelings are "normal" and "OK," that we will be able to see a change in the world and people around us.

This past year, I had major spine surgery. I was pretty upset because it not only took me away from my job as a teacher, but it kept me out all semester and away from things I really enjoyed, like sports and working out. The past 8 months, I have not been able to do much of anything physically. While I am gradually able to do more and more, like walking and swimming, for the first 5 months, I was homebound, lying in bed, and pretty much confined to the four walls of my room. I mention this story because, as I think about this experience, I realize that maybe this surgery was what I needed to stop the monotony of the every-day-routine that I was in, rarely taking time for what mattered, too consumed with work or other things. I asked myself, as I had much time to think and ponder, what was I really living for? What gave my life meaning? And those are questions I continue to ask today. But what I do know is that it was OK for me to feel that way; it was OK to be upset and scared, because there were a lot of unknowns. But through feeling these things, I was able to work through some of those feelings and begin to have an appreciation for what I could do. I know that now I can be more sympathetic to those around me who are much worse off, who can't breathe on their own, who can't walk, and who won't ever recover. So it is my continual prayer that God continues to allow me not only to heal, but to genuinely share the emotions I went through, because I know others can relate in some way, shape, or form.

MARIAN]·····[I made my decision years ago—feelings are too painful to be indulged in. Barriers are safely in place—how dare I feel? Perhaps my dysfunctional family background was to blame—a mother suffering with mental illness and in and out of psychiatric hospitals; father, self-centred and looking for relationships outside the home. How do I cope if mother hates me today? Or perhaps I would be the one in favour? What if I displease my father? I never could figure out what I did that was so wrong. No, feelings are not safe. Best to shut them behind iron walls. But as an adult . . . hear my cry, Lord, to be able to relate to You with a passion that responds to Your love. Is there hope, Lord? Can I once again find freedom in You?

But perhaps I am not so alone in being unable to really feel. Maybe the path to wholeness lies in being like Ben's friend and admitting to our struggle. There must be more to being a Christian than just working for You, Lord, and trying harder.

SARAH]·····[This view of emotions is one that has been taught to me since a very early age. I have been taught that worship offered in an emotional way leads to a worldly, tainted offering to God that is sensuous and self-centered—in other words, how wrong this was. I have been brought up not to feel toward God, in all my interactions and worship. But I also believed that God was One Who does not feel toward me. If God is unemotional, how can I interact on a personal level with Him?

JULIE]·····[I'm so looking forward to digging into this book, because I feel I'm "dead" inside. I know a lot of truths about the Lord, and I've been walking with him for 18 years, yet oftentimes I feel like I don't KNOW Jesus. I don't know the sweetness of his fellowship and communion. I'm a type A, list person by nature, so it's difficult to put aside my "to do" list to hear and respond to Jesus. There are so many other things vying for my attention and time. I long to replace the "deadness" with "life." I long to know the joy of my salvation.

I have heard many messages/sermons about emotions, and they have led me to conclude that emotions can't be trusted; therefore, it's just easy to stay in this "dead" state. It doesn't help that I was raised in a family that didn't deal well with emotions (conflicts were brushed under the rug, and most kinds of confrontation were avoided or sidestepped).

JARED]·····[Sometimes we do things that we do not feel like doing. Although this is an important lesson for the developing psyche of a five-year-old, I have noticed in myself that without the feeling, the result is bland. My most memorable achievements in life have been those things that I might have been hesitant about, yet sensed the inner urgings to proceed, to jump in, to go. I am still learning to listen and to heed, but I know that those feelings are God. Prodding and nudging, He garners a response: positive or negative. Those feelings, and that response, get us going toward the kingdom.

Enter the discussion at www.faithfulfeelings.com.

MY BLOG:

_____

_____

_____

_____

_____

_____

_____

_____

_____

_____

_____

_____

02 Discovery

As I walked from the gray cobblestone streets into the medieval stone-and-brick building that day in Tübingen, Germany, I had no idea that God was about to change my life.

Laura and I felt we had stepped back in time. Tübingen is a picture-postcard kind of place. We found ourselves surrounded by blocks of buildings that had been built hundreds of years earlier: an ancient cathedral, the duke's castle not far off, and then my home away from home—the University of Tübingen, founded in 1477.

As I walked into the lobby of one of the university's academic libraries, enveloped by its massive plaster-and-wood beamed ceiling, I was about to embark on a journey of discovery that I could not have planned or imagined. . . .

〈〈〉〉

I had been two years into my journey toward a PhD in the religion department at the University of Aberdeen, another ancient university, when the ground shook under my graduate plan: My advisor, the man responsible for directing all my studies, received a coveted scholarship in Tübingen and would be leaving for a year of study.

At almost the very same time, my wife, Laura, was struck by an earthquake of her own: She lost her job.

Aberdeen is the center for North Sea oil operations in Scotland and is full of transplanted Texans and their families. The children all went to the American school, where Laura was the sixth grade teacher. We had been so blessed and amazed that God had provided the only job in town where Laura could make a good living as a certified American teacher.

We had settled in and were quite content. Laura loved teaching, and I was fascinated by what I was studying—the role of emotion in the Bible. So far, I had not made much progress; the goal seemed elusive. But Laura and I believed that God had brought us to Aberdeen, and he was providing all our needs beyond our expectations.

When a new principal was hired at Laura's school, he wanted to bring in some teachers from the international school where he had worked previously. As the most recent hire, Laura was the first to be let go. She was crushed.

But God works in interesting ways.

If Laura hadn't lost her job, I doubt we would have left Aberdeen. But under the circumstances, and facing a less-than-certain financial future, I asked my advisor if I could join him in Tübingen. I liked him, and I had heard scary stories about changing advisors midstream. A new advisor might want me to change the whole direction of my research—I could lose months of hard work. And Tübingen, as it happened, was one of the premier centers on the planet for the study of the New Testament.

It was a great opportunity.

We set out in an old blue Honda Accord, purchased from our good friend Bobby Roundtree, who was taking his family back to Texas. During our time in Aberdeen, the Roundtrees had provided us with good, home-cooked meals and a family to be part of. Selling us their Honda on more-than-fair terms was their parting blessing to us.

So we committed ourselves to God's care. But at times we wondered . . .

On the ferry from England to Denmark, we experienced one of the worst of crossings. The North Sea was violent, and Laura and I did not dare to get out of bed during the night. Our porthole was forty feet above the water one moment and beneath a wave the next. It was incredible. I shouted out a running commentary about the size of the waves. Laura just closed her eyes and groaned.

Shaky on arrival, we drove south through Denmark into Germany in our British-outfitted, steering-wheel-on-the-right Honda, trying to remember which side of the road was right—or wrong. We had directions to Tübingen but little contact information once we got there—just the name of a student, Matthias Baumgartner, who would also be studying with my advisor.

We had no place to live, did not speak German, Laura had no job, and we didn't know a soul from the area. We were due to start language school in a couple of days.

Laura had an interview lined up at the International School of Stuttgart, a large city about forty-five kilometers from Tübingen. Near the location for the interview, we learned, was the European command for the U.S. military. On our way, we visited the base to check things out and find some English-speaking help. We learned from the military housing office how difficult it would be to find an apartment in the area. We soon discovered that a "furnished" apartment in Germany meant it had lights, appliances, and running water. An apartment with actual furniture was almost impossible to come by. The housing officer at the base couldn't help us, but he gave us the name of a local real estate agent who spoke English.

At the International School, Laura had the "best interview of her life," but she didn't get the job.

You can imagine how we both felt.

We wondered why God had led us here, yet we had faith that he was with us and that he would take care of us. It was the only thing we knew for sure.

<<>>

Driving on to Tübingen, Laura and I wondered how we were ever going to find our only contact at the university. Knowing almost no German, and realizing that most of the students were away on vacation, I got out of the car, overwhelmed and discouraged.

Approaching two students who were walking out the doors of one of the buildings, I asked them for help, hoping they might understand my English.

"Excuse me. Do you know Matthias Baumgartner?"

One of the students replied in fine English, with a crisp German accent, "I am Matthias Baumgartner."

That night we were eating at the Baumgartners' and staying with them overnight. They warmly assured us we had a place to stay for as long as we needed. We were overwhelmed by their generosity.

God was reassuring our hearts; he had a purpose for us.

Through several more God-ordained "coincidences," within one day we had a large, inexpensive two-bedroom apartment that was even nicer than the place where we had lived in Scotland. It came fully furnished

(with actual furniture), and even though the landlords understood no
English, they took us in anyway. It all happened in such a flash that the
Baumgartners were flabbergasted we could move into an apartment so
quickly.

A few short days after that, Laura found a job as a secretary at the U.S.
military base, complete with full on-base commissary privileges. Little
did we know that, even if Laura had been hired at the International
School where her salary would have been higher, it wouldn't have been
nearly enough for us to live on. It cost two or three times more to live in
Germany than in the United States and 50 percent more than it had cost
to live in Aberdeen. But with access to a military commissary, we were
blessed. Laura was making far less, but our standard of living actually
went up because we were able to buy gas, groceries, and clothes at
U.S. prices.

We had faced some big obstacles, and God had supplied in amazing
ways.

You would think that after this bountiful provision from the hand of
God it would be for some dramatic purpose, like studying with some
of the best German New Testament scholars in the world who teach at
Tübingen; or learning perfect theological German at the most presti-
gious of German theological schools—any New Testament scholar's
dream; or having access to any book I would ever need at one of the
three or four best theological libraries on the planet. But as is often the
case with God, none of these obvious things were in his plan. Yet
something else was. . . .

‹ ‹ › ›

Almost by chance, I was drawn to a library near the great cathedral in
Tübingen. It was not the modern, state-of-the-art theological library,
nor was it the cavernous main library of the university. In German
universities, they often divide different categories of books, with each
specialty having its own separate, focused library. It was a small
library off to the right of that wood-beamed entrance where I found
the books that would lead me on a journey of discovery. On one
section of shelving, floor to ceiling, I found all the major books about

emotion written during perhaps the past fifty years. For the next six months or so, I dug into those books, like a detective trying to unravel a great mystery. Eventually, they led me to hundreds of shorter articles on emotion as well.

So, by God's grace, my studies in Tübingen began with a total immersion in the history and philosophy of the study of the emotions. What are emotions? Can we trust them? Where do they come from? I quickly became fascinated by a very strange conflict that had begun as early as the birth of the Western world.

Plato, the great philosopher, insisted that there were two distinct parts in every person—*reason* (our capacity for thinking, or our mind) and *passion* (including emotions). He believed that reason was the higher (and better) part of our nature and should rule over and subdue the lower part, the emotions.

He believed that following emotions usually didn't take you anywhere good. In approaching life, reason should be front and center.

Another of history's most influential philosophers, René Descartes, agreed. He emphasized the concept that emotions came directly from the body—as actual products of bodily organs.[1] In other words, they were a kind of physical response. Emotions come upon you, and you have little control over them.

In the eighteenth century, David Hume echoed Descartes on the physical origin of emotions: "Bodily pains and pleasures are the source of many passions."[2] Again, emotions start in the body.

In the early twentieth century, Charles Darwin wrote that emotion grew out of the most basic instincts of survival. Emotions, to Darwin, are instinctual vestiges of early animal behaviors.

You almost get the feeling that emotions should be kept in cages, like lions at the zoo—nice to walk past and look at, but better left locked up.

The founders of modern psychology, such as William James and Sigmund Freud, shared this physical/organic view of emotions. To them, emotions were about what we feel in our nervous systems, completely separated and different from our minds, thoughts, or reason. Mostly, the leaders of the fledgling science of psychology subordinated emotions to what they thought was the better and higher authority of reason.

I am looking forward to taking a closer look with you at what some of these guys thought.

⟨⟨⟩⟩

So here was where the conflict began to strike very close to home.

These ideas about emotion were *very much in line with what I had learned from pastors and writers and teachers in the Christian culture in which I'd grown up.* And it also seemed as if the theologians and New Testament scholars I was reading believed this way too.

I knew a bit about these philosophers and psychologists: Many did not even believe in God, and some were downright hostile to Christians. That in itself was not the problem—because ungodly people can and do uncover truth. But the strange thing to me was that Christian teaching and Christian culture would so readily embrace *secular* philosophy.

Sure, preachers today are more modern than Descartes—they don't claim that emotions are generated from bodily organs or blood—yet they still view the emotions with some level of suspicion or concern. I recalled phrases and quotes from sermons and books suggesting that our emotions are powerful (and somewhat sinister) forces that must be controlled by reason and duty. And some speakers and writers teach that many of our emotions are sinful—that strong emotions such as anger and jealousy are "works of the devil."

The message is consistent and strong: "Your emotions are always getting you into trouble. You must control them and wrestle them into submission to the Word of God."

There was the church bulletin I'd read somewhere: "Pray that you and other believers will develop Christlike self-control: restraint over your own impulses, emotions, and desires."

Take a quick look online at the titles of the most popular Christian books about emotion. It is very revealing:

Deadly Emotions
Managing Your Emotions: Instead of Your Emotions Managing You
A Woman's Forbidden Emotion
Emotions: Can You Trust Them?
Those Ugly Emotions
Winning Over Your Emotions

Do I hear echoes of the Bible or echoes of Plato in these ideas?

‹ ‹ › ›

I wondered: Were these leaders right, or were they just running with stuff they'd learned in school rather than trying to figure out for themselves what God had to say about emotion?

I guess we all do that sometimes, but this seemed pretty important—to understand the biblical view of emotions and get it right.

The most common statement I read in these books was that the "love" Jesus commanded was not a feeling.

Yet, as I read on and on into what had been written by theologians—hundreds of books and articles, and finally a thousand—I could never find a single argument that rested on the Bible itself that said love or joy were not feelings. Mostly it was just stated as fact.

For example, Dr. Erwin Lutzer, a well-known pastor and author, writes, "Divine love is based on and dependent on the lover. It is not a feeling, for with it we can even love our enemies. Clearly, if love were a feeling, God would be putting a burden on us that we could not possibly bear."[3]

Kay Arthur puts the common argument like this: "Love is not merely an emotion, otherwise it could not be commanded. Love requires action. Love demands deeds."[4]

I heard pastor James MacDonald, who is now broadcast on more than six hundred radio stations, say that the problem in the church today is that "we think love is a feeling, [but] love is a choice." He also writes, "Faith is believing the Word of God and acting upon it no matter how I feel."[5]

New Testament scholar D. A. Hagner says of Jesus' command to love your enemies, "The love he describes, of course, is not an emotion . . . but volitional acts."[6]

Dr. Markus Bockmuehl, in his commentary on Philippians (Paul's letter focusing on *joy*), writes, "Joy in the Lord is not a feeling but an attitude, and as such it can be positively commanded."[7]

And Joyce Meyer, in her book *Managing Your Emotions: Instead of Your Emotions Managing You,* writes, "That is Satan's plan for our lives—to get us to live by our carnal feelings so we can never walk in the Spirit. . . . If we lack understanding about the fickle nature of emotions, Satan can use them—or the lack of them—to keep us out of God's will. I firmly believe that no person will ever walk in God's will and ultimately in victory if he takes counsel with his emotions."[8]

My purpose in citing these specific writers is not to single them out for criticism. I'm simply trying to illustrate how widespread and common these views of emotion are within our Christian culture.

For those who argue that love, joy, and hope are not feelings, the logic is usually quite simple: Emotion is this feeling we have little control over—and you cannot *command* a feeling. Therefore, the love or joy or hope that God commands in the Bible (nobody doubts that God commands love and joy) couldn't be emotions.

Were they unwittingly getting these ideas from Darwin, Descartes, James, and the psychology of our age that followed them? Or, put another way, does God think you *can* command emotion? And, if God thinks he can command us to feel a certain way, why does he think that? What does he know about the emotions that I didn't understand?

‹‹›

How is it that we want to convert the extraordinary passions of life in Christ into intellectual concepts? How can we redefine emotion into non-emotion?

As I read and studied at Tübingen, it seemed to me as if many Christian teachers and preachers today were resorting to some extraordinary word tricks to avoid the suggestion that what the Bible says about love, joy, hope, and other emotions is really something we are supposed to *feel*. And the so-called negative emotions, such as anger, jealousy, and hatred, were to be avoided in almost every situation—they were off-limits to the truly spiritual person.

The rhetoric about emotion in our Christian culture was starting to look like a gymnastics routine, redefining emotional words in non-emotional terms. I have read hundreds of these attempts and found none that is linked to any good evidence that the writers of the Bible actually believed this.

I'm a simple guy. Does it really have to be so complicated? Does such an important concept as what Jesus said were the greatest command-ments—to love God and others—need to be interpreted through philosophical glasses?

Or did Jesus say exactly what he meant—that he wanted us to really *feel* something toward God and toward other people?

‹‹›

My journey was not just intellectual. It was personal as well.

I realized that my own life and faith had been shaped by these views. I struggled with how I was to feel as a Christian. I had been taught that *love* in the Bible wasn't really an emotion; that it was more of a *duty* that I owed other people, and an act of selflessness—something that was *done* or *acted out*. *Joy* was not really an important emotion that I should be living in; it was a spiritual concept, a deep, inner reality that I might miss if I didn't really pay attention.

Many of the *positive* "emotion" words in Scripture were not to be
considered as real emotions but interpreted at a different, "higher" level,
a cognitive, rational level. With *negative* emotions, such as anger and
hatred, we should recognize them as emotions and then throw them out
with the other sins in our lives. If I was living with a heart of forgiveness,
how could I get really angry at somebody?

Was this right?

I didn't know, and I hadn't started my heavy biblical research yet; but I
began to have doubts. I found myself looking at things through a new
lens: Maybe modern-day Christianity had gotten something about this
all wrong.

My wife, Laura, had an experience growing up that perfectly illustrates
something here.

When Laura was in boarding school in South America, the students
were graded not only on their studies in math, English, or science but
also on personal stuff. One of these grades was for "emotional stability." A student received high marks if he or she kept an even keel
emotionally. In the context of that school, this was judged to be a sign
of spiritual character.

It was crushing to Laura in those years that she never earned a good
grade in "emotional stability." It was as if a more spiritual person kept all
strong reactions under the surface. But Laura was no good at that. She
was too honest. She had to express her feelings and emotions outwardly.
(Hey, that's one of the reasons I married her!) But for expressing her
emotions—for *feeling*—young Laura was marked down.

Recalling her story, I realized how often and in so many ways we give
ourselves emotional report cards. Why did I get so angry at that? Why did
I cry like that in front of the whole small group? Why did I get so upset
with so-and-so? We shame ourselves for having emotions. For *feeling*.

When we're honest, many of us would give ourselves an F on our
emotional report card because our emotions are not constantly under
control. And most often, our answer to this failing grade is to try to tone

down our feelings, to turn down the temperature, to pack it all back
inside and get on with life.

In Tübingen, I realized this idea was the prevailing Christian view of
emotions—and this "Christian" view was essentially platonic, a secular
perspective in line with the views of Descartes, James, and—if you can
believe it—none other than Charles Darwin.

And I began to understand just how deeply my own life and behavior had
been shaped by that. All my life, I had carefully controlled my emotions
according to some of these very ideas.

I realized I needed to read the Bible more deeply and see how God
communicates the truth of his design.

What did the Bible really teach?

I had to find out.

〈〈〉〉

When I began to dig into my studies, I was astonished. One of the first
things I did was read through the entire Bible, looking for and writing
down in lists every significant use of emotional words.

I found that the Bible is teeming with emotions. Passions abound.
Deep desires surface. There is anger, fear, love, joy, hate. Both the
Old and New Testaments are crammed full of people driven by
emotions—jealousy, anger, grief, as well as unconditional love, hope,
ecstatic joy.

There is the sexual passion of the Song of Solomon, the profound despair
of Ecclesiastes—and oh! the deep joy and peace of the psalms of David!

In the New Testament, the Gospels are packed with stories of how
Jesus encountered people who were trapped and bound *emotionally* by
patterns of sin, daily duties, or religious obligation. They see in Christ a
deliverance from their emotionless lives. They reach out. Christ touches
each one.

I reconnected with the story of the rich young ruler, a man who had "followed all the commandments," who had done his Christian duty, yet was missing something in his life and wanted the fullness of life he'd seen in Jesus.

There was the simple and sweet encounter of Jesus with Zacchaeus, who, unlike the rich young ruler, chose to toss away his sad life and follow Jesus instead.

And the account of Mary and Martha—Martha with her to-do list, stewing over Mary's lack of work and effort, while Mary sat at Jesus' feet, enjoying his presence.

Some of Jesus' most famous parables are about how we should *feel*— that is their main point.

Story after story tells how those who encountered Jesus walked away rejoicing or ran exuberantly to tell others. The Gospel of Luke is known to scholars as "the gospel of joy." Luke had a keen eye for helping us see that the gospel—the *Good News*—brings great joy to everyone who embraces it.

I can't wait to unpack some of these stories with you!

The Bible was telling me that people who simply pursue duty and follow the rules often miss the party. And the biggest thing they miss out on is the relationship.

I began to see particular patterns of how the Bible used emotional words, and it fit perfectly into the way I now understood emotions to operate. In the process, the stilted interpretations of so many theologians came down like a house of cards.

In all of these stories, I was impressed by the prominent role that emotions played. Not only that, but these stories were *about* emotion— how people could taste the vibrant life they saw in Jesus. Everyone who encountered Jesus began to *feel*.

And even more, these stories were about people like *me*—people who were stuck in their lives of obedience and duty—and how duty, while good in its own way, is not sufficient. The rich young ruler and Zacchaeus and Mary all wanted something more—the promise of the passion they saw in Jesus.

⟨⟨⟩⟩

About this time, I faced an intellectual crisis—almost more than that, it was a crisis of faith. Here I was, a mere student, yet I was beginning to feel strongly that many great scholars and teachers—people I greatly respected—were completely off base about some of the most basic ideas in the Bible.

How could that be true?

I really began to question whether what I was thinking, the conclusions I was reaching that went against what I had been taught, could possibly be true. I had too much respect for their depth of knowledge—far more than I had or ever will have—their command of the biblical languages, and their overwhelming unanimity in thinking, to just charge on alone. It was more than my confidence could handle.

During this growing crisis, I decided to stop my reading of modern scholars and dive into some of the classics. First on the list was *Religious Affections* by Jonathan Edwards, the great American philosopher and theologian. This book was a revelation to me, a fantastic breath of fresh air. It was like I was being pulled underwater by the weight of all who were arrayed against what I was starting to believe, and then Edwards single-handedly pulled me up again onto the shore. I remember sitting in the apartment in Germany reading Edwards, and literally line by line, this great intellectual leader (a central figure in the Great Awakening) was arguing for what I had come to believe—arguing against the same forces in his world that I was seeing in mine. It was a mind-blowing experience, and I have never looked back, never had a crisis like that again.

I was soon to find that Edwards and I were not alone. John Wesley, Thomas Aquinas—and, to some extent, people like John Calvin and Augustine—had views about emotion that were very different from what so many hold today. I also found a few great modern writers, such as

John Piper, who held similar views to those I found in Edwards. I cannot wait to share with you some of the things these giants of faith had to say.

The journey could continue. I was on firm ground.

⟨⟨⟩⟩

In my search in the library at Tübingen, one of the great revelations about emotion was so subtle, so natural, that I almost missed it entirely.

The Bible talks about emotion just like we do in everyday conversation.

There is no special category for "Christian love," that *agape* kind our Christian leaders like to talk about—intellectualizing an emotion into a philosophical ideal. Love, hope, joy—and even hatred—in the Bible are not lofty ideas and concepts; they are feelings and emotions, just as we know them in our own lives and talk about them with our families and friends.

There is a great example of what I am talking about in Romans 12: "Don't just pretend to love others. Really love them. Hate what is wrong. Hold tightly to what is good. Love each other with genuine affection, and take delight in honoring each other. Never be lazy, but work hard and serve the Lord enthusiastically. Rejoice in our confident hope. Be patient in trouble, and keep on praying. When God's people are in need, be ready to help them. Always be eager to practice hospitality. Bless those who persecute you. Don't curse them; pray that God will bless them. Be happy with those who are happy, and weep with those who weep. Live in harmony with each other. Don't be too proud to enjoy the company of ordinary people. And don't think you know it all!"[9]

See what I mean?

In these eight verses, Paul mentions emotions or uses emotional words a dozen times or so. They are mixed in naturally with the normal flow of his writing.

Really *love* people.

Hate what is wrong.

Love with *genuine affection.*

Delight in honoring each other.

Serve the Lord *enthusiastically.*

Rejoice in hope.

Practice hospitality *eagerly.*

Be *happy.*

Weep.

Enjoy.

Commands to love and to be in prayer and to be joyful and not to be lazy are all jumbled up together. In the midst of a plea to keep our spirits boiling passionately, Paul tells us to have great empathy for others, to *feel* what they are feeling. If we are going to be *enthusiastic* in serving God, we had better feel others' joy and pain as if it were our own.

It occurred to me that our spirituality is all about how we are *feeling*— whether we are *feeling* life or are numb to it. If we are not feeling as we should, something is really wrong with our relationship with God.

Paul takes no time to explain what he means by *love* and *joy* and *hope* and *hate* and *sorrow.* He doesn't try to tell us that joy is not a feeling or that love is just a choice. He speaks in plain language and assumes that emotions are simply recording our feelings—the stuff of life that God has given us. Paul assumes we will know what joy and love feel like, and he exhorts that if we live by God's standards, there are certain kinds of *feelings* that will fill our lives.

This is not rocket science to Paul; it's clear and normal. He has no embarrassment, no hesitation, no theological barrier to putting pure emotion front and center. He tells it like it is in real life.

I wondered at all the sermons I'd heard and if I'd ever heard a pastor say, "Feel!"

Without any qualifications.

Without any theological rhetoric.

Without any attempt to redefine the word.

Feel!

I wondered how I'd react if I went to church one Sunday and heard, "God is telling you that next week you should be filled with happiness and good cheer; you need to give genuine, warm hugs every night to your family; and if something really bad happens to a friend in the church, you need to be over at their house crying with them. No, I don't mean dropping by a card and a casserole for dinner, your Christian duty. I mean entering into their pain and really crying with them."

Paul is that preacher. And that is what I learned from him in Romans. To him, a Christian's emotional life is all rolled up in and with and around how we should behave and how we should think. For Paul, it's no different to say "cry with the grieving" than to say "don't lie." Duty is there, but not devoid of passion and true emotion. It's all one.

So *feel.* And feel *deeply.*

〈〈〉〉

This book is my attempt to bring you along with me on this journey of discovery. Are you ready?

We will look at what people are saying about emotions and why they are wrong.

We will discover how those wrong beliefs—both Christian and in modern culture—put us in a box and bind us up. And how this bondage does great damage to our souls.

My research also took me into the arenas of science, brain chemistry, and the most recent cognitive psychology. What is fascinating to me is how the latest research seems to be consistent with the Bible's understanding of emotions.

Together we will see how God created emotions to be powerful forces for good, powerful forces we can use to change the world.

We will see how love and joy and hope should define us.

I am excited to share more about what emotion is and to give you some key words to help you unlock your own emotional world, so you can understand what is going on in your heart.

If we can understand where our emotions are coming from and the stuff they are made of, I think we can stop giving ourselves an F on our emotional report cards and start living *with, out of,* and *in* our emotions— in harmony. I call this "living life in the heart of God," and I hope you will completely understand what that is by the time you reach the final chapter.

On my journey, I also discovered some simple ideas that made a difference to my understanding of emotions. We'll cover these ideas in depth. For example, one of my objectives in this book is to untangle the confusion between *emotions*—what we "feel"—and the physical sensations we have in our bodies.

Good science shows us that feelings/emotions are much more complex (and noble) than a mere, involuntary bodily response. And so does the Bible.

Another discovery I made is that our emotions are intimately connected to our thinking. Because our emotions are tied into our thinking and beliefs, every emotion has an object. We cannot think about nothing. We don't just love; we love *someone* or *something,* and we love it for some good reason. This truth, as it is understood by a new generation of philosophers and psychologists, has revolutionized our understanding of the emotions. Today, many have overthrown the flawed approach of Darwin, James, Descartes, and Freud, because their views simply do not stand up to reason.

God knew this from the start—the new approach just happens to be consistent with the Bible's understanding of emotion.

Well, really, there is no surprise here, is there?

⟨⟨⟩⟩

My experience in Tübingen was far more than an academic study for me. These are more than ideas. From the start, it was very personal. And very real. I can't wait to tell you how God had prepared my heart for this new understanding, even when I was a teenager, and how a passion for God in my early years led me to the study of emotion as a doctoral student. God is faithful, isn't he!

Laura and I pulled up all our roots from a promising job in Michigan, where I was already managing sixty people as a recent college graduate, and headed off across the ocean to an uncertain future. All because I had a passion, a call, to study the subject of emotion. The story of our move is amazing in itself, but I will need to leave that for another day.

This has been a journey of faith. Along the way, I discovered how much I had come to bottle up my emotions and put them in a box. I realized that much of what I'd been taught about emotions—that they were somehow bad and needed to be diminished and controlled—was hurting me. And I realized how I'd come to serve the cause of Christian duty at the expense of passion. The shock for me was finding out how wrong this all was.

I believe that Laura's and my amazing journey was not just for us. I believe God brought us here so that you could come too.

No, this isn't an academic exercise. This journey is all about transformed lives. . . .

BLOG 02: DISCOVERY

STEPHEN]·····[I have not often thought about what emotions are, where they come from, and why we have them. Having read this chapter, I agree that this may well be due to my acceptance of the general attitude toward emotions as lesser things. At the same time, the whole of my life has been one big tapestry of emotional experiences . . . it seems a bit bizarre to try to cover it up.

Since my teens, I have found myself becoming increasingly less willing to involve my emotions in my decisions and experiences. Sometimes, I am even embarrassed by them.

I feel I often concentrate more on being right, or looking "as I should" to others than on expressing what I want to communicate or what I am really feeling.

I remember visiting Africa and being taken aback by their willingness to express their emotions out loud and in front of everyone. Coming from a conservative evangelical church, I think I valued and envied their boldness to express themselves and let others see it.

REBECCA]·····[I think this chapter really hit home—not just for me, but for many of my friends. As I have been talking to them lately, it seems like we all feel the same—we are fed up with not being able to feel things, or having to live a life that is "perfect" on the outside but "miserable" and falling apart on the inside. We are tired of having to constantly perform or be on our best behavior because it's "wrong" or "inappropriate" to show emotion. Emotions are seen as a sign of weakness. But personally, I believe that it takes a stronger person to feel something than it does for someone not to show any emotion at all.

This past year, I was pretty upset with God for allowing me to have to go through major spinal cord surgery, in the middle of the year, taking me away from my 3rd grad-ers. And then, on top of it all, I was homebound for about 4 months, not being able to move, having to lie down a lot, and pretty much having little to no interaction with people. I was pretty helpless to even do the most basic things, like take a shower or dress myself. I got pretty mad and upset hearing the same things over and over again: "Don't let your feelings of anger control who you are," or "Don't let your circumstances dictate how you feel," or "Don't let your emotions run your life; there are people much worse off than you." And I was like, "Gosh darn-it. I do feel angry and I do feel sad. And just because I feel sad or angry doesn't mean I will lose my faith or become emotionally unstable."

But in spite of my anger and others telling me those things, I realized that it was OK to feel. It was OK not to be great or happy 100% of the time. It was OK to be sad and frus-trated. It was more about what I did with that anger and frustration, like not allowing it to control me, that was the most important.

TODD]·····[In my life, I have certainly gotten the sense that if I could just contain my emotions, I would have my act together spiritually. Having read this chapter, I'm amazed at how much of what I've heard in church reflects what Plato was saying, or could have indeed been influenced by what Plato said about reason and emotion. Glad we can attri-bute negative ideas about emotion to Plato and not God.

BOB]·····[Emotions are a gift from God. All my memorable experiences were filled with them. Why have many scholars cast them as only evil and deceptive? I can't wait to learn more about where thinkers have gone wrong, and how God and Scripture (rightly understood) can steer me in a higher direction.

JULIE]·····[A few things struck a chord in my heart as I read this chapter. Specifically: "The Bible was telling me that people who simply pursue duty and follow the rules often miss the party. And the biggest thing they miss out on is the relationship." I think I've got the duty part down in my life, but I'm missing the party and the relationship.

I know on a daily basis I feel many emotions, but don't quite know what to do with them. So, usually I just try to stuff them away. Where do they go, you ask? I have no clue. That's why I'm looking forward to reading on, so I can learn how to unlock my emotional world. So I can truly understand what is going on in my heart rather than just stuffing all of those emotions away to never-never land.

JARED]·····[It is almost as if we are led to believe that our lives will be easier without being led astray by our emotions. When does God ever ask us to do something easy—or, more accurately, easily? He asks us to follow Him, and what stymied the rich, young ruler was his adherence to reason above passion. It just does not make sense for us to impulsively rip up our roots and follow our hearts, so we find a way to calculate it away as "earthly desires." What Jesus wanted us to get was His need for an impulse for His will, a passion for His kingdom. I love that passage in Romans 12, where Paul pleads with us to not just love someone, but *really* love them. He knows we are prone to checklists, to-do lists, and trophies. The times in my life where I have "missed out on the relationship" tended to be when I did things for people out of a duty or a knowledge of what was expected. I think my "friends" could sense my rigid actions, and I lost the intentional intimacy of my feelings and thoughts for that person. I do have hope that God will use my emotions as a "powerful force for good."

Enter the discussion at www.faithfulfeelings.com.

MY BLOG

_____

_____

03 Breathe

Yes, the bride was beautiful, and the little mountain cathedral idyllic—built seamlessly into the pine-forest setting—but my little girl had no equal. When Cailin Rose walked down the aisle, all forty-and-one-half inches of her, she stole her daddy's eyes and heart.

Cailin wore a pale yellow gown with an ornate skirt embroidered with pink flowers and thin green vines. The simple silk top went down to a bouquet of silk roses, with green and pale yellow ribbons flowing down the front.

Her wispy, blonde hair framed her countenance with a natural, wood-fairy look. (Where she got those pale curls from two dark-headed parents we still have not figured out.)

Far from every hair in place, the yellow wisps of little girl could not be combed into submission. On her head, she wore a garland wreath of silk flowers and ribbons. Transparent, inch-wide green ribbons, set beside narrow, pale yellow and green ribbons, flowed down her back from the garland in a cascade of controlled chaos. I do not know that I will live to see another sight like my Cailin Rose on that day of celebration.

I am rather good at getting sentimental, rather good at feeling deeply the wonder and joy of seeing two people united into a new family. Rarely is there a wedding where I do not get choked up a bit sometime during the service. It is a time of reflecting on the great gift of my own marriage and the way that God brings couples together to share love and life.

On the other hand, I am rather bad at celebrating *with* other people. I am not so good at showing on my face and in my body language that I am sharing in their joy and festivities. I mostly feel like a fish out of water when the reception begins, unable to participate in the way that I wish I could. This time was no different. As people began to laugh and socialize, and later to dance and enjoy the music, it was no longer a place where I felt the joy of the wedding. It was now an alien world where I did not know how to behave, what to say, or how to let my guard down and enjoy.

I think others are like me—not really knowing how to celebrate. I realize some of this is due to differences in personality, how each of us has been shaped by experiences, and to a degree, how we were each born with unique characteristics.

But for many of us, I believe there are other factors that have caused us to be scared of celebration, of the expressions of joy and love and feeling. We have repressed our emotions for so long, leaving us as fish out of water when it comes to experiencing the joys and pleasures of life.

One factor is the experience of being raised in a church culture where we all too easily separate the sacred and the secular. Inside the walls of my own comfort zone, or my own heart, I can worship, rejoice, and get really pumped up about the good things of God. Outside that comfort zone— such as when I'm in a group of people—I have a harder time connecting in laughter, spirited conversation, and genuine, warm interaction. Oh God, burst my bubble!

Jesus was not like that. How else could he have gotten invited to the homes of the outsiders of his society, those who were outside the social and politically correct norms, those who had built a different kind of life than their culture accepted? People were no doubt drawn to him because he could laugh with them, and he could look them in the eye with genuine affection. He loved them, and I think he loved being with them. And that *showed.*

We bought a video for our kids called *The Miracle Worker,* a Claymation and cartoon version of the life of Jesus. It was produced by Mel Gibson's Icon Productions, which also made the movie *The Passion of the Christ.* The Jesus it pictures is full of God's joy in a way that I had not really understood before. The stories are ones I have always known, but when I see this Jesus bring them alive with a chuckle, a smile, or a hand to touch, somehow it brings his breath of life to me.

The Jews of Jesus' day knew how to celebrate. Passover was quite the festival. Hundreds of thousands of people descended on Jerusalem. One of the leading experts on Jewish customs at the time of Jesus describes it as "like Christmas: a blend of piety, good cheer, hearty eating, making music, chatting with friends, drinking and dancing."[1]

Now, does that sound like your church potluck?

There was no great divide for the Jews between the sacred and the secular. They did not go to worship at the synagogue on Saturday and then go out to the club to rock and roll on Sunday night. The joy of their relationship with God was all tied up with the joy of life, including the singing and—dare I say it?—the drinking and the dancing.

My stoicism at that wedding reception certainly is not part of a genuine Christian heritage, nor is it spiritual. Yet, somehow I have been conditioned to think that a mature Christian man does not celebrate by displaying outward emotion—except, perhaps, while watching football.

I have been teasing my wife recently about starting to have an occasional glass of wine in the evening just to help us relax and laugh. Both being from homes where alcohol was not part of our lives, this might push us outside our comfort zones. I've also suggested we join a ballroom dancing class. (I figure if we don't do something radical to change, we won't be ready for the Great Feast, the great celebration when we get to see Jesus face-to-face.)

C. S. Lewis put it best: "It is only in our 'hours-off,' only in our moments of permitted festivity, that we find an analogy. Dance and game are frivolous, unimportant down here; for 'down here' is not their natural place. Here, they are a moment's rest from the life we are placed here to live. But in this world everything is upside down. That which, if it could be prolonged here, would be a truancy, is likest that which in a better country is the End of ends. Joy is the serious business of heaven."[2]

Truth is, I really have no specific desire to drink wine, but I have a great need to learn how to celebrate. Of course, it's not about drinking wine, per se, or learning to dance; it's about doing anything that will break me out of my emotionally controlled stoicism and help me relearn the joys and art of celebration.

I have a whole lot of work to do to be ready for the great day when I will celebrate with God—and so do you. Of course, it's not just about preparing for the life after this one we are living in. God wants us to celebrate his presence in our lives *right now.* He wants us to be excited by his creation, by people, by life. Right now. He created us to breathe joy deeply from all the wonders of the people and the world around us—*today.*

Right now.

〈 〉 〉

I think we sometimes behave as if we believe there's something wrong with getting excited.

Things are white outside my office window; fresh snow has fallen twice this week. Christmas is just three weeks away, and my kids are getting excited. Evan, our six-year-old, is already dreaming about opening presents. Meanwhile, I'm thinking of all the responsibilities I have in the coming weeks—all the duties I have to friends and family—and it makes me tired. And I *know* I'll be tired by Christmas Day. But Evan will sit in front of the Christmas tree, and he'll be so exuberant and excited.

He hasn't yet lost his ability to feel.

I can think of spirituality in this same way. We spend so much effort "doing church," performing the duties to make events happen, that once we get to the celebration itself we're tired and numb. And in the service, then, are we excited? Probably not. We're already thinking of all the duties we have for the next spiritual activity. Likewise, in our lives in general, we spend our time doing the duties we've been taught we must do in order to be a good person. And in the constant checking off of items on that list, we miss the celebration entirely.

It's like that story of Jesus when he is on the way to Jerusalem and needs a place to stay. He is invited into the home of two women, Mary and Martha. Martha seems to be the older sister, the one in charge. It is "Martha's house." She was consumed with the event, putting on a great dinner for her honored guest, while Mary just sat there oblivious, in the eyes of Martha, listening to Jesus talk. She needed help in the kitchen!

"But the Lord said to her, 'My dear Martha, you are worried and upset over all these details! There is only one thing worth being concerned about. Mary has discovered it, and it will not be taken away from her.'"[3]

Martha should have forgotten her to-do list and just been with Jesus, enjoying the chance to laugh and hear stories. Martha thought loving Jesus was all about putting on a great dinner and being a stellar host, but Jesus knew that better loving was getting to know him, being with him, celebrating him.

People who *feel* for God are hot and bright. You cannot keep yourself from getting close to the fire on a cold winter day. Jesus was like that fire.

You will never get hot, providing others with warmth and light, by doing your duty, just following the rules.

Like Ben's friend in chapter 1, we become cold from duty, and we look at someone like my son Evan with envy for the simple joy and excitement in life he is still able to feel.

<<>>

The theme that emotions are somehow second-class citizens, things to be kept under tight control, resonates from our teachers and leaders. We're told it's part of being good Christ followers. It seems it's not only children in boarding schools who are being graded on their emotions.

What is so insidious about this is the way it is turned into a measure of maturity and character. Actually, the opposite is true: God created us with emotions, and the Bible tells us they are part of *his* central character. We can no sooner turn them down or turn them off than an eagle can clip its own wings.

And emotions *are* our wings. They are what carry us to a soaring Christian life—to the abundant life we were created to live. As the Bible says, "they will soar high on wings like eagles."[4]

God wants you to soar. He wants a "you" more full of vitality and spirit than you've ever imagined.

<<>>

Everybody feels. Men feel with the same intensity as women. They may feel about different things, but they feel. People from differing cultures feel, just as we feel. Adults feel as often as kids. We may feel for different reasons, but we all feel.

The differences in emotional expression that we see between age groups, genders, and cultures are often due to the unspoken "display rules" for emotions—the norms and cultural mores of societies, families, and belief systems that dictate what we are allowed to express and what we aren't. But however we display or don't display emotions, they are still inside of us. And we probably spend a lot of time and energy trying to deal with our emotions, whether others see the struggle or not.

In one conversation with an expert on emotion, I was told of a clinical study in which researchers showed a horrifically graphic film to audiences in Japan and America. The two cultures are very different in how they show their emotions. The American audience was horrified, nauseated, and very visibly shaken. The Japanese, on the other hand, sat stoically through the entire production. (This matched what is regarded as stereotypical: Japanese are unemotional; Americans are relatively more flamboyant and expressive.)

However, when the researchers ran the test again, they segregated the audiences by social status and age. This time, the responses of the two audiences—Japanese and American—were very similar, consistent with the intense responses of the American audience in the first test. What the researchers realized from these very different results was the strength and power of cultural display rules in Japanese society. In Japan, it is not proper to express strong emotion in front of your superior; this would be very disrespectful. With elders, leaders, and those of higher social standing gone, the Japanese were just as emotional as the Americans. So, in the first test, the *visible* reactions of the Japanese were kept under wraps—suppressed—by the society's display rules. But inside, everybody felt the same.

In other circumstances, American culture might very well have display rules that would severely limit our show of emotions compared to the Japanese.

Unfortunately, our Christian culture has built up a whole pattern of display rules that are strangling us as believers. Just think of how you display your emotions in church versus other places—such as at your team's big game or a U2 concert.

"Well, of course we're going to behave differently at church than at a U2 concert." And that's the point.

These unwritten rules are taking one of God's greatest gifts—the ability to feel—and making it a heavy burden to us. Like the church in Laodicea spoken of in Revelation 3, God desires for us to burn, to be hot again with the consuming fire of his love and joy.

The great tragedy is that as the church stresses what not to feel and how not to feel, we will and do find other things to feel strongly about.

We must find our emotional outlets somewhere.

Sometimes, I think the reason people get addicted to stuff is because they have worked so hard not to feel the things they were made to feel and enjoy. They become desperate to feel something—*anything*—and they find something to fill the emptiness. Sometimes it's something they need to keep secret. An illicit affair or some kind of dark sexual addiction is often sparked by such a need. And, for a time, it fills the need for the great passion they long for.

And it isn't just addictions. Sometimes it's a response that is inconsistent or out of proportion to the situation. Sometimes our emotions "leak out around the edges," despite our best efforts to keep them under wraps.

Each of us was created to love and love *mightily.*

We are either going to passionately love *stuff* or other people; popularity or Jesus; basketball or giving generously to fight AIDS in Africa.

Part of your essence as a person is your need to love and feel deeply. We must be careful in the choice of what our great loves will be, but we can't stop ourselves from feeling passionate about *something.*

Recently, I was talking to a friend. He told me of a situation in which he found himself complimenting a female coworker. He enjoyed working with her and felt she had done a great job on a project they were working on. In a natural and real way, he said, "I *love* that woman."

Almost immediately, he began self-censoring the remark, backpedaling to say that he "really enjoyed working with her" and she "really did good work." He was so afraid of people thinking the word *love* just had to mean something sexual or some kind of sinful attraction that he could not leave the comment dangling. It went against our society's rules.

But why is this censorship of our emotions necessary? Why can't we express more plainly how we are feeling? Can't we *love* a friend or colleague of the opposite sex with a full-hearted affection that doesn't cross moral boundaries? Or, why do I have such a hard time saying "I love you" to even my closest guy friends? Wouldn't that be a better thing, a better way to live much of the time?

When, why, and how should we express our emotions to others? How do we get to the place where what we feel is right and the expression of that emotion can communicate truth, and encourage and challenge those around us?

‹ ‹ › ›

I first met Jim, my men's small group leader, when I was a new member of our church.

Jim is small in stature but big on heart. When you talk to Jim, you feel listened to and cared about. You can see right away that Jim's passion is serving people and encouraging them in their walk with God. Over the last year or so, he has become an overseer of seven men's groups as his own group has multiplied several times over. I have learned a lot by watching Jim care for men. The way that he looks you in the eye and warmly, but directly and firmly, fingers something in your life that needs changing is an art I need to learn myself.

There was a man in his group who had struggled with an addiction to pornography. Jim went to the man's house and helped him install software to guard his computer, his mind, and his family. If someone is having trouble with discipline in spending time in God's Word, Jim is happy to call him every day to get him up on time—apparently even if it will wake up the man's wife! (In fact, from Jim's perspective, if waking up your wife motivates you to get disciplined and be a better husband, all the better!)

Jim once called me on the fly to ask me to join him in visiting a man from our group who was in the hospital with some serious health problems. Knowing I would someday be a group leader myself, he was showing me how to minister to the men who would be under my care. Jim is driven by ministering to the real needs of real men.

When I had my first one-on-one meeting with Jim, I was in a vulnerable state. Having recently left a church where Laura and I felt unloved and discouraged, I was skeptical and wary of forming relationships in a new church. I decided up front that I was going to be honest with this man about my feelings, dreams, and discouragements. I was tired of playing games with people who did not seem to care much about my struggles. I would find out quickly if this was the right church, the right group, the right friend for me.

I shared my discouragements, our recent struggles with church and friendships, and some of my most passionate spiritual goals. Jim and I had an emotional talk, and I even shed a few tears. I knew I had found a friend, as he faithfully cared for me and prayed for and with me. Jim's faithfulness was a special part of my getting over some hurts and discouragement.

Since then, as I have gotten to know Jim, I have learned some of his story. He grew up in a Christian home and was brought up in an established church community. He gave his life to Christ at an early age. In high school, he mostly stayed out of trouble. Jim performed a ventriloquist act for youth groups, camp meetings, and other groups. He and his puppet, Jude, would share the plan of salvation and words of truth from God's Word, which Jim had been taught by his parents and his church.

But Jim confessed to me, "I learned the four spiritual laws, but I never learned any passion for God." He learned to be a good person but did not see the power of God in his life.

Late in high school, he saw two godly men, close friends of his family, leave their wives for other women. A seed was planted in his heart that would soon bear rotten fruit. If these "godly" men could reject their wives and families, was God real?

Entering a top-notch religious college, Jim continued to see people proclaiming Christ on one hand and not living it out on the other. He felt rejected socially because he was considered weird and not cool. He expected more from Christian friends. The lip service they gave to God was obviously secondary to being successful and having fun. They did not *feel* for God, so maybe God was not worth living for. Jim told me that at this fine, religious school, the resident staff "never opened their Bibles to share God's truth with me."

Hurt and disillusioned, Jim soon left the religious college for a state school. During an exit interview, the dean of students told him, "The problems you have now you will just take with you."

"This proved to be 100 percent true," Jim told me. He was taking his wounded heart with him.

Jim began a search for truth and fulfillment. He thought that what he had learned in Sunday school was not it. An avid reader, he soon wandered far from the faith of his parents, reading lots of books and looking under every rock to see if he could find something real. He married his high school sweetheart, Cindy, and they embarked on a journey toward self-fulfillment, with Jim leading the way. Feeling good and living for the moment became their goal. This eventually led to some alcohol and marijuana use. Was truth to be found in self-fulfillment?

When his first son was born a few years later, Jim was on the fast road to success. Receiving five promotions in his first long-term job, he was successful in his career and earning more and more. Pulling back from some of the "bad" things they were involved with, Jim and Cindy set out to build the American Dream. Maybe being a prosperous, "white picket fence" family would fill the ache in their hearts. In Jim's own words, they were "self-absorbed, pleasure-seeking parents." When his son was six years old, Jim bought his first expensive, brand-new car as a symbol that he had made it. It was his prized possession and a great source of joy.

Jim started to grow fat (quite literally) because of his pleasure-seeking ways. He and Cindy set to planning the extravagant vacations they had always dreamed of and now had earned with the last years of success. Everything was paying off.

But under the surface, there was still an ache in Jim's heart. All this was not enough. At times over the years, he felt as if the God of his early life was somewhere out there waiting for him.

A few months after buying that luxury car, Jim was downsized due to his company's financial trouble, he was in an accident in which his car was nearly totaled, and he learned that Cindy was pregnant again (unplanned, for having more children was not a part of his intention or their budget). Jim told me that at this time he was an angry, arrogant, self-absorbed man who showed no kindness to his wife or family. (This is a far cry from the man who made dinner with a servant's heart for Laura and me the first time we visited his house.)

These setbacks sent Jim into a bout of wrestling with God. He realized that he was not in control of his own life. His well-churched family knew he was down like never before, and even his brother—who at the time was not following God—pointed him to Jesus for answers.

Jim's brother invited him to help on a business computer project for a few days, and Jim took him up on the opportunity. But after visiting his brother in Wisconsin and making a little cash, it was a broken and dejected man who drove home from that trip. The struggle intensified the closer he got to home. The promises of God, Scripture verses from his growing-up years, started going around and around in his head. "It is no longer I who live, but Christ lives in me. So I live in this earthly body by trusting in the Son of God, who loved me and gave himself for me."[5]

Would he give up control?

Late that night, God won the struggle. Jim yielded himself to the love of Jesus. He decided he would believe the promises of God. Jim told me, "I woke up and everything was different. My fear and anger were gone; I had no anxiety. I was at total peace. I finally found what I was searching for."

What the facts and events of Jim's story don't fully express is the depth and magnitude of the struggle that went on in Jim's heart—concealed from everyone else's sight. You see, early in life, Jim found himself in a Christianity that was rule based, passionless, and hypocritical. When he saw from the professing Christians around him that the "godly" were not feeling for God, he assumed that it was not going to work for him, either. He felt stifled by the Christian life he observed and experienced, and he turned to different pursuits that he thought offered him joy and pleasure. Jim had to feel for something. He needed life and breath. Duty-driven Christianity was not for him. Just knowing the right facts was not enough. Doing the right things was not enough.

So he burned for his own pleasure and sought the good life in the way the world defines it. Of course, this did not work either, although for a long time it was seductive in its promise.

When God finally got Jim's attention (or when Jim finally listened to God and gave him his attention), Jim decided that he would take on the new life that Jesus offered and feel for and love God.

Jim still has that car he almost totaled. His pride and joy was restored at the body shop, but now it's just transportation. Jim told me it is a symbol to him of God's provision, grace, love, and redemption. Though Jim was just starting a new business, and his financial struggles continued past that night of decision, God always provided the funds to make those car payments. The new life that coursed through Jim's veins provided far more fulfillment and joy than his success ever had.

And I could see that truth the first time I met Jim as the leader of my small group.

〈〉〉

Jesus met a man a lot like Jim. Like Jim before God touched his life, this young man did not really understand what God required of him. Not embracing God with his whole heart, he lived his religion by doing his duty, while at the same time pursuing success and the good life.

He asked Jesus this question: "Good Teacher, what should I do to inherit eternal life?"[6]

Jesus answered the question with a question, as he often did. "Why do you call me good? . . . Only God is truly good. But to answer your question, you know the commandments: 'You must not commit adultery. You must not murder. You must not steal. You must not testify falsely. Honor your father and mother.'

"The man replied, 'I've obeyed all these commandments since I was young.'

"When Jesus heard his answer, he said, 'There is still one thing you haven't done. Sell all your possessions and give the money to the poor, and you will have treasure in heaven. Then come, follow me.' But when the man heard this he became very sad, for he was very rich."[7]

We can easily mistake the point of this story to be about gaining a future life that will never end after we die. We see the word *eternal,* and we shut off our minds, thinking, *I'm already saved; this is not a story for me.* Eternity with God is part of it, but it's not the whole story. The phrase *eternal life* is as much about *life* as it is about eternity. And it's as much about *quality* as it is about quantity or length. We never hear the words *eternal death* in Scripture. *Life* is always tied up with the word *eternal* in the writers' thoughts. It is a phrase not only about *eternal,* but also about *life.* It's about the life of the new Kingdom of God that Jesus is ushering in *right now.* This new age of salvation will have a new kind of eternal *life.*

When this religious and financially well-to-do man comes to Jesus and asks about eternal life, he is asking about a full, abundant, new kingdom vitality that he does not yet possess. You might paraphrase his question like this: "How can I be truly alive *from now into eternity* as part of your new kingdom?"

Isn't that the question we are all asking of Jesus? "How do I get this life you offer *now*? How do I grab hold of the joy and fulfillment I am looking for *now*?" Not just for a moment, not just in the distant future, but *from now on* into all eternity.

Jesus first asks the man about fulfilling his duties, "Have you done all the right things according to God's requirements?"

Like Jim, growing up in a Christian home but not having authentic passion for God, the man has lived a moral life; he has done his duty. But Jesus fingers the problem right away. He is pointing at the man's heart, as if to say, "I know you have done the right things, but it isn't enough, is it?"

The well-taught religious ruler replies that, yes, he has kept all the commandments since he was as a boy. But Jesus knows that if the man had found fulfillment in doing all these things, he wouldn't have asked the question in the first place. Jesus knows that doing your duty is not enough. The rich young ruler (along with many of us) remains empty—his soul is cold. He wants to feel the overwhelming presence of the new kingdom that Jesus promises.

Jesus' second question strikes right to the heart of the matter—and to the heart of the man. Again, knowing exactly the man's problem, Jesus says in essence, "What do you love most, and what have you given your life over to? If you want to have the full eternal life of my kingdom, declare to yourself and the world that you love God more than money. Give everything away and come learn from me." What an invitation—give up a few worldly goods to learn at the feet of the Son of God himself!

But the man walked away "very sad," Luke tells us, and we think we understand. But this word *sad* means more than it seems. It is the same Greek word used when Jesus says, "My soul is crushed with grief to the point of death."[8] So the man wasn't simply sad when he went away. He went away grieved of heart, *heartsick*. This was no passing sadness. He may well have remained heartsick and unfulfilled for the rest of his days, knowing what he needed yet not able to bring himself to do it.

We meet another man, called Zacchaeus, just a few verses later in Luke's Gospel. He is also a rich man, but he quickly falls in love with Jesus. He reaches out to touch and embrace the new life that is offered him. This time, Jesus does not need to ask that Zacchaeus give all his money away. Instead, Zacchaeus joyfully, of his own will, offers half his money to the poor and declares that he will make it right with whomever he has cheated. Jesus' joyful response is, "Salvation has come to this home today, for this man has shown himself to be a true son of Abraham. For the Son of Man came to seek and save those who are lost."[9] Again, we should not think about salvation as eternal life in the future. This full life of spontaneous giving has come to transform sinners from misery to joy *right now*.

‹‹›

In these stories from the Bible, I see parallels to our lives today.

Many peoples' spiritual lives are actually killing them. They are living by
duty, by rote, by fulfilling their responsibilities to church and family. Their
goal is to get all their ducks in a row, to believe all the right things and
know why they believe it, and to act according to God's commands.
They think perhaps if they can get it all right, they will finally be fulfilled.
But eventually they find that it doesn't matter how well they can do "all
the right things." They still find themselves dry, cold, and empty. They
do not live by love as God created them to. Many are like Jim and
Cindy, who could no longer stomach the passionless duty of their
spiritual lives. So they reject their faith and pursue the pleasures of this
world. Perhaps this is a more honest response to our emptiness.

Living by duty to please God just doesn't work. It didn't work for the
rich young ruler, so why do we think it will work for us? And even more
important, God is not pleased with our efforts. He wants so much more
for us, his precious children. As he said through his prophet Ezekiel, "I
will give them singleness of heart and put a new spirit within them. I will
take away their stony, stubborn heart and give them a tender, responsive heart."[10]

So put off the shackles of duty, legalism, and your attempts to be perfect.
Jesus didn't call you to a life like that. Take on a life of delighting in God
and loving him.

Will you join me on this journey? Come on, you have nothing to lose but
your cold heart, your tired feet, and your lack of joy.

Jesus calls you now to unshakable love, to unspeakable joy, to hope in
sorrow, and ultimate delight as you dwell in his presence. Lift your voice
with me now and let's cry out to God that he would open our hearts to all
the abundance in life he longs to give.

This is a call for you to breathe and breathe deeply.

Stop holding inside all that God created you to feel.

Stop struggling to keep your emotions in check, and start living in and through and with them. Emotion is the only motivation that is able to propel us toward a radically obedient and abundant life.

BLOG 03: BREATHE

ANDREW]·····[You talk about being "conditioned to think that a mature Christian man does not celebrate by displaying outward emotion." You're right. But it is more than that. Within my emotionally controlled world, I am "normal." Things are under control. Life is managed and my spiritual walk is ordered. I like it that way—it's easier that way. I long for the joy of an emotionally free life. Yet I am bound by fear . . . insecurity . . . pride. And so I continue to obey the "display rules." I pray for the confidence to break those rules.

JAMES]·····[What a wonderful invitation—to take on a life of delighting in God and loving Him. I guess the scary part of that prospect involves those old emotional display rules that we learned in church and elsewhere. It is risky to venture into areas that some people think are radical or over-the-top or (heaven help us!) charismatic.

MEDINE]·····[I think the reason there are so many nominal Christians in Africa is because many are taught the dos and don'ts of how to please God. Instead, we need to love Him with who we are and what we have.

TODD]·····[I think I let a lot of opportunities slip by because I'm not breathing right. I let a person leave the room, and then a few minutes later I regret not speaking to them when I had the chance. I wonder if I would have been ready to respond to Jesus as spontaneously as Zacchaeus did. Breathing requires a letting go. Breathing is necessary for life. I need to link the words "eternal" and "life" to each other as Jesus is ushering in this new kingdom of God right now (Right Now). I can be as excited about Christmas as when I was 6 years old. I can love others and it will show, and it will all come as easily as breathing.

BOB]·····[There should be exuberance in our daily lives as followers of Christ. Not that I want or need to be giggly and giddy all the time (or ever: I am not a giggly person). But having two kids did teach me something: If you want to enjoy little boys, you've got to get down on your hands and knees and be with them. Tussle. Wrassle. Hug 'em and hold 'em. My little boys (now men bigger than I am) taught me to loosen up, let go, and love. That's what this chapter talks about, in various ways. I am convinced there are ways to relate to God in this way, too, and that it has everything to do with enjoying "life together" with God and others. Some will be like Jim in this chapter. For others, we can serve as their "Jim."

When Jesus said "the truth will set you free," I bet he meant a "truth" big enough to free us to celebrate and feel life's pain and joy with others.

JULIE]·····[I so desire to go from a dry, cold, and empty life to one where I'm loving Jesus, getting to know him, being with him, and celebrating him. I would love this life RIGHT NOW. I've got the duty thing down pretty good—serve in ministry roles and roll up your sleeves and work for Christ. I have such a difficult time understanding how to have this abundant life while doing the things I've been encouraged and taught to do—the things that get me all stressed out when I think of all the responsibilities (raise godly children by being a godly example, open up your home and show hospitality, serve my spouse and be his helpmate, and the list goes on . . .). I certainly know all the head knowledge of how to do these things, but the feelings certainly aren't there.

ANA]·····[My parents suffered the internment of Japanese citizens during WWII— meaning they were put in concentration camps for being Japanese. After the war, there were quite a few of us Japanese kids growing up in a small, rural community. It was pretty clear from our parents that it was up to us to bring honor to ALL Japanese and prove by our performance that we were great American citizens. That meant we'd better be outstanding in all our activities. That became my life strategy: perform at top level or don't try.

When Jesus finally really touched my life after college, I was totally sold out. However, I ended up transferring my "value based on performance" work ethic from my life activities to my walk with God. In no time, I became an outstanding Christian. My heart was truly engaged at first, but somewhere along the way the obligations began to outweigh the joy.

Enter the discussion at www.faithfulfeelings.com.

MY BLOG

_____

_____

_____

_____

04 Bound

All twenty hijackers died in the 9/11 attacks, except for one.

Zacarias Moussaoui had trained to be the pilot of a plane that some believe was intended to crash into the White House. Fortunately, Moussaoui was sitting in prison on the day of the attacks. Federal investigators had detained him on immigration charges after he had paid $8,000 to train on a Boeing 747 flight simulator. He was tried and convicted as a 9/11 conspirator, and today he is serving a life sentence in a federal penitentiary in Colorado.

During the penalty phase of his trial, Moussaoui took the witness stand and delighted in the tragic events of 9/11. According to AP reporter Michael Sniffen, "Moussaoui defiantly proclaimed he felt 'no regret, no remorse.' . . . He said heart-rending testimony of victims and relatives had disgusted him, and he wished they had suffered more. Watching a Navy officer sobbing in court made his day."[1]

A few days later, Rudy Giuliani, the mayor of New York City at the time of the attacks, testified at Moussaoui's trial. He said, "[9/11] was the worst experience of my life. I hope it was the worst experience I will ever have or the country will ever have. . . . Every day I think about it. Every day some part of it comes back to me. I can see a person jumping, see the body parts or see a little boy or girl at a funeral."[2] At one point, a video of the Twin Towers tragedy was shown in the courtroom. When Moussaoui saw the images of people jumping to their deaths to avoid burning in the inferno, it struck him as funny. He laughed out loud.

The day Moussaoui laughed, it was all over the news. I heard one reporter say, "The government could have closed its case right there." With that laugh, every juror knew the truth.

Moussaoui's emotions had betrayed his evil heart.

〈〈〉〉

We have been told by philosophers, scientists, and psychologists that emotions are unreliable impulses, leftovers from our evolutionary past that we have little control over. Our higher reason should trump or ignore emotions whenever they lead us down the wrong path. I have read and written a lot of arguments about why these scholars and scientists are wrong, but I have yet to hear a better argument than Moussaoui's laugh.

Emotion is not an illogical reflex, unreliable and fickle. Emotions cut through all our talk, all our spin, and take us right to the truth of the matter. That is what God created emotions to do, and that is why (as we shall see) God so freely commands emotions all through the Bible.

We know *intuitively* what we deny *rationally*. We understand what people are thinking by observing their emotions. We know some of the truth of a person's life from the laughter in their voice. We've all been hurt by someone expressing an emotion that told us the truth.

My first serious romantic relationship was as a senior in high school. She was a cheerleader; I was the starting center on the basketball team. She was valedictorian and homecoming queen; I was president of the student body. We thought we had it all together.

When graduation arrived, my grandparents drove all the way from New Jersey for the festivities. They rarely came to Chicago to see us, and when they did, it was only for a few days. Grandpa Elliott, "Pop-Pop" to me, was a Baptist minister on a small salary. He and my grandmother never had much. Having lived in a parsonage all their adult lives, it wasn't until they retired that they bought their first small house. Through college, I made a point of flying out to see them every year for a long weekend. I slept in the converted attic that Grandpa had renovated with his own hands. (I will always remember the carpet—all different rectangles of every color and variety that he had expertly patched together from free scraps he had picked up at the local carpet store. This carpet collage looked great, and you wouldn't mind having it in your basement family room—it was pretty cool.)

I was proud to be an Elliott and to have this godly couple as part of my heritage. To this day, my aunts and uncles on my mom's side think of my father's parents, Grandma and Grandpa Elliott, as Christian royalty. They set an example of grace and kindness for everyone who knew them.

But apparently this simple preacher and his wife did not meet my girlfriend's expectations. At the graduation banquet, she ignored and avoided my family and me while lavishing her attention on others. Her emotional lack of desire to get to know my grandparents may have been the beginning of the end of our relationship.

Looking back, I think her lack of emotion toward my family that night showed me the truth about what was important to her. As we began the summer and went on to college, I got to thinking, *Maybe she doesn't like me for who I really am.* Maybe part of what had drawn her to me in the first place was the image I seemed to project.

It took me several years to get over that ache in my heart, several years before I was ready to get close to another girl. This time, it seemed the girl thought I'd hung the moon. It was written all over her face every time she looked into my eyes. No girl had ever thought of me like that before. I now knew the difference between true love and just being cool. This girl knew I wasn't perfect, but she loved me for who I was—even my often too-serious demeanor, my spiritual discontent, and my sometimes off-the-wall sense of humor.

The next (and last) time my grandparents were able to make the long drive out from New Jersey, it was for a second graduation party—this time, my graduation from Wheaton College. I was amazed as I watched Laura greet my precious grandparents with a big hug, enjoy getting to know them, and even take time to hold my grandma's hand as she talked to her. Her emotion, genuinely expressed, revealed the truth about her. It told me a lot. She wanted to love the people I loved.

As you probably already guessed, Laura is now my wife and the mother of our three beautiful children.

Emotional moments and emotional understanding often lead to the greatest clarity in our thinking and understanding. These are the lightbulb moments. They capture the truth in a snapshot, as no amount of rational thinking can.

<‹›>

The problem is that we're taught by the church and our culture that emotions are not reliable indicators of truth. As a result, we are conditioned to believe that our feelings are trivial and useless.

My pastor loves to use the "train illustration." Have you heard that one? Many speakers like to use it. He said in one sermon, "Feelings don't take you anywhere good; they make a lousy engine but a wonderful caboose." (I always shake my head and wonder about all the things that the emotion of love motivated Jesus to do.)

"Enough about what my feelings are," he said. Yet, in the very same sermon he was unable to get away from his own emotional motivation.

He told a story about his sisters-in-law coming to faith after twenty-eight years of having family members faithfully praying for their salvation. Many nights, he and his wife labored in prayer for these women, often with tears of deep concern and emotion. What motivated those prayers? What powered the train? The love he and his wife felt for her sisters and the great desire they had to see them begin a relationship with God!

And what made for a great sermon illustration? What brought my pastor's truth home? What compelled eager ears and deeper under-standing among his congregation? Simply this: a story brimming with feeling and emotion.

〈〈〉〉

I feel we have been bound by our Christian culture. We have been conditioned to keep our emotions under control, strapped down, boxed away.

I was struck recently by a bulletin from the Biblical Counseling Center. In a feature article titled "Feelings or Faith?" Jeff Temple writes, "God never intended our feelings to guide our life or to gauge our commitment to Him. Over the decades in a godless culture, we have come to accept an extremely feeling oriented way of viewing life. We fall in and out of love based on our feelings. We marry people that make us 'feel good.' . . . We even join churches that we feel are good for us and where we feel happy. [Is that a bad thing?] When the feelings are no longer good, we feel depressed or move on to another 'feeling based' choice. Biblical living is not based on feelings but on God's unfaltering commitment to us as His children." He ends the article by saying, "Live by faith, not by feeling so that the end brings honor and glory to Him!"[3]

So, okay, let's go with this. Men, imagine this scenario: *You go home after work, sit your wife down at the table, look into her eyes, and tell her, "I just want to talk to you." After she picks herself up off the floor, you say, "Honey, I love you, but any feeling I had for you died several years ago. I am satisfied with our relationship, and you are a very good wife. My love is no longer about what I feel. It has grown into the true agape love of the New Testament, which is about my unfaltering commitment to you, not how I feel."*

Men, I said *imagine* this. Please, do *not* try this at home.

The point is that relationships, actions, marriage—life—are *absolutely dependent* on feelings and emotions, and they are very much a part of the truth of our lives. We know this intuitively—how can you talk about love apart from feeling?

Yet, pastors and Bible teachers and theologians consistently tell us that we can love—*agape,* that "special form" of Christian love we find in the Bible—without actually having to *feel* much of anything.

Isn't it fascinating that our Christian culture takes the emotion out of an emotion?

〈〉〉

Emotion was made to supply the energy and vitality in our lives. It was meant to work hand in hand with reason and logic to guide our decisions.

How do we make our greatest decisions? Do we marry a person because we admire his or her spelling ability? Do we choose to become a kinder-garten teacher because we get summers off, so we can go fishing? I'm not saying we don't employ logic in these decisions, but logic is always pulling our emotions and our emotions are always pulling our logic. On and on it goes, in a seamless interaction that only God could design. We cannot separate reason and emotion. They are linked in such a strong way that whenever we try to think of one without the other, the result is a mixed-up statement like "emotion is the caboose," a statement that doesn't hold up to logic or science—or the Bible.

If the teachings of our age are true, who should be the most scientific, most rational, most logical thinker our world has ever known? Wouldn't it be the wisest guy who ever lived? Well, of course. And that would be Solomon.

You may remember that Solomon was told in a dream that he could ask for anything in the world that he wanted. When Solomon asked God for wisdom, God replied, "I will give you what you asked for! I will give you a wise and understanding heart such as no one else has had or ever will have!"[4] This promise is immediately followed by a story to show us just how smart Solomon was. You might suspect that the story would be about science, literature, or mathematics. You would be wrong.

Emotion is at the center.

Two prostitutes come to the king and have a big dilemma; in fact, they are in a real knock-down, drag-out catfight. Each woman recently gave birth to a baby boy, and one of the boys has now died. The dispute is about which woman's son is dead.

One of the women explains the situation to the king: "She got up in the night and took my son from beside me while I was asleep. She laid her dead child in my arms and took mine to sleep beside her. And in the morning when I tried to nurse my son, he was dead! But when I looked more closely in the morning light, I saw that it wasn't my son at all."

Then the other woman, I'm sure, violently interrupts. "It certainly was your son, and the living child is mine."

Before she can finish, the other mother shoots back, "No . . . the living child is mine, and the dead one is yours."

You get the idea. This is a fight where the winner gets the most important prize—a healthy baby. The stakes are high.

Imagine if Solomon were a lawyer in our day and age, getting ready for the courtroom. It would be a *Law and Order* episode, and he would say, "Let's reconstruct the exact events. What was the timetable? When in the night did this happen? We need to take hair samples from the dead baby so we can match the DNA to the mom. Can we get a polygraph machine in here?"

Solomon doesn't have those sophisticated scientific tools, but he knows something else that will get right to the truth. He stops both women short with his authoritative voice: "Bring me a sword." And then he utters something really bizarre: "Cut the living child in two, and give half to one woman and half to the other!"

This slices right to the heart of the matter, just as Solomon intended it to. The woman who knows it is her boy that is still alive is overcome with motherly love. "Oh no, my lord!" she exclaims. "Give her the child—please do not kill him!"

The lying and jealous prostitute says, "All right, he will be neither yours nor mine; divide him between us!"

Her response made it clear to everybody in the room that the woman who loved the boy was the mother. The other mom's jealousy gave her away. All Israel was amazed at Solomon's ability to find the truth and do justice.[5]

So, the first story told about the wisest man ever is about how he made a *just* and *true* decision based on the *emotional* response of a mother who dearly loved her child.

Emotions tell us *a lot,* and they are so important in finding out the truth in life. Unfortunately, we are bound by a culture that tells us otherwise.

〈 〉〉

We have also been bound up and taken hostage by the rationalism of our scientific age.

Our culture is mesmerized by its own technical achievements. The power and convenience that have come from these inventions are really amazing. Scientists work full-time to unlock the mystery of the human genome; and teams of inventors work twelve-hour days, six days a week, to make the next generation computer chip faster and use less power.

My latest computer is a fast, wi-fi–equipped, wide-screen, mega-efficiency laptop—a first for me on all counts. I love it. I no longer have computer lust—which I felt for years when I had the cheapest desktop computer that would get the job done.

Who has bewitched us into thinking that all this makes any difference? If our family relationships stink, who cares that we have the coolest HD wide screen on the block?

Our technical achievements seem to crown reason as king and blind us to the importance of our emotions. If we can just get bigger, faster, better, and stronger, maybe *that* will satisfy us. Believing *in* science and technology keeps us bound.

But no matter what technical achievements we make, how tall we can build our buildings, how fast we can make our cars, or how energy-efficient we can make our dishwashers, our feelings will still be what really matters.

Psychologists, and those who dissect human behavior, have looked for a way to measure, gauge, medicate, and control emotions. What is their origin, what is their location, where do they reside in the human psyche? From Charles Darwin to William James, many intellectual giants of the modern age have tried to disengage and belittle our emotions as a lower evolutionary trait than our reason.

Darwin taught that our emotional responses were leftovers from our animal past. You know how you tend to clench your teeth when you're angry? Or how, when you're really mad, you may even bare your teeth and just want to say *Grrrr*? According to Darwin, these responses come down to us from a distant ancestor that actually defended himself by biting. So now, when we get mad, our body naturally prepares itself to battle with its teeth.[6]

When was the last time you bit your best friend in an argument?

Amazingly enough, these kinds of ideas eventually led to the neglect of emotion in psychology. According to J. J. Campos and K. C. Barrett, "by 1933, some psychologists were predicting that the term *emotion* would eventually disappear from psychology . . . a prediction that almost came true in the 1970s."[7]

Because they believed that emotion was a lower evolutionary impulse that could not really be measured or understood, psychologists of the last generation essentially said, "Let's get on with studying something that we can look at scientifically." According to Ronald Koteskey, psychologists often considered emotion as "disorganized processes" that "interfere with the orderly behavioral laws they are trying to study."[8]

‹‹›

The idea that emotion is a lower, less important part of our human nature and that science and logic should prevail over emotion is alien to the worldview found in the Bible. Biblical definitions of words such as *heart, mind,* and *know* all have the sense of a *totality* of mind, will, and emotion. When we're told to "know" this, or to have the "mind" of Christ, or to do something with our "heart," the particular emphasis may be different from word to word and verse to verse, but all refer to a totality of our humanness—logic, thinking, and emotion.

In the most recent studies, we're beginning to find that science actually agrees with the Bible's way of looking at *mind* and *heart.*

Antonio Damasio is a guy who studies the anatomy and function of human brains. He wrote a book called *The Feeling of What Happens.* Damasio has studied people with really crazy brain injuries. One patient he calls S has a brain that cannot recognize fear. She cannot produce a look of fear on her face, nor does she recognize fear on the face of another. S was unnaturally positive in demeanor, very forthcoming, and had little caution in her relationships. She formed bonds easily, often with people who took advantage of her.

Damasio ran a test in which people with a normal capacity for fear were asked to rank a series of human faces according to how trustworthy they appeared. Most could instinctively tell who the really dangerous people were, but S could not tell any difference between the faces; all were equally trustworthy to her. S had good intelligence and good skills, and she was a caring mother. But her lack of emotional sensitivity to fear left her vulnerable to a sometimes cruel and dangerous world, and this was borne out in her life.[9]

Another patient, Elliot, was intelligent, smart, and skilled. Sometime before he came to see Dr. Damasio, Elliot began getting headaches and was diagnosed with a brain tumor. After a skilled team of surgeons removed the growth and Elliot regained consciousness, it was clear that he had retained his intelligence. His family was happy that he was okay. He was a good husband and father.

However, as he returned to normal living, he was no longer able to order his life. Faced with going to work, he needed to be told what to do. At work, he could not keep on task, and he easily became distracted by trivial things. He could spend all afternoon trying to figure out whether to organize a file by date, subject, or size. He could not prioritize one task above another. He could perform any single task just as well as ever, but to figure out how much time to give to it was beyond him. He was fired from his job. And fired. And fired again.

Elliot was eventually forced to apply for disability because he could not work successfully. The psychologists who interviewed Elliot saw that he had a great memory of the events of his life, was intelligent, and could make meaningful conversation. At first glance, Elliot seemed very capable. The reviewers declared him mentally competent, and his claims for disability were repeatedly denied.

His troubles continued. Lacking discernment and ignoring the warnings of friends, he lost his life savings in a failed business venture with a man with a bad reputation. His wife divorced him, and a second marriage soon ended in divorce as well. He could make no good plans for the future because he had no capability of judgment.

Enter Dr. Damasio and his team of brain researchers. After numerous mental tests, Damasio determined that Elliot possessed a very high IQ and a very good memory. Puzzled by this in light of Elliot's history, Damasio realized that he had evaluated only Elliot's intellect and intelligence while ignoring his emotions. He found that Elliot could tell his own tragic story with only detached interest. There was no anguish over his firings, failed marriages, and inability to lead a normal life. After hours of talking, there was no hint of sadness, or frustration with the endless questions, or any emotional reaction to the process. He felt no love for music he had once enjoyed; he felt no sorrow when shown gory images of destruction or devastation.

Elliot knew just as many facts as he had before the tumor was removed, but he felt nothing for anything. Next, Damasio tested Elliot's social and moral reasoning with a battery of problem-solving tests. He came out totally normal or even above average—that is, on paper tests.

Elliot could *reason* out what the moral choice should be, but with all the variable choices of real life, he was totally incapable of making a good decision between right and wrong. His lack of emotions prevented him from attaching any significance to a particular choice. With no emotion to guide his reason, he could not choose. Elliot was no longer a rational person.[10]

Damasio draws some powerful conclusions: "The powers of reason and the experience of emotion decline together, and their impairment stands out in a neuropsychological profile within which basic attention, memory, intelligence, and language appear so intact that they could never be invoked to explain the patients' failures in judgment."[11]

In other words, science tells us that emotion is necessary to make right and true and practical decisions. Without it, we are like Elliot.

〈 〉〉

I read a book review recently with the subtitle "Biographies of three influential Americans who put heart above brain." As if the conservative critic were somehow above these liberal icons who were driven by their passions. Let me tell you, this guy was as passionately conservative as the three subjects were passionately liberal. They were all passionate about what they thought was the truth.

Occasionally, I'll catch a few minutes of the number one radio talk-show host, Rush Limbaugh. As infrequently as I listen, I have often heard Rush go on at length about how conservatives follow the facts and liberals just follow their emotions. But here's the funny thing: Listen to Rush for more than twenty-eight seconds and you will know why he is successful. He's passionate and emotional like few others. He cares greatly about the conservative cause. You may disagree with his ideas, but you could never accuse him of being less passionate than his opponents.

Have you ever heard a football coach say something like this after winning the big game: "Their team played with heart, but we did not allow our hearts to get in the way of our superior brain power. We decided to forget about our feelings and just concentrate on the *X*'s and *O*'s." Absurd, isn't it?

Any basketball diehard like me would say that March Madness is the best time of year on the sports calendar. That is when sixty-four college teams square off to settle the national championship. We enjoy watching the top-flight schools showcase their talent, but what we really love is the big upset. When a smaller school—say a fourteenth seed—knocks off the number three perennial basketball powerhouse in their bracket, the commentators can't seem to stop talking about it for days on end. That kind of upset is what brings us up out of our chairs with a spontaneous cheer. The number three powerhouse has the better players, the larger crowd, and probably the bigger-money coach. But the fourteenth seed wins on tenacity, diving for every loose ball and leaving their guts out on the floor on every possession. A winning team may have a good strategy and a good heart. But a great team will have a good strategy and a *great* heart.

Despite what our culture teaches, we do not claim the moral high ground by claiming that our brains rule our passions while our opponents rely on their feelings.

We claim the high ground when our passions clearly match our convictions. That's when people can see the truth in our eyes and hear it in our voices. That's true heart. And that's what wins games, makes good radio talk-show hosts, and decides close elections.

〈〉〉

One of my favorite writers on the subject of emotion is a man named Robert C. Solomon. If you were to go to your local college library, access their philosophical database, and search for the word *emotion,* about fifty bazillion books and articles written by this guy would pop up. (Well, maybe only a few dozen—but that's *a lot!*) Solomon says, after spending much of his adult life thinking about how emotions work, "The brunt of this theory is the total demolition of the age-old distinctions between emotion and reason, passion and logic. . . . What we shall find is that emotions turn out to be far more logical, far more complex, far more sophisticated, and far more a part and parcel of reason than most philosophers have ever imagined."[12]

Emotion serves to guide us in every aspect of decision making and daily life. A life led only by reason or logic is impossible. That is not how God created us. Emotions are an essential part of the engine, whether we like it or not.

We all remember the pointy-eared, green-blooded half Vulcan named Mr. Spock in the science-fiction series *Star Trek*. The Vulcans spent generations training themselves to eradicate their emotions and embrace pure logic and reason. This allows them to achieve great things in the sci-fi series as they walk unsmiling through life, looking at the pros and cons of every situation in order to make the best decision possible.

In the movie *Star Trek II*, Admiral James Kirk is inspecting a refitting of his beloved Starship *Enterprise*, and Spock is training the new crew. In an early scene, Kirk is with a new Vulcan captain-in-training and makes a joke. The Vulcan says in response, "Humor . . . it is a difficult concept . . . it is not logical."

As we laugh, we are struck by the awkward emptiness of a life without emotion.

During the inspection, Kirk receives a message that a top-secret science project called Genesis is in trouble. Responding to the distress call, Kirk tells Spock to take command of the *Enterprise* so they can go investigate the trouble. Spock knows that Kirk is longing to take command, but Kirk insists that Spock be the one to captain the mission. Spock knows that, logically, Kirk is the better captain. What follows is an interesting dialogue.

SPOCK: "Jim . . . you proceed from a false assumption. I'm a Vulcan. I have no ego to bruise."

KIRK: "You're about to remind me that logic alone dictates your actions?"

SPOCK: "I would not remind you of that which you know so well. If I may be so bold, it was a mistake for you to accept promotion. Commanding a starship is your first, best destiny. Anything else is a waste of material. . . . In any case, were I to invoke logic, logic clearly dictates that the needs of the many outweigh the needs of the few."

KIRK: "Or the one."

Spock's foil on the show was always the ship's doctor, the volatile Dr.
McCoy. During a discussion of the power of the Genesis project to create
and destroy life, Spock says, after a typical emotional outburst by McCoy,
"Really, Dr. McCoy, you must learn to govern your passions. They will be
your undoing. Logic suggests—"

McCoy cuts him off mid-sentence, "Logic? My God, the man's talking
about logic! We're talking about universal Armageddon! You green-
blooded, inhuman—"

Just then, the conversation is cut off by a vicious surprise attack by Khan,
Kirk's archenemy, who had been banished to a barren planet. Severely
damaged, the *Enterprise* is breaking apart, and the proud Kirk seems to
have no choice but to surrender himself to the revenge-seeking Khan.

In what follows, Mr. Spock puts the needs of the many above the needs
of the one and uses his immense Vulcan strength to enter a radiation-
containment area to make essential repairs to the ship's power genera-
tor. The *Enterprise* zips to warp speed just as the Genesis machine goes
off, obliterating all life in the quadrant.

Admiral Kirk rushes to the main engineering area and finds Spock
dying of radiation poisoning, his face rapidly disfiguring. Kirk is now
faced with losing his best friend and comrade. Before their hands
touch through the Plexiglas of the containment area, Spock and Kirk
have one final conversation.

SPOCK: "Ship—out of danger?"

KIRK: "Yes."

SPOCK: "Do not grieve, Admiral—it is logical: the needs of the many
outweigh—"

KIRK: "The needs of the few."

SPOCK: "Or the one."[13]

Faced with a choice between his own death and the death of all on the
ship, Spock easily and willingly gives up his life without a tear or any

regret. He ends with the Vulcan blessing, "Live long and prosper." As Kirk slumps to the floor in utter grief, all he is able to say is a weak "no."

For the eulogy, Kirk is barely able to get the words out. He says, "Of all the souls I have encountered in my travels, his was the most human."

I believe our culture has made us into a bunch of Mr. Spocks. We have been told we must aspire to our "best nature"—that we are "most human" when we are thinking, reasoning, living by logic. Spock, so we're told, used logic to face death head-on and do his duty for humanity.

But Spock is a figment of this generation's imagination.

Overcoming our emotions in order to become fully human is something that cannot be done. God did not make emotions to be ruled by logic; he made them as something we use to make decisions and understand the world.

The character of Spock is impossible in itself. The example of Elliot tells us that much. Without emotion, Spock would be the most useless person on the Starship *Enterprise.*

〈〈〉〉

We are faced with a choice: Will we choose the Jesus of our rational age or the Jesus of history?

Who is our Jesus? The Spock-like Jesus who overcame his emotions in Gethsemane to logically choose the many over the one? The Jesus who did the right thing no matter how he felt? Do we embrace the words of author John Eldredge, who writes, "Equating the heart *with* emotion is the same nonsense as saying that love is a feeling. Surely, we know that love is more than *feeling* loving; for if Christ had followed his emotions, he would not have gone to the cross for us"?[14]

No. Without a great motivating love, Spock would never have chosen that radiation chamber.

And Jesus would never have chosen the cross.

In the Bible, we are faced with a different Jesus, motivated by *deep love*. For the *joy* set before him, he endured the pain of the cross.[15] Do you choose a Spock-like Jesus, with rational and logical thought taking the lead, dying on that cross having done his duty? Or do you choose the Jesus whose love held him to the cross when at any moment he could have called down a legion of angels to take him directly to God the Father?[16] Love propelled him through the horror for your sake.

The choice you make may decide how you live out the rest of your Christian life.

If we really believe that Jesus' great emotional love is what motivated the Cross, we will live differently. Instead of just talking about how we can love people, our love will motivate self-sacrificing service. Instead of serving others out of obligation, we will be driven to serve with *joy*. Instead of pursuing just deeper knowledge, we will pursue a new and deeper *heart*.

As John Calvin writes, "How can the mind be aroused to taste the divine goodness without at the same time being wholly kindled to love God in return? For truly, that abundant sweetness which God has stored up for those who fear him cannot be known without at the same time powerfully moving us."[17]

BLOG 04: BOUND

STEPHEN]·····[It's easy to look at the Spock picture, laugh, and think, "Well, I don't sign up to that really." But in my heart there is this desire to be "free of all this" using my own strength. To be the hero who overcomes his own "pathetic little emotions" to do great deeds for the good of all and to do it all on my own.

JAMES]·····[I have known the story about Solomon and the two mothers for decades. But I never looked at the story as proof that our emotions reveal the true nature of our hearts. Emotion really was the surest means that Solomon could utilize to discern truth and justice. Sounds like emotion is an engine and not a caboose to me!

MARIAN]·····[We are truly fearfully and wonderfully made. And what is more, God has made us in His Image. He is a thinking being Whose thoughts created the intricacies of the universe. He is an emotional Being Who loves and relates. Those two attributes are held together in perfect harmony in Him. Why should we be any different?

I desire to be loving and caring. I desire to see people made whole because they relate to God, to others, and to themselves in love. I ask God to guard me against thinking my way through life rather than really living. Like a rainbow, He puts colour and variety into the darkest day. I see emotions as the colour of life set against the grey facts of logic. We need both, and I bless God for that truth. God's Word says we shall know the truth and the truth shall set us free. Jesus is the Truth, as well as being the Way and the Life. I ask for help to listen to my own heart, my reactions, my attitudes, so that they may be challenged by the truth. I thank Him for the Cross, His love expressed through obedience to the Father's will, for our salvation. I choose for my heart to be brought to life as I consider the Cross and the great cost of His love.

BOB]·····[Great Calvin quote! This chapter makes me wonder at a perhaps hidden motivation of those who fear emotion and belittle feelings. It strikes me that if you can limit people's basis for decision to one thing, like "reason" or "facts," then it is easier to control that person. You can come at that person with more compelling logic (there's always someone out there smarter than we are), or more pertinent facts, and you can discredit what that person thinks so he will think what you think instead. If this is true, then emotion might be part of a very important defense mechanism. You may not need to give in to what someone says they can "prove" with certain facts or arguments alone. What "reason" dictates needs to square with other considerations too, including "feelings." What we're talking about here, then, is not "truth" dictated by feelings rather than fact, but "truth" that consists of both "factual" or "reasoned" components and components arising from our emotional faculties.

SARAH]·····[Honestly, I think that a point made in this chapter heads back to my fear of people. Often, my emotions are not "in check." What if I don't feel like taking the trash out? Often, I won't show my emotions to my husband—fearing what he will think of me if I let him know I don't want to take out the trash. Sometimes that is why my emotions stay "hidden." I need a heart change to get my emotions "out of the box." Or remove the pride and let people know exactly what is inside—surely I would be quicker to change.

Enter the discussion at www.faithfulfeelings.com.

MY BLOG

 Release

This past weekend, my good friend Dave told me about the movie *Pride and Prejudice.* Have you seen that one? He characterized it as the ultimate chick flick. You know the definition of a chick flick: a movie that your wife or girlfriend wants you to watch with her, curled up on the couch, snuggled under a hand-knitted afghan, sipping a warm cup of hot chocolate.

Well, with or without the hot chocolate, it turns out that *Pride and Prejudice* is a pretty good movie.

This classic Jane Austen tale has all the elements of a great story, a story that pushes all your buttons. A beautiful young woman, Elizabeth, longs for love and wants to get married. The suitable suitor who fits her station in life is dreary and boring to her. Instead, she finds her heart taken with a serious-minded nobleman, the dashing Mr. Darcy. Darcy, of the landed gentry, scorns love and finds no woman worthy of his affections until meeting the feisty Elizabeth.

All his misconceptions about women fall flat in the spell of her oversized personality and simple, unadorned beauty. She is utterly spellbinding and mysterious to him. His total existence becomes tied up in being found worthy by her. There follows a string of missteps, misunderstandings, and missed moments where Elizabeth and Mr. Darcy could have declared their true feelings to each other and been free to pursue love. As you watch, your whole heart is overtaken with a desire that they find the words to express to each other their deepest feelings.

Guys, no matter how hard you try to hold it inside, you're going to cry. Just get over the macho thing and let a tear or two streak down your face. For one thing, the woman in your life will love you all the more for your sensitive side. But more importantly, for a couple of hours you will be pulled out of your box of emotional control and made to feel deeply. It's not just a chick flick. It's a heart-wrenching tale of true love that applies to all of us.

Pride and Prejudice is a good movie because it grabs your heart. That's why we are drawn to many things in culture and the arts.

How do you choose your favorite songs? Isn't it because they awaken something in your heart, something you connect with on a deep emotional level? Why do you love a particular photograph or painting? Because they are images that make you *feel* something.

Our relationships, of course, are driven by feelings. A person can grab your heart as much as a song or a movie—although that passion can be anger as well as love.

Our biggest decisions are guided by our emotions.

If you follow professional football, you heard all the talk during the 2006 season about the impending retirement of Brett Favre, the superstar quarterback of the Green Bay Packers. "Will he retire or won't he?" The speculation filled the sports pages of many newspapers. After an ultrahuman number of consecutive games started—237 and counting at the beginning of the 2007 season—this future Hall of Famer is now well past the age when most football players retire. How long can his body hold up to the brutal nature of professional football? I heard one commentator say that the only thing that could make Favre continue to subject his body to being hunted down by 342-pound linemen would be his passion for the game. His heart would drive him to play—or to retire. His decision would be guided by his deepest feelings.

Emotions also drive our relationships with God. Indeed, God wants our emotions to drive us toward him, just as passion drove Brett Favre to suit up for another year of football in 2007. God wants our hearts to long for him like Elizabeth Bennett longed for Mr. Darcy. God's desire is that we can do nothing else, think nothing else, be nothing else, until we are completely his.

So much of this seems so obvious, and yet we don't get it. We do so many things to *stuff* our emotions, to push our passions down, to fight the feelings we experience in daily life. We repress ourselves constantly, daily, mastering our emotional states so they don't show, don't affect us, and don't reveal us.

We put our feelings in a box.

Let me tell you about the box. The box gets stuffed when we think too hard about our emotions—what they should or shouldn't be—instead of allowing ourselves to feel freely. The box is about being paranoid to tell those closest to us when we are hurting, angry, or afraid. When we are in the box, it is all about control. When we are trapped in the box, we would never think of letting loose with a hallelujah or an amen at church, let alone giving a big bear hug to a friend we haven't seen in years.

We all live in the box at one time or another.

But the box is not always about *controlling* our emotions.

People whose emotions are totally out of control are in the same box. They're in the box when their tantrums, outbursts, or steamrolling of other people are their *modus operandi*. They are surely in the box when their desire for material things takes over their lives and their credit card debt is piling up fast. They're in the box when any kind of compulsion or addiction takes over their lives.

Does this sound contradictory? Perhaps. But the problem is the same. Addictions, compulsions, and emotional flashpoints are behaviors that come out of emotional repression and damage. They can be evidence of a person who has lived in an emotional box for a long time—either someone who bursts out periodically or one who acts out through some sort of secret, driven behavior.

The compulsive or explosive person and the repressed or controlled person represent two sides of the same coin. The scary truth is that those who seem out of control and those who seem completely *in* control are in the same box.

〈 〈 〉 〉

Two great thinkers of our age have looked at emotion in two different ways. Both views make the same mistake and end up in the same box.

The first view is that of German philosopher Immanuel Kant. Entire courses in college are devoted to Kant's ideas, and some believe that he is the most influential philosopher of our age. If you read people who have studied his writings, those that can understand them will tell you that he believed that obeying and loving God was all about *doing our duty.* Kant believed that love was about *doing an act of love* even if the emotion of love was absent. God commands us to love, and this love is obeying his command and doing our obedient duty. The feeling of emotion is separate and not even necessary. To Kant, love is the rational intention of love acted out by the will, regardless of the feeling of love.

To Kant, reason is king.

As I studied Kant, it came to me that the way this kind of thinking plays out in our churches is in the teaching that what is important is "doing the loving action" from which, supposedly, our emotions will follow. Many teachers, when talking about marriage, say, "Don't get hung up on the fact that you don't love your wife like you used to. Just keep working at doing nice things for her and eventually your emotions will catch up." Or, you might also be told how dangerous our emotions are, that they are always getting us into trouble and we cannot listen to them. To do otherwise is seen as being irresponsible and out of control. We're taught that it's better to do our Christian duty, to perform the act of love or joy. The actual emotional feeling is not so important—and is actually a bit dangerous.

I recall a church situation in which a man, Steve, had been assigned by the church as a spiritual mentor to a friend of mine named Carl. Steve's job was to bring mentoring wisdom and spiritual guidance into Carl's life. One time, Carl was sitting in a discipleship meeting, and Steve said to him, "I have this word I have been praying for your life, Carl. I have found over the years that God will give a specific word to me that characterizes people I mentor. This may be just what you need to be encouraged and strengthened."

But whatever the word turned out to be, it wasn't helpful to Carl. Not because of the word itself, but because Carl realized that Steve was offering it apart from any real feeling toward him. It was meant to be a deep, spiritual moment, but the spiritual word had little to do with what Carl was struggling with or who Carl was as a person. Steve spoke this word of encouragement because it was something on his to-do list. It was a "should." Steve was doing a Christian duty, but he had never taken the time to get emotionally close to Carl and love him as a person. Sure, all the formal requirements set by the church were fulfilled, but Steve was not genuinely loving enough to be a true mentor. Carl was left hurting and alone.

Like Kant, we Christians focus so much on duty—fulfilling the list of things we are supposed to do—without honest and genuine heartfelt emotions behind the actions. We elevate reason and duty above true emotion and compassion. That leaves us, and those we are trying to love, empty.

And we push ourselves into the box.

Another German philosopher, Friedrich Schleiermacher, came on the scene around the time of Kant's death and was one of the many academics in the early 1800s who were talking about and reacting to the new, radical ideas thought up by Kant.

Schleiermacher (a good German name—almost impossible to pronounce!) believed that *feeling* was what was most important in living out God's Word. The true essence of religion was to be found in religious experience that was not weighed down by science, facts, or argument. An authentic relationship with God must be found by looking within ourselves and finding a true meaning that is greater than what our minds know.

If we say that, for Kant, reason was king, then for Schleiermacher, emotion was king.

But there are problems with both of these views.

When emotion is king, what we believe can too easily be diminished into something of low importance. We tend to think that we can just follow our hearts, against all facts to the contrary. Just love others, and it will work out fine. But many a sad marriage has been built on that kind of thinking. Sometimes, people say things like "your passions will lead you where you really belong." For some, the need to find emotional peace by "knowing" they are in the center of God's will is more important than following God's simple moral commands. As if we could please God with a passionate heart yet live however we want.

I have a friend, Marie, who has suffered through two failed marriages to men who claimed to be Christians yet lived like the devil. They were unfaithful, dabbled in drugs, and even abused her and her children. She has been so hurt. For the first two years after her second husband left her, she cried every day.

You could very well assume that her husbands made carnal desires king in their lives, pursuing the satisfaction of their need for temporary pleasure at the expense of what reason would tell them was their responsibility and the "right thing to do" as a godly husband. But now

Marie is making the same mistake. She is sleeping with a man who is kind to her but will not marry her. She has actually said, "He is the best husband I have never had." Her emotion—fear—is keeping her from doing the right and godly thing, and it is causing her to disobey God's will regarding sex outside of marriage.

Without regard to truth, she has chosen to live by her emotions—in this case, her fear of a marriage commitment and her desire to be in a loving relationship. You can understand why these emotions are there, but you can also see the pain that is coming into her life as a result of her disobedience to God. By making emotion king in her life, Marie is violating what God knows is best for her. It cannot end well.

Emotion is not meant to rule our lives. Living impulsively by our feelings and following whatever desire we have is a sure way to be stuck in the box.

The problem with both Kant and Schleiermacher is that neither emotion nor reason is supposed to be king. People do not work that way. God did not create a higher us and a lower us, a ruler and a subject. He just created *us*. Reason and emotion are so totally intertwined and inter-dependent that anyone who tries to separate them will end up with spiritual dwarfism, never attaining true maturity or emotional fullness.

God made us emotional *and* rational beings. The two go hand in hand. They support, define, and clarify each other. Emotion and reason *together* are what make us complete and make our lives full.

So we should not diminish either one or make either one subordinate.

The problem is that our culture and our scientific era emphasize rational thought at the expense of emotional expression and encourage us to put our emotions in a box. So we tend to live more on Kant's side of things. God never intended that.

He wants us to get out of the box.

Getting out of the box means living with emotion and reason working *together,* instead of having them jockey for top position. This balanced approach is the harder road. It requires that we never ignore what we are feeling—or what we are thinking. We have to search ourselves and the Bible to make each decision in our lives.

We cannot shove our feelings into a box and forget about them. Emotions always mean something, and they will always be with us. Part of living with our emotions means that we must treat them like any other thing in our lives. If they are good, we treat them as good. If they are bad, we need to deal with them accordingly. But we should never shut them out.

〈〈〉〉

Sometimes we stay in the box because we are afraid that strong emotions might embarrass us or hurt others.

But freedom from the box does not mean that if anger propels us to start screaming, we scream. It *does* mean that we listen to *why* we want to scream.

Freedom does not mean that if we feel jealous of our boss who lived off our work and got the big bonus, we stab her in the back. It *does* mean that we listen to our jealousy and try to understand what is fueling it, so we can work toward change.

Freedom does not mean we try to attain whatever we desire. It *does* mean we need to think about what we love, why we love it, and if God wants us to love it.

Strong emotions are not bad in themselves. We often equate them with "being out of control," yet for most of us, what we feel as "over the top" is not at all extreme or inappropriate. We have conditioned ourselves to live in such a narrow, limited range of emotional expression that nearly any strong emotional response feels like it's too much to us.

I had to learn this lesson the hard way, and it really hurt my marriage. Raised in the church, going to a Christian school, living in a home where my parents never talked about sex very much, I had a right theological understanding but a damaged heart. I grew up living in an emotional box.

And it hurt me and my bride when we entered into marriage.

For every one message in my life that talked about God creating sex as good, there were thirty that said, "Be careful," "Don't touch," "Don't look," "Don't allow yourself to feel deeply." I began marriage unable to separate sex from "thou shalt not" on some deep level.

I enjoyed our physical relationship, but often I found myself "too tired" to fulfill Laura's desire to be loved. I just didn't allow myself to desire her too much. I was afraid it might get me into trouble.

About eight years ago, after seven years of marriage, I started to realize that by not allowing myself to desire my wife deeply, I was hurting both of us. Laura felt that I did not really want her, that she wasn't desirable, and that I was not finding the physical fulfillment I needed and deeply desired. I finally began to understand that a sexual desire for her was not, as I had been conditioned to think, the same sinful desires of lust. A desire for sex was not the same as adultery or using pornography—which was the equation I'd learned—but rather a desire for sex in my marriage was something good. I was in an emotional box, and being there was, in fact, a sin—a sin against what God intended, and a sin against Laura.

I confessed this to Laura one night and committed in myself to confront this sin whenever it came into our relationship. I then sought to build a new kind of physical relationship with Laura. I started to work on getting out of my box, on sharing with her how much I desired to be one with her.

It has taken years—yes, years—to repair what I had broken. I had hurt Laura deeply, and in so doing had hurt myself. I had damaged what God had planned for my marriage and had missed great blessing. But step-by-step, we have taken back the passion that sin had stolen from our lives. Every stage of working through the fear and hurt, working through my sin, has been worth it. We are beyond where I ever thought we could get and continue to grow in our marriage. Am I ever glad I climbed out of that box!

A great side benefit of learning to love with more passion is just the opposite of what I expected. In learning to express and feel total desire for my wife, I have decreased my desire to sin, to lust, to view anything that is not pleasing to God. As righteous passion grows for the wife God blessed me with, sinful desire grows less day by day. As I learn to unleash, unchain, and let go in my relationship with one specific woman, desire for being with any other woman fades.

I believe the behaviors of pornographic sin and adultery are often the result of people living "in the box." Such sexual sins are wrong and hurtful, not because of the really strong sexual feelings themselves (which God created), but because the sexual feelings have not been expressed in a good, God-ordained way. They've been repressed to the point that they've burst out in a wrongful expression.

The pain of emotional repression takes many forms and hurts us (and others) in so many ways. Sometimes it's sexual; other times it comes out through anger, withdrawal, compulsive behavior, or spiritual and emotional numbness.

I know of a woman named Claudia who has terrorized her family with her anger. On a bad day, it's like living in a powder keg with a bunch of matches lying around. Everyone walks around on eggshells because they don't know what might set her off. Dirty socks on the floor, a missed deadline, or the wrong — "disrespectful" — word could lead to an explosion that lasts for hours, an explosion that is totally out of proportion to the offense. But, you see, Claudia has many wounds of her own that she has not yet dealt with — childhood memories and abuses that are buried deep. Her insecurities and perceived failures are always in her mind, but it's all bottled up because she hasn't worked through the pain and frustration of her woundedness by sharing it with someone who could help her. When the stress in her life gets too high, she lets it all out by raging at those she loves most. She feels mysteriously separated from everyone in relation-ship to her, but she doesn't know why. Sure, she gets mad, but she lets it out and gets over it. The next day, everything is "back to normal" — at least for her. But the explosion has wounded others, and they know it's only a matter of time before she needs another release.

Other people have been similarly wounded and share similar hurts to Claudia's, but instead of becoming explosive, they withdraw, strangling their emotions. The coldness they feel and project to others is not a *better* way to deal with it than Claudia's outbursts of anger. Both ways hurt others deeply, break relationships, and keep the person from becoming emotionally mature.

We must understand that emotions are great, God-given gifts, but we live in a sinful world that has perverted every part of God's good creation. What God planned for our good, sin has hijacked.

Just as in our gardens we deal with dandelions (where too many pop up year after year), in a sinful world, we must deal with harmful emotional tendencies that will pop up time and time again. Like weeds, the trouble comes in all shapes and sizes. Some, like the dandelions my daughter picks and gives to Mom as beautiful presents, will soon take over the yard if left untouched. Others, like the spiny sow thistle, we immediately recognize as dangerous because they are so painful to touch that we must wear gloves to pull them. In my yard, I pull weeds, occasionally spray poison on them, and pull them up again, but they just keep coming back in the same places.

As we shall see, emotions are like a garden full of flowers and shrubs, which often grow alongside harmful plants and weeds.

Emotions, good and bad, flowers and weeds, must be dealt with. But they should never be ignored.

We bought our house in late winter and had no idea what our garden would be like in spring. Within a few months, a huge chorus of plants, flowers, and ground cover was coming up all over. Spring bursts out in our yard in a chorus of green and color. I can see a flowering crabapple tree from my office window that drapes over the deck like a natural open arbor. On many branches, I cannot see any green poking through the white flowers. That first summer, all I did was try to figure out which plants were actually plants and which were weeds. Every two weeks, some plant I was skeptical about would start blooming, and more than once I realized that I had pulled up something beautiful in another part of the yard a week or two earlier.

Our neighbor explained that the parents of the first owners of the house ran a nursery. For a moving-in gift, they had given the young couple twenty thousand dollars' worth of landscaping. So, we do not have just a few more flowers than most of our neighbors; I'd guess we have six to ten times more than just about anybody on our block.

There's a guy where Laura and I walk that we refer to as "the neatnik." His garage floor is coated with some kind of sealant, and everything is in its place. When you walk by his garage and the door is up, it looks like an advertisement for Home Depot: "If you buy this shelving system, your garage could look like this!"

His lawn has a built-in sprinkler system and looks like a golf course green—literally. I can't recall ever walking by his house and seeing that his lawn needed to be mowed. The sidewalk edges are so well kept that they have developed a distinctive, tiny ditch of separation where no blade of grass dares to grow within a quarter-inch of the concrete. I have never seen a dandelion in his yard. Every shrub is groomed and spaced exactly eighteen inches from the next. The neatnik's garden is perfectly ordered but would never end up in *Better Homes and Gardens* magazine.

Some people believe that God desires for us to live our lives in such a way that every belief is in place, every situation is handled just right, every reaction is calibrated according to a preset mechanism. Boy, is that living in the box.

God designed the wildness of the earth and the wildness of our souls.

I think the most beautiful gardens are tended but also allow the surprises of the past to bloom and populate the garden in a kind of glorious chaos.

The perfectionist's ordered garden has all the beauty of the neatnik's immaculate, well-ordered garage.

We must glory in the ordered, flowering chaos of our emotional lives. We need to allow our emotions to bloom in fullness and beauty. And like me with my overflowing garden that first summer, we must also learn to tell the difference between a weed and a flower—not always as easy as identifying a dandelion!

‹ › ›

I've always been drawn to the person of David in the Bible. David lived out of the box, and God loved that about him.

In fact, God declared that David had a heart like his own.

What does that say about how emotional God is?

When the Ark of God entered Jerusalem in a triumphant procession, David danced before the Lord with all his might. He showed such passion that his wife Michal ridiculed the public display as unfit for a king. And David, this man with a heart like God's, wrote much of Psalms, the most emotional book in the Bible.

When David's traitorous son, Absalom, died, David's life seemed to blow apart for all Israel to see. Instead of celebrating the return of the kingdom to his hand, David took a nosedive into grief.

"The king was overcome with emotion. He went up to the room over the gateway and burst into tears. And as he went, he cried, 'O my son Absalom! My son, my son Absalom! If only I had died instead of you! O Absalom, my son, my son.'

"Word soon reached Joab [the commander of David's army] that the king was weeping and mourning for Absalom. As all the people heard of the king's deep grief for his son, the joy of that day's victory was turned into deep sadness. They crept back into the town that day as though they were ashamed and had deserted in battle. The king covered his face with his hands and kept on crying, 'O my son Absalom! O Absalom, my son, my son!'"[1]

There was no hiding of emotions from public display for King David, the man with a God-like heart. The people on the street were fully aware when their king danced or when he cried.

David was a man of emotion. He had a heart like God's.

Maybe you've lived in the box for a long time, hiding your true feelings from your spouse, your kids, your parents, your closest friends. Yourself.

You know I did for a long time.

The only way to get out of the box is to allow yourself to feel again. And that can feel good, or it can feel bad. The only way to get to the joy of David's dance is to allow yourself to feel the grief of loss in its full fury.

But whether the feelings are good or bad, God wants you to *feel*. To be emotionally full. To embrace life emotionally.

He wants you to get out of the box.

BLOG 05: RELEASE

STEPHEN]·····[It's easy to talk about the big picture, but at ground level the way I am called to respond to specific situations or make decisions with my emotions involved is a really difficult and risky process. As a child, I had an incredibly short fuse. I could move from being totally content to being totally, uncontrollably angry within a matter of seconds (usually with a small provocation from a brother, classmate or colleague).

In my adult life, I generally keep myself under control, but on a number of occasions I have lost my temper with people, resulting in a messy scene and some difficult apologies afterward (some so difficult that I never got around to making them). Releasing emotions in a healthy way seems so far beyond me. I feel I have to be all or nothing, I just can't be this well-rounded man that everyone wants to see, both passionate and controlled. Either I am all emotions or I'm no emotions; sometimes it doesn't feel like there is much ground in between.

ANDREW]·····[I regularly tell my wife that I love her. And I am learning to express to her my joys, frustrations, and desires. But that is about as far out of the box as I climb. By not understanding, expressing, or dealing with my emotions, I am dealing with sin. You have to admit that ignoring emotions is easier. No, you don't experience the pleasure of the chaotic emotional freedom. But I have security. How do I allow myself to feel? No more hiding. No more fear. No more box.

TODD]·····[I never would have thought that being totally out of control would put me in the same exact box as when I'm totally controlling my emotions.

Good chapter. Keep me from making a king out of emotions. "Reason and emotion are so totally intertwined and interdependent . . ."

Like David, to release some weeping or some dancing would not be a burden to a neighbor on the street.

BOB]·····[It is reassuring to read that to give emotion its due does not mean to lose hold of reason. Rather, the two work together. And the suggestion is compelling that the right use of emotion (the example used in this chapter was marital passion) does not promote dangerous growth of that passion (in this case, lust for women generally). Rather, it enhances enjoyment of that emotion where it belongs, and minimizes it where it does not belong. I am reminded of Paul's statement, "Walk by the Spirit, and you will not fulfill the desires of the flesh." If this chapter is correct, that to have a heart like God's is to feel deeply and to live out of the space where that feeling roams wild and free, then the enjoyment of emotion in ways God approves is the best defense we have against the misuse of emotion that would constitute sin. Robust expression of emotion is key to robust pursuit of a fulfilling relationship with God.

SARAH]·····[I appreciate that emotions and reason work together. I had never thought of that before. I long to know how to always have both at the forefront of my mind, indicating what is going on in my heart. In chapels at our school, we began to sing the song "Undignified" by Matt Redman. Students began jumping around in their seats, of course, but I was flabbergasted by what I was seeing, and the worship leader was continuing to encourage it. I thought immediately how wrong they were for doing this. However, after my husband and I discussed this with each other, we realized that worship, as long as it is taught in the right way, can be expressed with our total being, our entire selves. I now jump and fully participate with these students. I love them and I love worshiping with them. I look forward to fully participating in Heaven's worship.

TOM]·····[My son Ben recently had a birthday. Though he was born in July, he likes to begin talking about his birthday somewhere around December 26th. My wife and I lay down rules about how he can't discuss his birthday until at least summer; however, deep down I love it because I really admire his genuine enthusiasm for life (and it reminds me of myself when I was his age!). He loves everything Star Wars and Lego. And since Star Wars and Lego like to partner up, life is just grand! Ben received three very nice (and expensive) presents this year: a Lego Star Wars collector set; a Star Wars video game; and a Green Machine! I'm not sure who was more excited, Ben or me? What really made the day was his reaction. There were a lot of people present as we celebrated Ben's birthday (as well as a few others) at a family reunion. There was a lot of noise. But Ben grabbed everyone's attention with genuine shouts of joy as he discovered what he received. As adults, we don't do that because it's undignified (I guess?), but I hope and pray that I can still be that enthusiastic.

JARED]·····[I can totally identify with the feeling of Christian male sexual repression. There are times when I love my wife so easily, yet times when I am bound to feel wrong for wanting her. Many times the church, in an effort to keep sexual sins under control, has mentally castrated men from following their desires with their wives. My usual reaction is to tell us that we should not focus on sex so much, or that we are doing well for spending time loving each other more "practically." It is encouraging to hear these thoughts. It is also important to hear the sides of emotions, such as not letting emotion be king. Often the conservative criticism I hear of the emergent church is that "feeling" is too paramount and the Bible is not being followed. My experience has not been that of ignoring Jesus' words, but instead really trying to experience His love for us, and expressing His love to others as sacrificially as He did.

Enter the discussion at www.faithfulfeelings.com.

MY BLOG

_____

_____

_____

_____

_____

_____

_____

_____

_____

_____

_____

_____

_____

_____

_____

_____

_____

_____

_____

_____

06 Power

Emotion is God's provision for powering through the tough stuff.

It was the first time I had run for exercise in a long time. One foot in front of the other, step after step. My body was not liking it, but on I went, pounding the pavement. I knew I would pay for this—the hard concrete unforgiving against my aging bones and joints—and I did not want to keep going. I did for a while, but I stopped too soon, winded, tired, bored.

This past Saturday, I felt really good playing basketball. It was the best I have felt in a long while. We had both courts going, rotating and playing hard. For two hours, I ran and jumped and played defense. My shot kept hitting the back of the rim, which was frustrating, but I did have at least one twirl-around-my-defender, under-the-basket, left-handed-reverse-off-the-backboard layup that was really sweet. The game was sheer fun. Yes, my muscles cried out under the strain; yes, I got tired— but no, I was never bored. Because the game was sheer fun, I loved it. I even loved the pain.

Effective, long-term discipline is driven by passion. Whether it's a desire to keep in shape, a lifelong relationship with a game you have come to greatly enjoy, or an insane need to be bigger or faster than the next guy, the love of something propels you through the sweat, the practice, the work.

The *love* of something . . .

Emotion. A personal passion. The more you love something, the harder you will work for it.

My muscles ached five times more after those two hours of basketball than they did after my pitiful, aborted attempt at running. For me, exercising through basketball is driven by love; jogging is just something I think I should be doing to keep in shape when I cannot play ball—a duty.

〈〈〉〉

Passion/emotion gives us the power to do things we don't otherwise want to do. Passion also gives us the power to achieve great things.

In *Good to Great,* Jim Collins observes that great companies have a fanatical culture of discipline built around their *passion for accomplishing something really great.*

Collins tells the story of Dave Scott, a six-time triathlon winner. The triathlon is that insane event where they swim 2.4 miles, bike for 112 miles, and then run a full, 26-mile marathon. (No normal person does this.) And Dave Scott had *won* it six times!

His average *day* of training included running seventeen miles, biking seventy-five miles, and swimming two thousand meters. Dave did not have any problem burning fat, as you can imagine.

Wanting every conceivable advantage over his opponents, Dave would *rinse* his cottage cheese in order to reduce extra fat intake.

Yes, you heard me right.

Jim Collins says it well: "Much of the answer to the question of 'gooc to great' lies in the discipline to do whatever it takes to become the best in carefully selected arenas and then to seek continual improvement from there."[1]

Passion drives fanatical discipline. The driving desire and love to win triathlons is the only thing that could have driven Dave Scott to rinse cottage cheese. Emotion is God's provision for helping us do what it takes to achieve. We are strong enough to run the race when our emotions drive us to the finish line.

⟨⟨⟩⟩

Emotions not only power us to greater discipline and achievements, passion also produces in us the commitment to help others, sometimes at great cost to ourselves.

At the end of World War II, many former Nazis took refuge in South America. Some ran from justice, while others just tried to forget the past and forge a new life. One Nazi party member in particular fled to Argentina and tried unsuccessfully to establish a farm there. Finally destitute, he moved back to Germany to be near people who would take care of him during the final years of his life. You might think that the people he sought out would be his family, or perhaps fellow Nazis. But they were neither.

The people who took care of Oskar Schindler as he lived out his fina days were Jews.

Before the Nazi invasion, there were about two and a half million Jews living in Poland—380,000 in Warsaw alone, about one-third of the city's population. Today, after the mass murder of their relatives by the Nazis, only about four thousand Jews remain in all of Poland. Six thousand others of Polish descent are alive today because of Oskar Schindler.

His story is all about the power of emotion.

Steven Spielberg's Oscar-winning masterpiece, *Schindler's List,* opens with Schindler, an enterprising and profiteering German, taking every advantage of the Polish Jews for his own personal gain. With the Jews losing everything they own and being herded into the infamous Warsaw Ghetto, Schindler takes a luxurious house, formerly owned by a wealthy Jew, and barters for a Jewish-owned factory, hiring Jews instead of Poles because they are cheaper labor. Soon, his factory is turning out goods for the German army, and Schindler is living the high life, enjoying fine wines and exquisite food and dining with German officials in order to procure lucrative contracts. Life has never been better.

At first, Schindler is despised by many of his Jewish workers. Their terrible loss is his great profit. He is all about status, money, and woman-izing. His success is built on courting the favor of the Nazis and taking advantage of desperate Jews who will work for anything in order to avoid starvation in the Warsaw Ghetto.

One day, Schindler's Jewish accountant allows a one-armed man into Schindler's office. The man thanks him for the job and livelihood he is providing. He says to Schindler, "You are a good man. You saved my life. God bless you, God bless you."

These haunting words begin to break open Schindler's heart.

Leaving the building, he says to the accountant, "By the way, don't ever do that to me again. Did you happen to notice that that man had one arm? What's his use?" Like the Nazis, he tries to think of the Jews as animals to be used and discarded. I say *tries,* for "he doth protest too much" an effort extended to give cover to his own conscience.

When a group of Nazis finds the one-armed factory worker among a group of Jews shoveling snow, they shoot him down in cold blood.

Schindler's heart is further awakened by this atrocity. He sees that the
Nazis have acted on the echoes of his own thoughts.

As his eyes are opened to see this one murdered Jew as a person of
worth, he begins a 180-degree transformation.

The power of the compassion this one man's death brings into
Schindler's life cannot be stopped or contained. Every senseless act of
brutality, every Jew imprisoned or tortured for no reason, becomes an
affront to his own humanity and a torment to his soul.

Then Schindler's workers are moved from the ghetto to a labor camp.

The commandant of their camp uses the prisoners for target practice
from his high balcony, shooting them down at will. He enjoys it as sport.
He sees their lives as worthless, except perhaps as a source of entertainment. His life is utterly empty.

This commandant has a Jewish maid whom he uses and forces sexually.
In a Shakespeare-like soliloquy, she tells Schindler of her master's total
disregard for human life: "One day he will shoot me. . . . I know, I see
things. We were on the roof on Monday . . . and we saw the Herr
Commandant come out the front door and down the steps by the patio
right there below us, and there on the steps he drew his gun. He shot a
woman who was passing by, a woman carrying a bundle, through the
throat, a woman just on her way somewhere. She was no fatter or thinner
or slower or faster than anyone else. And I couldn't guess what she had
done."

Schindler responds, "He won't shoot you because he enjoys you too
much. He enjoys you so much he won't even let you wear the star. He
does not want anyone else to know that it is a Jew he is enjoying. He shot
the woman from the steps because she meant nothing to him. She was
one of a series, neither offending or pleasing him. But you, Helen . . ."

The Jewish maid is safe because the commandant has developed
feelings for her. He needs her. Later, he wonders at the fact that he has
such feelings for her, saying, "Is this the face of a rat? Are these the eyes
of a rat? 'Hath not a Jew eyes?' I feel for you, Helen. No, I don't think so.

You're a Jewish bitch." He goes on to give her a savage beating, hating himself for loving a Jew.

It is upon these words that the story turns.

One man lets compassion take over his life, following his emotion in the face of Nazi lies. The other man lets go of all compassion, regarding even his Jewish lover as a "rat." He feels nothing after shooting Jews for sport. In fact, he shoots them just to see if he is still able to feel anything at all.

Oskar Schindler remakes his factory into a lifeboat for Jewish survivors of Nazi atrocities. Under the guise of business and profit, he negotiates with the commandant, paying a high price for more than a thousand Jewish workers to continue their lives working at his factory instead of being shipped to the infamous Auschwitz death camp.

At the end of the war, we see Schindler break down while clasping hands with his Jewish accountant, who is now a beloved friend. "I could have got more," he cries. "I could have got more." Weeping, he says, "I didn't do enough." He reaches toward the automobile he owned that had transported him. "This car . . . why did I keep this car? Ten people right there. Ten people. Ten more people." His selfishness has been replaced by selfless love.

When Schindler came face-to-face with the physical suffering and its gruesome consequences, it awoke in him a holy horror that forced him to utterly reject Nazi dogma. Emotion rose up and declared false every ounce of Nazi indoctrination he'd taken in. Love and compassion made him risk his life and give all he had for those who were most despised and hated by the Nazis.

The power of emotion is powerfully illustrated through stories of people like Oskar Schindler. What compels someone to risk his life for someone else? What drives people to do things that put their lives in harm's way? C. S. Lewis, in his book *The Four Loves,* says that this is the uniquely human emotion of sacrificial love.

Emotion becomes a great force for good, a power that drives us to altruistic action, moving us beyond ourselves toward helping others.

‹ ‹ › ›

Ed and Denise Aulie are church planters in rural Mexico. They've spent much of their adult lives living in a mud house.

Soon after the birth of their first son, Eric, Ed became fearful for his young family's safety. His mission involved traveling to remote villages with Mexican evangelists. In these areas, a rebel movement was growing, and government officials looked at Ed and his work as a threat. As the rebel groups gained strength, law enforcement became hostile to evangelism in the remote villages.

Ed said, "I could handle being thrown into prison by local officials in the villages now and again. They only beat you with pipes, leave you overnight, and then they let you go. What I was afraid of was being thrown into the Mexican federal prisons." An American born in Mexico, Ed holds a Mexican passport and has spent more time south of the border than in the United States. It was his home. He knew what the federal prisons were like, including the torture and sexual abuse that went on there.

With the violence increasing, he felt that his effectiveness in preaching and his witness were not what they should be because of his fear. He wanted to be an effective father for his kids for many years to come.

But Ed's worst fears were about to come true.

The governor of the state issued a warrant for his arrest. The charge was having forged documents. Ed had a Mexican passport and a Mexican birth certificate; his documents were as official as official gets. Still, the trumped-up charges stuck, and Ed found himself on the way to a federal prison in Mexico City. If convicted, he would be sentenced to eight years in prison. Ed thought it would be easily straightened out with the help of a lawyer, but nothing is as it seems in the depths of a corrupt legal system.

Meanwhile, Denise and the kids were alone in their mud-brick house, knowing little about the situation.

Ed spoke on the bright side: "God had decided to free me of my fear of being thrown into federal prison."

The cell where they placed Ed had eight concrete bunks. The undisputed kingpin of the cell was Don Amaro, a man who ran most of the brothels in northern Mexico. Amaro was dripping with gold chains from his wrists and neck, the picture of a powerful pimp who used people as sexual play toys.

The guard said to the pimp as he put Ed in the cell, "I have brought you another man to play with." Amaro was an experienced sexual predator.

Ed said later, "I remember wishing at that moment that a crack in the ground would just open up and swallow me up."

Amaro looked at him and asked, "What are you doing here?"

The Holy Spirit took over Ed's tongue, and he said, "I am a preacher of the gospel. We go out to the villages preaching about a Christ that sets men free. In these villages, there is no way out of the poverty, so people turn to alcohol and immorality and adultery. We tell the people that there is a different way, that Jesus Christ offers a way out of that bondage. Jesus can set them free. When a man is saved, it shows that there is a different way, and other men hate that." (That was why Ed was really in prison—for teaching a different way out of spiritual bondage.)

Don Amaro screamed back at him, "Shut up and don't ever talk to me about this thing again. I've read the Bible, and it's only literature." He pointed to a slab of concrete and said, "Go to your bunk. We have two rules here. Bathe every day, and don't touch anything that isn't yours."

Little did Amaro know the truth of his own words.

You see, Ed Aulie was a child of the King of kings, not Don Amaro's sexual toy. The evil of sexual abuse would not touch him. Amaro stayed away from him for the rest of Ed's months in prison.

The bunk that Amaro chose for Ed was right below the only lightbulb in the cell. It was the bunk nobody wanted because the light would keep them up all night. As he lay down on that concrete slab, Ed told me that he knew God had prepared a place just for him, the only place in the cell where he would have enough light to read his Bible.

Earlier in the day, they had taken Ed's backpack and all his possessions. Allowed only one set of clothing but no shoelaces, books, or any other object that could be used as a weapon, he knew he would lose his New Testament with Psalms and Proverbs. He decided he could not live without the Bread of Life and stuck the book in his pants.

When they entered the prison, everyone in the line was searched. Except Ed.

He read the Scriptures that night on the bare concrete slab under the only light in the cell. He understood how *good* God was as he read the words from Psalm 34: "I will praise the LORD at all times. . . . I will boast only in the LORD; let all who are helpless take heart. Come, let us tell of the LORD's greatness; . . . I prayed to the LORD, and he answered me. He freed me from all my *fears*. Those who look to him for help will be radiant with *joy*; no shadow of shame will darken their faces. In my desperation I prayed, and the LORD listened; he saved me from all my troubles. For the angel of the LORD is a guard; he surrounds and defends all who fear him. Taste and see that the LORD is good. Oh, the *joys* of those who take refuge in him!"[2]

Ed knew right then that Don Amaro, who hated anyone who preached the gospel, would never touch him. "I had never known God's Word and his presence to be so sweet; there was tremendous joy in that. The place of worst fear became the place of greatest joy."

Life in prison was hard. They had just one cup of coffee per day. Those who were not disciplined and drank from the tap got terribly sick. Ed had managed to hide a water filter he'd had in his backpack, so every day each man in his cell had a cup of healthy, clear water.

Ed was the source of water for their bodies as well as sharing Living Water for their souls.

They were given one cup of rice one day and one cup of beans the next. "That was their idea of a balanced diet," Ed said with a chuckle. Some men were literally going crazy with hunger and becoming enraged at the conditions. Some days, Ed gave his single cup of rice or beans to someone who was suffering. He felt really bad for these men.

After one month, Ed was able to talk to the U.S. consul, who was visiting another American prisoner. The consul told Ed, "It will take a miracle to get you out. This other man was just working without a permit and has been here for months. You are charged with fraud and forgery."

Ed's family prayed for a miracle. His father, communicating through a lawyer, asked if Ed needed anything. Ed responded that he needed a box of New Testaments, tracts, and plastic spoons. (The men were not allowed spoons; everybody ate with dirty fingers.)

When the lawyer visited the prison, Ed got the box. Though no one was allowed to bring anything into the prison, Ed walked back, carrying his box with confidence past the guards. One prisoner yelled out, "Guards, stop that man! He's turning this place into a monastery!"

A guard came out and asked Ed, "What is this?"

Ed answered, "This is the story of Christ. This is what changes a man's heart. Had these men known Christ they would not be here."

Hearing this, the guards wanted a copy of the gospel also.

On Sundays, Ed held church in the courtyard. It grew to a meeting of about sixty-five men. One Sunday he told everyone, "I love each one of you. You know that I love you because I have lived here with you for the last two months. I would give my life for any one of you. It has not been easy being separated from my family, or having little food, or sleeping on cement. But I have come to love you."

"I have a little baby boy at home, and even though you know how much I love you, I would not give him up for all of you together. God in heaven also has a Son. God the Father sent his Son, gave him up for your life. Some of you have missed special moments with your family and feel so alone, but God so loved the world that he was willing to send his Son away for you."

There was a great response to God's love among those men; many who came to the service gave their lives to Christ that day.

Soon after Ed finished the message, the guards came for him, and he was whisked away to the airport and put on a commercial flight to Texas. He later remarked, "You should have seen the looks I got from the other passengers on the airplane when they sat me down in handcuffs."

The miracle of release had come.

So how did Ed endure the agony of prison? How did he overcome the daily hunger and poor conditions? How did he triumph over fear?

He did so because of the passion of his life—Jesus Christ. In Christ, he became filled with the *emotions* of hope and joy, emotions that sustained him through the most difficult circumstances and *helped him help others.*

The power of emotion helps people overcome adversity. Whether you're a persecuted Jew in a concentration camp, an evangelist for the gospel in a Mexican prison, a cancer patient fighting for your life, a parent dealing with the loss of a child, a person overwhelmed by financial hardship—adversity focuses you on the essential passions of your life, and it is those emotions that have the power to pull you through.[3]

〈 〉〉

If passion and emotion are the powers that can drive our lives in positive ways, then the opposite is true as well—the lack of passion and emotion deprives us of the power to live whole and healthy lives.

Without passion, our lives become dependent on sheer will—the mental grit to persevere. A life that is an endless effort of sheer will is a life of drudgery, tedium, infinite list making. A life that makes relationship with God merely a process of logic, a rational understanding, is a life that "embraces" God and "relates" to him only in mental concepts.

No wonder we get burned out. No wonder we become spiritually dead.

I recently heard a sermon on a passage in James: "Dear brothers and sisters, when troubles come your way, consider it an opportunity for great joy. For you know that when your faith is tested, your endurance has a chance to grow. So let it grow, for when your endurance is fully developed, you will be perfect and complete, needing nothing."[4]

The preacher waxed eloquent about the tough stuff of life and how we all face some big and difficult trials. But I was afraid the bait and switch was coming. (As you must know by now, my ears are specially attuned to such things!)

He was passionate about how God has given great reasons for us to have joy in these hard times. He gave a fantastic list of all God has done to give us the strength to pull joy out of the fire of testing. But I was getting a knot in the pit of my stomach; I was afraid the turn was about to happen. Then, about two-thirds through his exposition of God's promise of joy, it came. This great sermon with the possibility of such a powerful climax made a U-turn.

The pastor was suddenly defining the emotion of joy as a kind of "biblical" joy. "It would be a big problem for me personally," he said, "if this was *emotional* joy James was talking about."

The pit in my stomach grew as he continued, "No, the word *count,* or *consider,* in Greek precludes emotion; instead it's about mental work. 'Consider' is saying 'think of it as joy,' even if you are not joyful in your heart. It is believing the right things."

If that weren't enough, this nationally known preacher added, "The biblical concept of joy is not laughter or being happy, but the knowledge that down deep inside all is okay."

Yes, he really said that.

I wanted to scream. (I should have—it would have been a great example of the power of emotion!) I should have shouted, "Where is the power in that?"

When we don't believe that God is big enough to provide joy even on dark days, we rob our faith of its transforming power. This preacher, like so many others, converts true emotion into "mental work," stripping it of its power and leaving us with . . . well, *work.*

What does it mean to constantly work at maintaining joy as an idea but not experiencing it as a true emotion?

What people see is a life that is all mental, all rational—simply a set of beliefs that, like an array of plates spinning atop poles, are constantly, manually refreshed, spun, and kept going. So our lives are not really about *feeling joy*, but about keeping the *idea* of joy afloat in our minds. So we do not allow ourselves to really *feel hope*, but we constantly spin the hope concept in our heads to keep it going. And we don't really open ourselves to *genuine, passionate love*, but we do "love-like" deeds and other to-dos in daily life, which keeps the *idea* of love spinning.

It's a lot of work to keep those plates spinning. After a while, the mental work becomes utterly tedious. Devoid of real emotions and yet compelled to constantly spin our mental belief plates to keep them going, we lose the power of emotions and the richness of life that God intends to provide through them.

What's that Scripture? "Having a form of godliness but denying its power."[5]

And after we've lived that way for *years*, what do other people see in us? Do they feel our love during a difficult hardship; do they see real joy? Or do they develop a sense that we're "just doing the right thing," that they're on our mental checklists, that we're tired and weary and don't feel much of anything?

Here's what others see: the futility of a bunch of spinning plates.

⟨⟨⟩⟩

The realization that he was merely spinning plates is what helped to turn Mike Singletary's life around. This great Chicago Bears middle linebacker, Hall of Famer, ten-time Pro Bowler, and two-time defensive player of the year is a real hero in my hometown. But after growing up in a Christian home, living a picture-perfect life, and achieving wild success in sports, he still felt something was missing. He was going through a hard time after the end of his playing career, and he knew something was missing in his Christian walk because he did not *feel* the joy in trials that the Bible talked about. His faith was not the reality in his life that he wanted it to be.[6]

This was not the kind of faith, or the kind of God, that Mike wanted— a God who talked about joy in hard times, but a joy that was really just a list of things we were supposed to believe. No way—he wasn't taking that bait and switch either. He figured out that the bait was God's promise of joy in trials, and the switch was that this joy was somehow not about really being happy, but rather about the theology of joy.

Mike Singletary—a player who will forever be known for the intensity of his eyes staring out through his helmet at middle linebacker—realized the passion he had in playing football was missing in the game of life.

Here's the thing: It is easier to believe that joy in hard times has nothing to do with our feelings. It is easier to obey the command of Jesus to love our enemies if loving has nothing to do with God really changing our hearts. The Christian life is easier to conduct when it is separated from real emotional heart change.

Emotional transformation is hard, and for most people it's easier to avoid it. Why?

I think in part it's a lack of faith—faith that God is big enough to provide for us the fully emotional spiritual life he promises. When we keep God in the realm of rational thought, separate from other parts of our lives, we don't have to test his greatness. When we make our spiritual lives dependent on our duties and lists, we don't have to trust God to be as awesome as he claims he is or trust him to do hard things like give us real joy in suffering.

By barring God from the real emotional places of our lives, we rob him of his power. It's as if we tell him, "God you won't do this in my life. I just know you won't. I can't have joy in this difficult tragedy. You won't be big enough to bring me to a place of contentment. I'm afraid you'll disappoint me or fail me, and I can't take that chance." In this, we keep God small.

There is great sin here—the sin of denying that God is powerful enough to break through our greatest struggles and trials—the prisons of our daily lives—and lead us out singing, with uplifted hands and full-hearted joy.

So it is harder to have the Big Faith that God can bring real emotional joy through pain. And it's hard to believe that in our very moments of struggle, our lives can be more emotionally alive than we have ever felt before.

Yet, this is what God is promising us.

Can we let go of our "forms of godliness" and open ourselves fully to the power of emotional transformation in Christ?

〈〈 〉〉

Laura and I have coined the term "alarm clock spirituality."

Like many, Laura grew up in a very duty-driven Christianity. When I first met her, she was excellent at setting her alarm clock in order to have the proper time in the early morning for her dutiful devotions and Bible study. Truth is, she was afraid her spiritual life would fall apart if she skipped even one day.

After we married, we set about exploring together what made daily devotions important to God. Interestingly, we realized devotions should be about *devotion,* which is defined as "feelings of ardent love." We should love God so much, and desire being with him so much, that we long to find times to be with him.

But how does God feel (and, yes, he *feels*!) when our "devotion" is about the duty of setting an alarm clock each morning, dragging ourselves to the Bible, and feeling guilty that it winds up being fifteen minutes instead of half an hour? Where are the feelings of ardent love in that?

Well, I wasn't sure my own spiritual life was all that great or that my view of daily devotions was exactly on target, but I was adamant that devotions should not be about Laura setting an alarm clock. She eventually agreed, stopped setting the clock, and worked through the difference between duty and true devotion.

For a few years, she neglected devotional time in the mornings. There was a barrier there: She was convinced that to have any kind of regular devotions would send her back to a duty-driven, joy-killing spiral. Yet, she also wanted to spend time with God—and it was difficult, especially with two babies, to make time.

Eventually, Laura promised God she would always respond to his call in the morning. If he would wake her before the babies were up, she would love to spend time with him. She just needed his help.

And God faithfully did that for her, giving her just enough time to spend serious time with him in prayer and study.

Laura's times with God are now totally different. How do I know? All I have to do is listen to her pray. The power and passion of her prayers is something I'd never heard from her before. Her remade heart toward God now empowers her spiritually; her previous, duty-driven obligation to God is no longer killing her spiritually. Now her time with God is true devotion and expression of her ardent love to be with him. And he is giving new power to his daughter.

What happened to Laura is captured by the psalmist in Psalm 119:

> I am always overwhelmed
> with a desire for your regulations. . . .
> How I delight in your commands!
> How I love them![7]

But I think how we approach our devotional time with God each day is just a small example of a larger issue in our lives.

One of the things we sometimes get confused is the difference between being duty driven and obedient. God calls us to obedience, but somehow we make that into a rote thing. It's as if we don't consider it real obedience unless it feels hard and tough and bad.

It's so much easier to obey when you want to!

Sometimes, just to tease my kids, I will call them over in a stern voice and say something like, "You must go to the freezer immediately and get a Heath Bar Klondike ice cream bar, go into the backyard and eat the entire thing. I do not want to see one single piece of chocolate left and absolutely no drips of ice cream on the deck!"

Let me tell you, there is no need to repeat the instruction. It is carried out with great vigor, and as fast as possible.

Contrast that with the fundamentally different response and energy level that greets another of my signature commands: "Go downstairs and clean up all your toys in the basement!"

Having positive emotion for doing what we've been asked to do makes all the difference in how we obey the command. When we see the reason for it, when we enjoy doing it, or when we want to please the one giving the instruction, we are much more likely to obey, and to obey with energy and enthusiasm.

The difference between duty and godly obedience is *passion.* Just as Laura set her alarm clock out of a sense of duty that had become disconnected from a feeling of passion for God's presence, so we tend to convert God's calls to obedience into rote and passionless routines. God doesn't want that.

He's commanding us to eat our ice cream!

As we grow in our faith, we will be driven more and more to obey God's commands, not because they are things we should do, but because they are what we *want* to do, and we desire in our deep places to do them. As we learn how good they are for us and those we love, we will see how it is a joy to obey. As we grow closer to God and know more of his great love for us, our desire to please him will grow deeper and wider and all-consuming in us.

Not only will it be easier to obey, but we will obey more fully with greater passion and results.

That is the kind of obedience God longs for us to have, obedience that is fueled by our deep passion and desire for him. That kind of obedience is what brings God's power into our lives.

〈〈〉〉

Lack of emotion and passion saps us of power to live and enjoy life fully. It also makes us destructive, especially self-destructive.

So many of us today are emotionally repressed to one degree or another. And when we repress emotions, we become crippled. We limp through life, making the best of it that we can, but really experiencing very little of it. And in our fractured state, in our partial emotional paralysis, we try to compensate in various ways, trying to fill the emotional void inside. Our lives become twisted compensations for a lack of passion.

In fact, many of the problems we see in modern society are the result of people compensating in unhealthy ways for their repressed emotions.

I think of the "flashpoint person," who is explosively emotional, whose sudden outbursts may be a compensation for a childhood of hurt and imprisoned emotions; the "traumatic," who compensates through addictions to alcohol or drugs or pornography—substitutes for emotionally whole experiences that are otherwise lacking; the "depressive," who is constantly down on life, perhaps in an effort to control a fear of experiencing disappointment; the "wanderer," who moves from one thing to another without purpose and whose aimlessness is a product of emotional detachment; and the "control freak," who dictatorially manages events and other people.

Yes, the world is filled with people who are not emotionally whole and who need to compensate.

The good news, I believe, is that God promises emotional fullness, the very thing the world so desperately needs. The bad news is that many Christians don't experience emotional fullness themselves, much less provide it to others.

This is what makes me cry out. The Bible provides us with God's good path to emotional fullness. Yet so much of what is taught in Christian

books, in sermons, and in the church rewrites the Bible into yet another
form of emotional repression. Christians walk away repressed like everyone
else, powerless to carry God's promise of emotional fullness to the world.

〈〈〉〉

What can we do? How can we reclaim the power of passion in our lives?
I have four simple ideas.

First, *read the Bible,* but with new eyes. Focus on how emotionally full the
people and stories in the Bible really are. As you approach the Bible with
a fresh perspective, set aside what you've been taught about emotion
(that it's not really *emotion*) and think about real, *passionate* love when
you see the word *love;* think about real, *exuberant* joy when you see the
word *joy;* think about real, *faith-inducing* hope when you see the word
hope; think about real, *flaming* anger when you see the word *anger;* and
so on. In other words, read the Bible as the story of real people feeling
real emotions in their real lives in connection to a real God.

Second, *take a walk in the woods.* But don't just walk. Talk. Talk to God.
Talk to him out of your deepest emotional places. Cry out to him, yell at
him, shout for joy before him. Pour out your hurts, fears, troubles. Put it
all out there and let God respond. He will.

By the way, you know what that is? Prayer. Real, vibrant, passionate
prayer.

Third, *find something outside of yourself, or someone outside of your
common world, to love.* Find something bigger than yourself that you can
pour your heart into. There's nothing like caring for someone else in need
to help us feel again, overcome our own numbness, and reach out in
power to help and love.

Finally, *let go.* Stop trying to control everything in your life. Stop trying to
keep your emotions in check. Just stop trying, and instead, open yourself
to feel.

For ten years, I have been pouring my life into trying to meet a small part
of Africa's huge need for Christian books and Bibles. Estimates are that
well over 200 million Christians in Africa do not have a Bible. I am really

passionate about finding long-term solutions to the church's needs in this area. I have poured my time, my life, my best working years into trying to figure out creative answers that might really solve the complex problems of printing and distribution, so that my brothers and sisters in Christ might be able to have the Bibles and books they need to grow in their faith.

But I had been struggling. I was really discouraged about some of the problems we were facing. I found myself in church, listening to an amazing sermon from 2 Chronicles. My pastor began to talk about the hopeless situation of King Jehoshaphat when three nations' armies were arrayed against Judah. The king cried out, "O our God, won't you stop them? We are powerless against this mighty army that is about to attack us. We do not know what to do, but we are looking to you for help."[8] Everything led to this moment of hopelessness and helplessness. My pastor said, "At that point, God had them right where he could work."

With that, my heart just opened up within me. The message that day hit me like a sledgehammer, breaking through years of accumulated layers of dependence on myself, trying hard, and doing all the right things.

I thought, *I have done everything I know to do, I have tried everything I could think of, I have looked under every rock, I have climbed every mountain that seemed good to climb, but it is never going to be enough. No matter what I do, no matter how good my ideas are or how hard I work . . .*

At that moment, I just knew for certain that nothing I did would ever be enough.

I have always known in my head that God is the answer, but somewhere deep inside I must have really believed that if only I could figure out the solution to the next problem, if only I did just a little bit better, if only I worked just a little bit harder, if only I . . . I . . . I . . .

In that moment, that illusion was crushed beyond recognition. I would never be good enough to solve these problems. They were totally beyond me, even after *years* of trying.

My only hope—*our* only hope—is God's provision. That's not a place I was comfortable being in. Would God really come through when there was no other hope?

I found an elder from our church, a friend whom I trust, and I poured out my tears and grief about working so hard, investing so much of myself in this great challenge, and how afraid I was that I would fail. And I recounted the sermon and how it had spoken to me: *What I can do will never be enough.*

Are we ready to take God at his word? Are we ready to believe that whatever comes, whatever we have to deal with, he will take care of us, he will provide for us, he will bring us through—rejoicing?

Jehoshaphat's army went out praising God in joyful worship, in the face of insurmountable odds. They went out to battle in the strength of God's promise: "This is what the LORD says: Do not be afraid! Don't be discouraged by this mighty army, for the battle is not yours, but God's."[9]

The people listened to the prophecy, and the army marched out praising God—literally. It's a scene of incredible emotion. "After consulting the people, the king appointed singers to walk ahead of the army, singing to the LORD and praising him for his holy splendor. This is what they sang: 'Give thanks to the LORD; his faithful love endures forever!'"

And the Bible says, "At the very moment they began to sing and give praise, the LORD caused the armies of Ammon, Moab, and Mount Seir to start fighting among themselves."[10]

Joy came even *before* the victory as they declared their total dependence on God.

Of course, you can see the incredible irony: The power becomes real only after we recognize how utterly powerless our own efforts and duty-driven actions really are.

BLOG 06: POWER

STEPHEN]·····[I love to make lists. I love ticking things off. It gives me closure and makes me feel like I've achieved something. But like Laura, I've also found that it places a massive burden on me. I find it very hard to believe that God wants good things for me.

I feel like I should just be strong and take up this huge burden that I have made for myself, and run with it; whilst, in reality, God is offering to take it from me.

I can't remember the time it happened (definitely the latter part of my teenage years), but there came a point when doing the washing up after dinner changed from being almost a punishment (it wasn't meant to be, but that's what it felt like) to being a joy. The difference was that I wanted to please my parents, to show my appreciation to Mum for cooking, and to hear a word of thanks from my dad. I think I'm still very much a pre-teenage Christian in the way I relate to God.

JAMES]·····[For some reason, this chapter got me thinking about a song we sang over and over in Sunday school and youth group meetings as children. "I've got the joy, joy, joy, joy down in my heart. Down in my heart. Down in my heart. I've got the joy, joy, joy, joy down in my heart. Down in my heart to stay." Now, I'm curious. What kind of joy were we singing about? The belief "joy" of the preacher in this chapter? or emotional joy? I think we knew that this joy was true emotional joy. At least I hope so.

MARIAN]·····[Has my life really been reduced to plate spinning? What futility! To have a passion for something, someone, to be fully alive—God please help me get there. I see so clearly that I am not emotionally whole. I need to compensate for that, but that is not where I choose to stay. I may not do great exploits like Oskar Schindler or Ed Aulie, perhaps, but I see that I can make a difference where I am, in my church, among the members of the ministry team. If only I can lead with passion and love, God will do the rest.

Duty can be tedious and stale. Discipline is somehow harder. I know I need to keep both, but if God breathes through them, they become privilege and opportunity. Lord, I am going to take a long walk by the river this afternoon!

SARAH]·····[I run to stay in shape. And my passion is for staying fit; I don't run for the love of it. I have heard that when a person trains for a marathon and they reach the end of themselves physically, their mind (motivated by a passion) drives them to the finish line. I desire to run this race for Christ with a passion that drives my actions—a love for Him.

I was challenged where you wrote that "selfishness has been replaced by selfless love." To allow myself to really feel love and to act selflessly would be freedom. To see love as an emotion moves me beyond myself toward helping others. I look forward to seeing how the power of emotion helps me overcome adversity in my future.

JULIE]·····[We can experience God's power over our negative emotions, such as feelings of failure, inadequacy, fear, or whatever emotion is trying to pull us down. We need to focus on the BIGNESS of God and WHO he is. What I've always heard when our negative emotions want to pull us into depression, hopelessness, or whatever it may be, is that we need to take the lie that we are believing (and feeling) and replace it with the truth of God's Word. This seems to be the gist of this chapter if I'm understanding it correctly. And you give us ways we can stir up passion in our lives for God and for others [read God's word with new eyes, take a walk and pour out your heart to God, find something or someone outside of your common world to love, and let go).

JARED]·····[I totally agree that our output is only as good as our passion for the thing we are focused on doing. The question that still seems to remain for me is making that transition from duty to joyful obedience. How does something remain a passion for me in this world of changing focus? If I start to become spent at one topic, my desire is to try something new and to mix up my focus. Often, I really enjoy this quality because it has enabled me to try so many different opportunities. But what happens when one of those topics that I take a break from is an essential part of my life in Christ? What happens when I do take a break from prayer and try to experience God in other ways, when prayer is so important? God wants us to talk to Him and He can always find ways to talk to us. I suppose it does come down to a release of control to Him to show us that He can connect with us however He wants. As long as we are open to hearing from Him, and always listening, He brings the passion by connecting with us in His timing for us.

Enter the discussion at www.faithfulfeelings.com.

MY BLOG

_____

_____

_____

_____

_____

_____

07 Friend

God created emotions as part of us, just as they are part of him, to empower, encourage, and strengthen us. Rather than seeing emotions as an enemy that trips us up and causes us to stumble, we must learn to embrace them as a friend.

Just as we get to know another person and what makes them tick, we need to understand more clearly what emotion is and how it operates. More than that, we need to discover how emotions come alongside us and help us.

That's what these next chapters are all about. In these pages, we will get to know our own emotions and understand ourselves by exploring four simple words: *Focus, Know, Value,* and *Believe.* We will discover what the Bible says about the emotions we should *grow, keep,* or *be done with.*

But first, let's explore the core of what emotion really is and discover how we can depend on it as a friend.

‹ ‹ › ›

You have read about some of my intellectual journey at the University of Tübingen to understand God's purpose for emotions. But my spiritual journey toward a God-view of emotions started much earlier than that. That earlier spiritual journey was why I chose to study emotions in the first place.

When I was a young teenager, I connected with the music of Keith Green. Seeing the passion in his life and hearing it in his music challenged me to get really turned on for God. Listening to songs about a total commitment to Christ, I learned that as I filled my mind with truth, I gained a desire to be holy in my spirit.

That growing desire led to a crucial decision. All my friends were starting to listen to rock music. Now, I think a lot of contemporary music is great; I really enjoy a good love ballad—especially if it is sung by Johnny Cash—or a rock song that talks honestly about the struggles of life. However, I found that many of the groups and lyrics that my friends were starting to get into seemed to glorify things that God hates. When I talked to church friends about the disconnect between our faith and the lyrics to some of their favorite songs, the most common answer was "The words don't affect me; I just love the music."

I wasn't sure this was true.

As I wrestled with their argument, it occurred to me that if what they said was true, the consequences were even worse than I had imagined. If lyrics glorifying sexual immorality, for example, do not really affect us, aren't we saying that we are hardened and insensitive to evil things—things that wreck relationships, tear families apart, and destroy the most intimate of relationships?

Being unaffected—wouldn't that be the worst thing that could happen to your heart?

If my friends were listening to songs about having sex with a girlfriend, I knew God's teaching on that—it really hurts people. Shouldn't we hate the things that bring destruction to ourselves and others? Shouldn't we be grieved that Jesus Christ died to pay the penalty for that kind of sin? God wants us to hate sin like he does. It's not good to be unaffected by it.

"God," I cried out, "teach me to grieve over evil like you do, to see it clearly for what it is."

Let me be careful to say here that I don't lump together all music or movies or aspects of pop culture. There is good rock music, there are good movies, and there is positive television. But one must be discerning. I'm just as excited as any red-blooded guy to enjoy a good action flick or, more seriously, a movie that deals with the grim realities of our world, where you see a struggle with evil that actually portrays it as bad, and good can triumph and redeem. But we need to avoid things in our media-driven society that *glorify and celebrate evil*.

As a teenager, I came to a point where I determined I wanted to love God and love the things he loved. At the same time, I made a determined choice not to fill my mind with what I knew God hated. When I heard or saw something that glorified sin, I chose to concentrate on the painful consequences that sin produced and the fact that this is what sent my beloved Savior to the cross.

An interesting thing happened in my life as a result.

I found as I focused on loving what God loved, it became much easier to obey him; when I was in sync, the things that were important to him were also important to me. And when sin and evil were glorified, it grieved my spirit just as it grieves God's.

I was learning that our emotions, rightly focused, can be a guide for us, pointing us toward right things and away from wrong things. In this way, emotion does what a friend does—it counsels and advises.

Have you ever had a best friend you were so close to that you confided in her about other people in your life? You might say, "I don't know about Joe. I don't trust him." But your friend says, "You know, Joe is struggling right now, but he's basically a good guy. I think he's okay."

Or you tell your best friend how excited you are about a new employee at work. "He's so experienced, and he's going to make my job so much easier." But your friend cautions you, "Be careful there. I sense this guy has problems; you might get burned."

Emotions are best friends whom we should often trust to counsel us about the people and situations we encounter.

〈〈〉〉

When I got to college, I understood more about how God wanted to mold my emotions. I asked him how I might learn to pray and be more passionate about what he was doing in the world.

I began to take long walks at night, just learning to pour out my heart to God, telling him exactly how I was feeling. I spent some of the time singing—sometimes too loudly for the sleeping houses I was passing, I am afraid. I learned that prayer was not about a specific place or position or time (although those things can be useful and there *is* a place for them); it was not about a list. It was about pouring out to God what I did not understand, what I struggled with, what I desired. It was a longing to feel what he felt. If I did not know how to pray or did not want to pray, I told God how I felt and let him take it from there. On my long walks at night, all masks were off.

At the time, one of the realities we faced in the world was the great Iron Curtain of Communism. On my walks, I prayed so many times, probably hundreds of times, that God would open these Communist countries to the gospel, that he would free my suffering brothers and sisters.

Every night, my roommate Solomon made sure we watched the
MacNeil/Lehrer NewsHour on PBS. On one of those nights, my room-
mates and I watched the amazing sight of the Berlin Wall, the great
symbol of Communist oppression, being physically torn down by
German students. I can remember the waves of thankfulness and awe
that swept over me as I saw God answering so many prayers. I remember trying to communicate to the guys how I felt, how God had done
this awesome thing.

They kind of looked at me like I was having a "weird Matt moment."
One remarked, "Yeah, of course we know that God did it," and that
was that. It was a news story to them, not something they felt really
emotional about. But I was so amazed, so full, so in awe at what God
was doing.

It was through this combination of passionate, honest talks with God—
fervent prayer—and seeing God's hand in history through these current
events that I experienced God in a fully emotional way.

As we are conformed to Christ, we can learn to rely on emotions as we
might rely on a friend.

‹ › ›

And so it was that I went, first to Aberdeen, and then on to Tübingen,
to explore emotions.

I learned that psychology, philosophy, culture, and the church have led
us to believe that emotions and the mind are separate. What I started
to put together was that our Christian culture tended to do one of two
things: It either banished emotions, sidelining them from serious
engagement, or it rationalized them, turning emotions into rational
ideas or theological concepts. But that's not what God designed. *He
made emotions to be emotions, thoughts to be thoughts, and both to
be partners, working hand in hand.*

Rightly understood, our emotions are connected to what we focus on,
what we know, what we value, and what we believe. What we *think* and
how we *feel* work together to point us to the truth.

Emotions are a complex judgment or evaluation of someone or something in light of the past, present, or future. Hope, for example, is the
expectation that something good is going to happen in the future to
something or someone we love; whereas joy is felt when something
good has happened in the past or the present.

Emotions can do what a wise counselor does, what a veteran mentor
does, or what a spiritual advisor does—help you make right decisions
from complex information. Emotions carry truth and wisdom, just as a
good friend does.

Philosophy professor William Lyons, in his classic study on emotion,
defines emotions like this:

> The evaluation central to the concept of emotion is an evaluation of some
> object, event or situation in the world about me in relation to me, or accord-
> ing to my norms. Thus my emotions reveal whether I see the world or some
> aspect of it as threatening or welcoming, pleasant or painful, regrettable or
> a solace, and so on.[1]

Separating thinking and judgments from emotion is like trying to ride a
tandem bike with one rider. It is awkward, your balance is off, you tire
easily, and you will not reach where you want to go. Add a second rider,
learn to work together, and it becomes a well-oiled machine that accom-
plishes what it was made to do.

Yet most of us ride the tandem with just one rider. We attempt to drive
our lives by rational thoughts while we repress emotions and the complex
truth they have to offer.

The interdependence of thoughts and emotion has been denied by
some of the great psychologists and philosophers of history and our
generation. We can trace the lie that emotion is not related to our
thinking as far back as Plato, as we noted briefly in chapter 2. Plato saw
these two parts of man as warring against one another in a constant
battle for mastery of the human soul. He especially did not like poetry,

plays, and the arts because he thought they made us more vulnerable to our destructive emotions:

> In regard to the emotions of sex and anger, and all the appetites and pains and pleasures of the soul which we say accompany all our actions, the effect of poetic imitation is the same. For it waters and fosters these feelings when what we ought to do is to dry them up, and it establishes them as our rulers when they ought to be ruled.[2]

One of the strong themes that runs through the classics (you know, those great plays of ancient Greece that you hated to read in high school) is the supposed battle between the passions and reason that Plato talked about.

Plato's views may even have been influenced by earlier Greek poets and playwrights, such as Euripides, who wrote *Medea,* a dramatic tale of destruction unleashed by unbridled passion.

In the play, Medea and her aristocratic husband, Jason, are banished from their hometown and end up as political refugees in Corinth (yep, the same city that Paul visited). There, Jason befriends King Creon and ends up abandoning Medea in order to marry the king's daughter.

Undone by Jason's treachery, Medea hatches an awful plan that will make her notorious throughout theatrical history. After her initial violent reaction results in her banishment from Corinth, she feigns an apology and "makes up" with Jason and the king. Then she sends her children to the king's daughter (Jason's new wife) with a gift of a dress and a diadem. The dress is laced with a deadly poison that kills the princess—and it is so potent that it also kills the king when he embraces his dying daughter.

Medea's next act is even more gruesome and is what earned her a reputation that is synonymous with violence and deceit. Throughout the play, the chorus and the nursemaid have been making comments about the children's safety—and their prophetic words are about to come true. Upon the children's return from their deadly errand, Medea lures them into the house and brutally kills them as they scream for mercy. To the poet, a mother killing her own children is the height of all moral depravity. Denying her maternal instincts, Medea slaughters her precious sons without mercy in order to exact revenge on Jason, their father.

The chorus that narrates the play and the dialogue of the characters show us clearly that much of the play is about the war between reason and emotion in the human soul. At one point, Medea says, "For I have reasoned with my soul and railed upon me thus, 'Ah! poor heart! why am I thus distraught, why so angered 'gainst all good advice?'"[3]

For those who believe that passion is at war with reason, the message of *Medea* is that when passions win the day, we are in grave danger of losing all restraint and morality.

I began to understand that this was like two people fighting over who should ride the tandem bike. How could anyone win? In the Greek plays, the hero can almost never win (that's why the plays are called *tragedies*); passions inevitably lead to great harm and often to the hero's downfall and death.

But did God really create two parts of the human soul that are at war within us? Is there any evidence in the Bible of such a dichotomy? Does the Bible ever speak of emotions generally as *dangerous*?

If so, I haven't found it.

‹ › ›

During the Renaissance, Plato's ideas were picked up by the leaders of a new generation of thinkers and philosophers. René Descartes, the brilliant mathematician, who some say was the father of modern philosophy, echoed Plato in separating reason and emotion.

Many modern psychologists have also followed Plato and Descartes in separating emotion and thinking. They argue that emotion is almost like a reflex reaction of the nervous system to an object or stimulus, much like the "knee jerk" response a doctor gets by tapping your knee with that tiny rubber mallet. So, they believed, it is possible to have a certain feeling without any input from your mind.

This idea was championed by psychologist William James in the late 1800s. He puts it this way:

> Our natural way of thinking about these standard emotions is that the mental perception of some fact excites . . . the emotion, and that this latter state of mind gives rise to the bodily expression. My thesis on the contrary is that *the bodily changes follow directly the* PERCEPTION *of the exciting fact, and that our feeling of the same changes as they occur* IS *the emotion.* Common sense says, we lose our fortune, are sorry and weep; we meet a bear, are frightened and run; we are insulted by a rival, are angry and strike. The hypothesis here to be defended says that this order of sequence is incorrect, that the one mental state is not immediately induced by the other . . . the more rational statement is that we feel sorry because we cry, angry because we strike, afraid because we tremble, and not that we cry, strike, or tremble, because we are sorry, angry, or fearful. . . . Without the bodily states following on the perception, the latter would be purely cognitive in form, pale, colourless, destitute of emotional warmth. We might then see the bear, and judge it best to run, receive the insult and deem it right to strike, but we could not actually *feel* afraid or angry.[4]

So, in James's view, if your mind realizes that your skin is hot, you feel agitated, and your heart is pumping faster, it concludes that you are angry. The emotion *is* the feeling.

Can you believe that this crazy idea became the most dominant understanding of emotion in modern psychology? It's almost as if James's hypothesis says that I am angry *because* I am punching somebody in the face. What sense does that make? The body's reaction that results from our emotion can't be the cause! Yet, this same basic assumption is prominent in the writings of many who have shaped our modern world, from James to Darwin to Freud. But if it is true, it leaves us grasping at straws as to what emotion really is.

Nobody who believes that emotion is the sensation of feeling itself can explain their feelings of love or joy or any other emotion in a way that makes any sense. If emotion is the sensation itself, we are left with no concrete concepts by which to define what emotion actually is.

⟨⟨⟩⟩

The idea that emotions are not connected to thinking is especially important to understand when we think of the words we often use for emotions: *feelings* or *how I feel.*

We often use the words *emotions* and *feelings* interchangeably. We refer to emotions as "feeling something" because most often when we get emotional, our bodies react with physical feelings. You can see, however, the importance of understanding the difference between emotions and feelings. Emotions are things that originate in our minds. Feelings, on the other hand, can refer to anything that our bodies sense or perceive, such as a stomachache or pain when we stub a toe.

To Plato, Descartes, Darwin, James, and Freud, emotions *were* a certain type of bodily feeling experienced in the nervous system. They believed that the emotions *were* the feelings.

However, more recent scholarship and science support what I have come to believe: Emotions *produce* the feelings that are associated with them. If I get up to speak and feel sick to my stomach, it is because my mind is telling my body that I'm nervous.

Emotion, from this perspective, is clearly different from what we feel in our bodies or nerves. There is no better explanation of this idea than the one given by theologian Jonathan Edwards in *Religious Affections*:

> The other faculty is that by which the soul does not merely perceive and view things, but is in some way inclined toward the things it views or considers. . . . The soul either views things with approval, with pleasure, and with acceptance, or it views things with opposition, with disapproval, with displeasure, and with rejection. . . . These are those vigorous and sensible exercises of the faculty that we call the affections. . . . The body of man is not directly capable of thinking or understanding. Only the soul has ideas, and so only the soul is pleased or displeased with its ideas. Since only the soul thinks, only the soul loves or hates, rejoices or is grieved at what it thinks. The bodily effects of these emotions are not the same thing as the affections, and in no way are essential to them.[5]

Edwards gets it right when he says, "These are those vigorous and sensible exercises of the faculty that we call the affections."

The important thing to remember is that we cannot get emotional without making a judgment, without evaluating, without thinking.

The healthy soul is like the tandem bike, on which both thoughts and emotions are pedaling.

〈〈〉〉

Another thing I learned on my journey is that the connection between emotions and thinking usually happens subconsciously.

Obviously, we do not sit down and decide to have an emotion in the same way that we might sit down with our spouse to make a major decision. To say that emotions are connected to thinking does not mean they always come from conscious, intentional thoughts. Rather, emotions have a wisdom all their own, which is naturally informed by our circumstances, situations, and relationships. They speak to us about truth that we cannot always know rationally or even think thoughts about.

I love the famous quote from Blaise Pascal: "The heart has its reasons which reason knows nothing of."

In other words, emotion has a level of "thinking" that is not conscious or "reasoned." Yet, it is wise and complex in its perceptions—a very smart friend, and one we should listen to.

It's not uncommon for people to feel fear when they enter their house while it is being robbed, even when they have no direct knowledge that someone else is in the house. They step inside, and all of a sudden they're afraid. They know something is wrong. This feeling has saved many a person from harm, as they have acted on that fear. When questioned at length after the fact, often the people can identify why they felt afraid. Perhaps a picture was moved out of its normal place, or maybe they knew the door to the dining room was shut when they left but it was open when they returned. Some perceptions they may never be able to identify, but their wonderfully complex minds (which God designed) picked up something that said there was reason for fear, without their even having to think about it. That is the realm in which emotions operate, which can make it difficult to figure out exactly why we are feeling what we feel.

Our tendency when emotions surface is to decide that we shouldn't feel them, so we dismiss them, ditching them in the first mental trash can we can find. But our emotions often tell us things that our rational processes cannot get to, things we desperately need to hear.

I think this idea is the essence of *Blink,* the best-selling book by Malcolm Gladwell. The book's subtitle gets to the point: "The Power of Thinking Without Thinking." Gladwell asserts that our first impressions on subjects we are intimately familiar with are usually right. We have an innate instinct about what's true that completely bypasses conscious, rational thought. These instincts are wise, informed, and usually accurate—but they're most often not a conscious act of reason. They are packets of wisdom that come to us in a flash. Gladwell's advice? Pay attention to them.

I'm not sure I want to equate emotion with instinct or intuition, but I believe they're related and interdependent.[6] And emotion works similarly to instinct: It carries a very intelligent, subconscious thinking that comes to us in a flash—a "packet" of awareness and truth and knowledge that instantly equips us to respond in a situation.

When my wife was in college, she spent a summer working with youth in the Philippines. She lived with a pastor and his wife and their five-year-old daughter. The first nine weeks she was there, she felt really uncomfortable and afraid. She knew of no good reason to be struggling and feeling at risk, but she was. She felt guilty for her lack of trust and her emotional distance from others. She remembers asking her roommate, "What is wrong with me? Why can't I connect with the people here?"

One day, she went into the house to get an aspirin, and the pastor followed her into her room and tried to kiss her. She pushed him away and escaped, her summer ministry shattering into hurt, disillusionment, and disappointment. A tragedy now faced this broken man and his young family. Laura was immediately removed from the situation by the

agency, and through loving care and wise counseling, her sense
of peace was restored.

One reason God gave us our emotions was to aid us in our decision
making by giving us impressions and information that are outside our
conscious thoughts. Laura knew there was something wrong in that
home in the Philippines, though she had no way to truly identify it. Our
emotions tap into things we just can't get our minds around, things we
cannot understand like we would understand a map or an instruction
manual. We cannot always explain *why* we feel as we do about something or someone, but we just have a sense about it.

After fifteen years of marriage, I would say that Laura has a 65 to 75
percent accuracy rating on her woman's intuition. There are times when
I have to say, "Laura, this does not fit the facts; there is no possible way
that is true." But more often than not, if I am willing to listen, I gain
valuable insight about a person or a situation. Intuition occurs in both
men and women, of course, but with women's God-given role as mothers
and nurturers, they seem especially able to see truth about other people
through the window of emotion.

When you think of emotion this way, it becomes clear that it's "higher-
order" stuff—a complex faculty within us that God has provided to help
us, guide us, and counsel us—all the things that a good friend does.

This "higher-order" understanding is in stark contrast to the historical
understanding that emotions are physical sensations that are part of our
animal nature and cannot be trusted.

〈〉〉

Another thing I learned is essential to our further discussion of emotion.

Emotions are always *about something*. They have an object. When a
woman falls in love, it is not just a vague experience of falling in love
generally. She falls in love with *someone*. When a man becomes angry,
he is angry at *something* or *someone*. I'll admit that sometimes we
don't consciously know the object of our anger or fear or love; yet
there's always an object. We have become so out of touch with our

emotions, so repressed and confused, that the object of our emotions isn't always as clear to us as it should be. That's why we often use friends and pastors and therapists to help us pinpoint the object of our emotion.

Emotions are verbs that must have nouns.

Hope is an illustration of this. A farmer can hope he will have a bumper crop of corn next year, but that is dependent on factors beyond his control—such as rain. There are no guarantees. I can hope that tomorrow will be sunny because I am planning a trip to Brookfield Zoo with my kids—the wolves being a special favorite of my eldest. If I listen to the weather report and hear a good forecast, my hope is on pretty good footing. With Christian hope, it is like the sun coming up tomorrow. That hope is something so grounded, so hard, so true that we can bank on it every second of every day.

The nature, intensity, and duration of the hope we feel are totally dependent on the object upon which we are setting our hope.

The difference is not in the emotion of hope itself, not what hope *is*, but rather what is hoped *for,* the noun that is attached to the emotion.

The same is true of joy. This is apparent in Paul's famous phrase, "Always be full of joy in the Lord. I say it again—rejoice!"[7] He doesn't tell us just to "have joy." Our joy is "in the Lord." There are few things in life that we can always rejoice in. God is one of the few. We can do the always rejoicing part because it is "about" the always-loving, always-holy, always-good God.

Or how about the best-loved verse, John 3:16: "For God so loved the world that he gave his one and only Son, that whoever believes in him shall not perish but have eternal life."[8] I'm just not big enough to love everybody in the world, and thankfully God never tells me to do that. Love is personal, toward a specific object. God is the only one who knows every person intimately. He is the Creator. He loves the world personally and intimately in all its complexity, and every individual within it. God is the only one who can love in this way, because he is the only one who knows the world fully. It really means something special that he loves the whole world.

What emotions are telling us is information — wisdom — about the
nouns in our lives.

⟨⟨⟩⟩

Whenever we build a friendship, we start by being interested in the
other person. We begin to evaluate what they say, consider what it
means in our life, have fun with them, trust them to give valid input, and
begin to interact with them — hopefully in a way that builds both of us
up. Over time, a strong friend becomes an anchor in the storms of life
and someone who really celebrates our triumphs and grieves our pain.
Sometimes a great friend needs to show us where we are wrong or
encourage us where we are right.

Emotion can work like that in our lives.

Jonathan Edwards, arguably America's greatest Christian philosopher,
faced much the same problem in his generation — people thought
emotions were something to conquer rather than embrace. Edwards
became one of the leaders of what we now call the Great Awakening, that
great revival that swept North America. With an eloquence more common
in his day than in ours, he said that emotions should be our friends and
strongly criticized those voices that wanted to push them to the sidelines:

If the great things of religion are rightly understood, they will affect the heart.
So the reason why men are not affected by such infinitely great, important
and glorious things as they often read in the Word of God, is undoubtedly
that they are blind.

To devalue all religious affections is the way to harden the hearts of men
and to encourage them in their folly and senselessness. This keeps them in a
state of spiritual death, as long as they go on living, and at last brings them
to eternal death. So the prevailing prejudice against religious affections today
has the awful effect of hardening the hearts of sinners and of dampening the
grace of many saints and reducing all to a state of dullness and apathy. To
despise and cry against all religious affections is a sure way of shutting all
religion out of the heart and of ruining souls. . . . Those who have little religious affection have very little religion.[9]

When we start seeing our emotions as friends, we look for what our emotions have to offer us. We begin to see that they help us identify what we truly believe, what is truly important to us, and what we value.

Like friends, emotions can add such dimension to our lives. Who would ever want to live without laughter, for example, or even the ability to grieve? We would be so flat and dull.

As we familiarize ourselves with our emotions as friends, we realize that they tell us the truth. Sometimes we can be in the middle of a hard situation, and suddenly we feel a sense of futility. When we realize that our situation is not going anywhere good, we are motivated to action, to live life differently.

That is the beauty of true friendship. True friends don't let us stay in the same, comfortable rut. They encourage and exhort us to move somewhere new by something they say or do. How often in conversation has a friend said something that gets right to the heart of your struggle? How often has a friend's perspective opened a whole new way of thinking for you? Emotions can act as tremendous catalysts in our lives if we will only listen to the truth they reveal.

Kate is a natural perfectionist. Everything needs to be just so, or her world seems out of balance. Some of this works; we need people like Kate to keep an ordered world. But some of her perfectionism goes over the edge to dysfunction. Like when she must start a project over from scratch when there is just one mistake that nobody else would even notice. Recently, she was vacuuming the house and felt so overwhelmed and upset that she just lost it—to the point that she didn't think she could finish. Finally, she pulled herself together and sat down to think about it. Why was this simple task feeling like it was just too much?

She used the emotion of feeling overwhelmed to help her focus on her unhealthy level of perfectionism and change her faulty thinking. She understood that she felt overwhelmed because she was trying to do the task perfectly, and she just did not have the time or energy to do it perfectly. But then she realized that getting into every corner, under every piece of furniture, and finding every speck was not the goal. She had company coming the next day, and all she really needed to do was get the main traffic areas clean before they came. Once she recognized that, Kate was able to finish the job feeling just fine.

Kate turned to her feeling for counsel and advice, as she would a friend. She used emotion to help her identify what in her life was making a simple task so difficult—her need to clean perfectly—and then deliberately refocused herself on reality. That is when her emotion became a true friend.

All of us have seen that sometimes a friend's direct comment or honest assessment can take us to a new and better place. The same is true of emotion. Whether it is showing us our brokenness or our strength, it still is our friend.

When viewed rightly, emotion becomes a strong friend that pulls us through the tough stuff in life, of which there is plenty. I remember finding out that our son Jackson, nine months old at the time, needed immediate heart surgery. He was so small, and this was our first really big challenge as parents. His surgery would take about six hours, and they believed that he would recover fully and require no further treatment.

During that time, friends asked us how we could be so calm when we were taking our only child to have open-heart surgery. I remember thinking that this was not hard compared to what other people were going through on our same floor at the pediatric cardiac unit at Christ Hospital. Other parents were learning that their children would die or that keeping their child's heart pumping was going to be a lifelong struggle. I was overwhelmed with gratitude that our doctor gave us the name of a top surgeon; that there was a great local hospital that specialized in children's heart surgery; that the hospital would take Jackson; and that once the surgery was over, his heart would enjoy a long and totally normal life. I could choose to be thankful and trust God. As I did, a peace came over me, showing that what I thought about and what I felt were close together. Being thankful for the good things—and the emotions that came with that—powered me through that tough time.

God provides us emotions as friends, not enemies. It's wrong that our culture teaches us to mistrust emotions, to diminish them, and to convert them into abstract, rational ideas.

⟨⟨⟩⟩

What about negative emotions? Like that anger that takes you to a place you do not want to be; or the jealousy of somebody else's success that you cannot even admit to anyone; or the hatred of something about another person? We have all been there.

What about these emotions? How can they be your friends? Well, if you can believe it, negative emotions can be some of your best and closest friends. Remember, emotions have an object, and negative emotions are attached to things we value and believe. Just as best friends are typically the most honest with us, negative emotions often give us the most help to let us know when we are out of whack and when it is time for a change. Negative emotions demand a response; they compel us to enter the dialogue—to grow. Negative emotions are often tied to deep realities within ourselves. And we must deal with these realities, even when they're not so pretty.

The root problem behind negative emotions is not the emotion itself; it's you—your mistaken beliefs, your unhealthy values, your faulty thinking.

Emotions will point you back to what needs clarifying or changing. They help you identify where you need to grow.

God truly wants us to embrace all of our emotions as companions, as friends, as dependable counselors in our lives.

BLOG 07: FRIEND

ANDREW]·····[It is hard to trust Emotion as a friend when I am only meeting him for the very first time. He's like that cousin you had never met until the awkward family reunion. The only thing we have in common is the same last name. Knowledge has been a good friend for a long time. It will take time to trust Emotion for direction. You say that "emotions carry truth and wisdom." But can't emotions also carry lies and ignorance? I have been there when Knowledge fails to explain what only Emotion can discern. But Knowledge stands by my side when Emotion is skewed by tiredness and disease. I think you are right though—Emotion will be a valuable friend. But it's going to take some time to learn how (or when) to trust him.

REBECCA]·····[One of the things I really liked about this chapter was how it equated emotions with being our friend, our best ally, instead of our worst nightmare. About mid-semester last fall, I had my world turned upside down. For a period of 3 weeks, I was in excruciating back pain until finally I said, "Enough." That was the athlete in me not wanting to do anything about it. In mid-November, I finally went in to the doctor, and after some examination, he told me that he wanted me to go immediately to the ER because he thought I had appendicitis. I was so scared and just started crying. Now, keep in mind I am not a person who cries and shows much emotion, so my mom and doctor were caught a little bit off guard. As the night progressed, after 8 hours and lots of tests, we found out that it was not appendicitis but instead a grapefruit-sized cyst growing on my spine, as well as a 10 cm ovarian cyst. Part of me was incredibly relieved because it meant I would not have to have immediate surgery. That was my first reaction—relief. But as time went on, I came to find out that not only was my condition more serious than we originally thought, but it was one that would require major surgery; in fact, it would be a case that was a rarity.

I realized I was pretty scared, but I was afraid to show that I was scared. I didn't know how to respond. However, when I did let on that I was scared, more like terrified, then I began to have a little bit of peace. I know, ironic I say that I had peace about it because I knew I couldn't change the situation. I knew that it had to be done or they would cause worse harm. So it was through my coming to terms that I needed to have surgery and then depending on God for wisdom as to when the surgery needed to be done and other details—like my job—that I was able to fully give the situation over and have peace. It didn't mean I wasn't scared. But it did mean that I allowed my emotions to guide me into a place where I was comfortable being scared but in the peace of knowing that God was there every step of the way.

JAMES]·····[Aha. There is the better analogy: a tandem bike. Reason and emotion working together to make progress through life. And in my experience with a tandem bike, it really doesn't matter which person is in the front doing the steering. Either one can do it well. What a refreshing way of looking at the problem.

MARIAN]·····[How easy it has been for me to distrust emotion. I, like so many, have been conditioned to do so. My emotions were simply too painful, so I shut them off—in my infamous box. But I see their value and worth. I choose to embrace them as friends. To learn to trust them. To let them do their work of revealing truth, even when they challenge me about my unhealthy beliefs. I see their purpose and value— like verbs that need nouns—that bring wisdom. Teach me Lord to trust my heart as much as my mind.

TODD]·····[I'm a believer in love at first sight. I liked the reference to Malcolm Gladwell's book, *Blink*. It's affirming to me, to assert that our first impression is usually right. I understand Jonathan Edwards when he said, "The other faculty is that by which the soul does not merely perceive and view things, but is in some way inclined toward the things it views or considers." It's the way God nudges me along in life, past my faulty rationale.

What changes my thinking in this chapter? The idea that my negative emotions can really act as dependable counselors, or even go as far as best and closest friends. Rather than lead me down the path of destruction, these emotions want to call out the faults that I need to change.

JULIE]·····[These past 6 months for our family have been the most intense and most challenging time we've ever experienced. Our third child was born in January, and four weeks after that our second child, Joshua, was diagnosed with cancer. Immediately, he had to have surgery, and then twenty-five weeks of treatment. Soon after Joshua's surgery, there were three deaths in our family back-to-back. My husband lost his godly grandma, whom our firstborn is named after. She lived to be almost 101! Then my grandma died, and then our 52-year-old brother-in-law died of a rare disease that he was suffering with for many months, but wasn't diagnosed with until everything was going on with Joshua. As a Christian, this period in my life was to me my first real taste of "trials and tribulations." Sure, I had experienced difficult circumstances or inconvenient things in my life, but nothing like this.

But time and time again throughout these 6 months, my family and I have seen God at work and we've experienced His peace and presence in amazing and humbling ways. We've been able to truly say God is good ALL the time. We've never questioned "why us?" We have clung to God's promises found in His Word. The Lord reminds me when I start to fear about our son's future that He has ordained the number of our days. He will not give us one day more or one day less. God is not surprised by cancer, disease, or death. He is in control, even when things seem out of control. He holds the future, and we can rest in Him. Yes, there have been times when we were exhausted. Yes, there have been times when we shed tears. But God remains good all the time. There is nothing like having His sweet peace in the midst of such uncertainty.

TOM]·····[I also connected with the music of Keith Green. I would say that I wanted to love what God loved, but my commitment was not strong enough. It's funny when I think about it now. I would listen to Keith Green and other Christian artists because their songs encouraged me to worship God, echoed what I read in Scripture, and made me aspire to more excellent things. But then I would turn right around and listen to lyrics that were morally bankrupt and somehow think they did not affect me. Luckily, as I grew older, the Spirit convicted me about what I was listening to, and I cleaned it up. Part of the problem was that I was also too young to pick up on a lot of the hidden and double meanings in songs. I say that, hoping it does not come across as an excuse—I am responsible for what I allow before my mind. But it's a great lesson for me as a parent as I remember that my kids need a lot of guidance. It's going to be harder for them to make good decisions about the so-called "big issues" such as underage drinking, premarital sex, drugs, etc., if they are careless about what influences they allow to shape their attitudes about living for God.

I once heard a preacher say, "Our conscience is a great gift from God. It is a dark day when we play fast and loose with it." I have never forgotten that.

Enter the discussion at www.faithfulfeelings.com.

MY BLOG

_____

_____

_____

_____

_____

_____

_____

_____

_____

_____

08 Truth

Emotions help us navigate life better. They empower us to accomplish remarkable things for God, ourselves, and others. They carry wisdom and intuition about situations and people beyond the mere facts. They are the source of the pleasure that God wants us to have. They serve as guides to help us understand what we believe and how we need to grow.

No doubt you are reading this book as a way to understand emotion, but I hope you can begin to see emotion as a way to understand life.

As a parent, I have occasionally had to deal with a bawling or screaming child who has entered the meltdown stage. Sometimes, I've had to say to one of my kids, "Stop your crying right now." I stop the expression of the emotion because I am committed to training my children to handle their emotions well. They need to stop the meltdown and take some time to refocus and evaluate what they are upset about and how to communicate it. We've all been there, and often it's because we are just tired and weary and can't handle things. We have to stop ourselves and figure out what is going on.

Of course, you and I know that a child's emotions are windows into what's going on deep inside. Mothers are specially attuned to this—they can hear their infant's cry a room away and know from the particular character of the cry that the baby needs to be fed or needs to be changed or is in some danger. Most of us can read a child's emotional expressions and have a pretty good idea of what's going on.

Despite the fact that we sometimes stifle our children's crying and screaming (in order to train them), we understand that the emotions expressed are not always wrong. They provide us with valuable information about our child's state of being, mind, and heart.

Unfortunately, we aren't always so adept at reading and understanding and interpreting our own emotions. Often, our emotions burst out, and we don't really understand why they're there. Sometimes we think they're about one thing, but actually they're about something else. Sometimes, we hold one emotion in, but it's still there, and it comes out in other outbursts or behaviors that we don't like or want. We don't always have a parent's intuition about ourselves—why we feel what we do.

This is why there are psychologists, counselors, therapists, pastors, and friends—people who help us interpret our emotions and what they mean.

I believe we can do better at reading and interpreting our own emotions, just as we can learn to read the emotions of a child. One reason we can read the emotions of our children is because we can remember how we felt as a child before our understanding grew to where it is now. Likewise, I think we can learn how to use emotion as a way of understanding the truth about ourselves.

But how?

⟨⟨⟩⟩

I want to provide a simple set of tools to help you understand and interpret what your emotions are saying about you and others. We'll label these tools *Focus, Know, Value,* and *Believe.* It's a simple toolbox that may help you immensely.

It's helped Bob and Dianne. In fact, they've experienced a revolution in their lives.

When Laura and I first met them, we were immediately drawn to their passion and vitality. Whatever is in front of them to do, they go after it with energy, enthusiasm, and hard work. In the few years they've been our friends, this go-get-'em attitude has included everything from teaching Sunday school to leading a small group; from starting an afternoon kids' club at their boys' school to running the sound system for kids' programs; from Dianne being on the planning committee for a women's retreat to Dianne spending each church service with a little boy with special needs so that his parents could attend the service. (Are you tired yet? I sure am!)

This is their story. Ten years ago, the energy that they now spend on serving others was spent on serving themselves. They were all about self-indulgence. They purchased the house where they live because it had a pool, a great big yard to play volleyball in, and a fire pit. They wanted a place where they could really party and have fun. They had what they considered to be a good marriage, and they enjoyed living it up, traveling, and drinking together. Bob told me, "We used to put the kids to bed early so we could go out to the garage and drink together." Dianne added, "I told a friend that I would never live my life without alcohol."

The TV was always on because the quiet desperation growing in Dianne's soul could not take silence. "With all the drinking," she said, "as much as I loved Bob, I knew somehow that my marriage was headed in the same direction as that of my parents, who were selfish and miserable. I just remember praying that God would show me truth." She became desperate to find something solid to live for. She decided to stop drinking until she found truth.

One day, she was driving in her car, and she felt a touch of God, as if Jesus himself were saying to her, "Come to me." She did not want to believe that Christians had an edge on truth. She did not want to admit that Jesus was the Truth, but at that moment there was no denying it anymore. She knew that the Bible and all Jesus said were true, whether she liked it or not. She would just have to get past her own bias and jump. Dianne surrendered—completely, totally, without any holding back. It came like a flood. The joy and hope she was looking for were upon her in that car in a way she could not have imagined a few minutes before. The Truth, Jesus himself, had stepped into her life, and everything changed.

Bob's resentment of Dianne's new faith grew as he lost his best drinking buddy and understood that Dianne was not just passing through another stage. This change was for keeps. Dianne focused on Jesus and prayed for her husband. Not only was resentment growing in Bob's life, but he was struggling with a deep fear of death.

Sometime later, they both went through a process of being instructed in the responsibilities of a godparent by his brother's pastor. Bob thought, *I am not even doing that for my own kids, let alone my godchild.* Bob and Dianne started checking out services at local churches so their kids could be brought up with some religious training.

When Bob and Dianne went to a service at a large church in their area, it was baptism Sunday. Baptism is a symbol of new life, a reminder that death has been conquered. Bob knew he needed new life. When a man got up and told the story of his life before Christ, Bob saw himself in the story. The man told of how he lived now, joyfully pouring his life out for Jesus because his past sins were forgiven. Soon after, Bob gave his life over to God.

I tell this story because, of all the people in my life, Bob and Dianne are probably the best at taking God's Word and simply believing it enough to actually do what it says. As they have poured themselves into learning about God, their emotions have been transformed. They have gone from a fruitless pursuit of pleasure to joyfully serving others.

Bob and Dianne have put the principles in this chapter to work, and it has been part of the recipe for their changed lives. They expect that if God says you should feel a particular way, they can and should feel that way. More than that, they believe that God is big enough to empower them to feel it.

During one period in Dianne's life, she struggled with anger. She found that stuffing her anger down and pasting a Bible verse on top was not helping. There was no victory in that. She found herself eating too much and organizing her house and life like a crazed clone of Martha Stewart. Something was wrong.

Eventually, she embraced some of the ideas in this book, particularly the toolbox of *Focus, Know, Value,* and *Believe.* It has really helped her gain a window into her life.

Likewise, Bob has learned to use the toolbox to deal with a number of stressful situations over the years. Recently, I observed a situation between Bob and his sons, Karl and Alex. We were enjoying a relaxed after-dinner dessert in their backyard. Our combined total of four boys were all play fighting with swords and light-sabers, running around, throwing balls at each other. Karl, their eight-year-old, was in a hard-fought dodgeball battle with his big brother, twelve-year-old Alex. The battle did not go well for Karl; he lacked the skills of his brother, who is four years older and a much larger combatant. Do you remember that feeling as a kid? No matter how hard you fought, how well you did, it was never enough, and you were desperate to prove you were just as good, if not better? Overwhelmed with frustration, Karl was soon really upset and angry.

I wondered how Bob would have handled the situation earlier in his life. This time, he used the principles of *Focus, Know, Value,* and *Believe* and came to a good resolution in that moment with Karl.

I'll explain how these situations turned out in a moment, but first let me show you the four tools and how they work.

Focus

First, we need to understand why we are feeling what we are feeling.
That takes *focus*.

The familiar story of Jonah is a great illustration of someone who was
completely out of touch with his own feelings. He had no clue.

I'm sure you remember the first part of the story, but do you recall the last
part? God tells Jonah to go to Nineveh to preach a message that is very
simple: "Repent or die." Going to the most prosperous and powerful city
in the world, standing on a corner and shouting "repent or die" does not
sound like Jonah's idea of a good time. So he hops on a boat headed in
the wrong direction.

You know the rest: God sends a storm; Jonah is thrown overboard and
is swallowed by a giant fish. In the fish's belly, Jonah decides that it
must be pretty important that he get to Nineveh as soon as possible.

After the fish spits him out, Jonah arrives in Nineveh and—would you
believe it?—this powerful and rich city responds rather well to the
message of "repent or die." Everyone from king to beggar gets dressed
up in old burlap sacks and sits down on ash heaps. They decide that
not only are they not going to eat, but they will not even feed their
animals. Better yet, they pledge to "turn from their evil ways and stop
all their violence."

God listens to their plea and decides they can all live. The Bible says,
"This change of plans greatly upset Jonah, and he became very
angry." He says, "I knew that you are a merciful and compassionate
God, slow to get angry and filled with unfailing love. . . . [But] just kill
me now, LORD! I'd rather be dead than alive if what I predicted will not
happen."

Here is the key—are you ready? God says, "Is it right for you to be angry
about this?" God does not say, "How dare you be angry!" or "Do not be
angry" or even "Just get over it, okay? This is what I am going to do."
Instead, God asks a question. And not only does he ask a question, he
gives Jonah a teaching aid so he can actually get the right answer.

Jonah goes up on a hill overlooking the city, perhaps still expecting God to destroy it in some kind of cosmic, fiery explosion. The sun is hot, so Jonah builds a lean-to. God causes a plant to grow up and over the structure, providing wonderful, cool shade on that hot, Middle Eastern day.

The next morning, a worm eats through the stem of the plant, and the plant dies. Not only does the plant die, but it is an incredibly hot day, with a baking sun and a hot wind that only make it worse. It is so hot that Jonah says, "Death is certainly better than living like this."

Then God comes out with his questions again: "Is it right for you to be angry because the plant died?"

"Yes," says Jonah, "even angry enough to die."

God replies, "You feel sorry about the plant, though you did nothing to put it there. It came quickly and died quickly. But Nineveh has more than 120,000 people living in spiritual darkness, not to mention all the animals. Shouldn't I feel sorry for such a great city?"[1]

Do you see the point? God is taking Jonah to an understanding of why he is angry. He is questioning the thinking that is creating the anger, digging out the root. Eventually, God has to walk Jonah through the whole thing. God's initial response is not to denounce Jonah's anger, but to examine it.

He literally prompts Jonah to ask and answer the question of why he is angry.

The first aspect of the *Focus* tool is why. What is behind this thing I'm feeling?

The second aspect of the *Focus* tool has to do with the MP3 downloads we play in our heads about the way we see the world, who we are, what we have to offer, and what we believe about other people.

Our emotional response to anything is a collage of our personality, upbringing, self-image, worldview, experiences, and beliefs. What we concentrate on, what we dwell on, what we run over and over again in our heads is what we get emotional about. So we need to stop and think about what we are always telling ourselves. If it does not line up with what is true, we must cancel the download. Then we need to reboot our thought patterns with godly values and beliefs. Only then can our emotions reflect a godly perspective.

Whatever podcast you play in your head is what you will eventually believe about God, others, and yourself. It will determine your emotional starting point and the place out of which you will respond. You can spend most of your life at a single spot emotionally because you pitched your tent on one thing that you relive and rehash every day. Sometimes, you have to make yourself pack it up and move on to something new.

Sometimes grief can be like that.

If we lose a friend we loved dearly, the first few months are the hardest. We're used to having that person around, talking to them on the phone regularly, meeting them for coffee, or seeing them at church. As we go about our days, we are reminded that the loss has left a gaping hole in our lives.

But as the months and years pass, the grief normally dissipates. The daily reminders are not as fresh; we have developed a new routine. The love we feel for the person is no less, and we can still grieve when we are reminded of their death, but time and distance have given us relief from constant grief. Now we simply don't focus on it all the time.

Emotion is shaped by what we focus on, by what we consciously put before our minds.

I sometimes share words from Deuteronomy 11 as perhaps the most powerful words in the Bible about emotion:

> So commit yourselves wholeheartedly to these words of mine. Tie them to your hands and wear them on your forehead as reminders. Teach them to your children. Talk about them when you are at home and when you are on the road, when you are going to bed and when you are getting up. Write

them on the doorposts of your house and on your gates, so that as long as the sky remains above the earth, you and your children may flourish in the land the LORD swore to give your ancestors. Be careful to obey all these commands I am giving you. Show love to the LORD your God by walking in his ways and holding tightly to him.²

These verses ask us the questions, What do we put before our eyes? What do we concentrate on? What do we spend our idle moments thinking about? If we want to have the emotions that God promises to give us, we need to fill our lives with his words, his truth, his thoughts. We need to go to Scripture regularly when we face a decision in the middle of the day, when we gather for a meal around the table, and when we're with our spouse before we go to sleep. God did not tell us to do this just to make our lives more complicated. He told us this so that we could live the abundant life that he wants for us, "so that . . . you and your children may flourish."

We will never be able to deal with the triumphs and tragedies of life as God intends until we have studied and memorized his ways, putting them before our minds constantly and focusing on his truth about our lives.

A recent study on the average Christian's Bible-reading habits found that twenty- and thirtysomethings are not reading their Bibles all that much. It will be impossible for this generation, a generation that prides itself on living out of their emotions, to ever come to emotional balance or fulfillment if they do not know the Word of God. If you say to me, "I do not feel God, and I do not feel excited about my faith," I'd ask you if you are immersing yourself in his truth. Is it living water to your soul?

My grandfather, a Baptist minister, gave my dad his Bible, the Bible Grandpa had used his whole life. Every page is well-read, every margin has notes, and the binding is failing. My grandfather has faced lots of trials, trouble, poverty, and death. His father abandoned him; his strong-willed mother raised the family on her own; he lived through the Depression; and he never owned a house until he reached retirement. My dad never met his grandfather until he was engaged to my mom and his grandfather was on his deathbed. Grandpa has told me the story of how as a little boy they did not have money to buy coal to heat the house. He would walk along the railroad tracks, looking for coal that might drop from the steam locomotives or hoping that a kind fireman might shovel some out to him.

Grandpa has a happy heart; I have never seen bitterness in him, nor have I ever known him to feel sorry for himself. Even after Grandma's death, his beloved wife of more than fifty years, he is very quick to tell a joke and has an easy smile. The well-worn Bible has made all the difference. He has lived by dwelling on the truths of God rather than focusing on the hardships of life.

Without a worn Bible, we will never get through the troubles of life with a glad heart.

We must choose to fill our minds with the right things. As Paul teaches us in the book of Philippians, "fix your thoughts on what is true, and honorable, and right, and pure, and lovely, and admirable. Think about things that are excellent and worthy of praise."[3] The *Focus* tool asks, *Why I am feeling what I'm feeling?* and *What is preoccupying my mind and heart?* Answers to these questions focus us on something in our lives and past that is generating a behavior and emotion right now. Sometimes, those answers require a change in our thinking and focus. This is the first step to understanding our emotional lives.

Know

The plain facts often determine how we feel. The *Know* tool is our assessment of the world around us, a determination of what is *actual* and not just *imagined.*

Recently, our son had his first dentist appointment. It was a simple checkup, but Jackson felt a lot of apprehension about it. What he imagined was pain and blood. We sat him down before the appointment and talked about what can happen to your teeth if you don't take care of them. The knowledge that cavities, drills, and Novocain are much worse than his idea of the checkup, and the fact that checkups help prevent the worse stuff that he was imagining helped him get through the experience. He did great, because the new knowledge gave him the courage he needed. When he came to *know* why he needed to go to the dentist, he discovered that he could overcome his fear.

Sometimes, our emotions are based on wrong knowledge. We often make the mistake of saying our emotions are wrong, when much of the time they're perfectly right—just based on the wrong information. The *Know* tool helps us check to see if our information is right.

If I tell you there's a five-hundred-pound grizzly bear fifteen feet away from you, you would be terrified, your heart would beat like crazy, and fear would overwhelm you.

Now let me add one little piece of information: zoo.

Knowing more of the context, your feelings now change. Were your feelings wrong before? No, but they needed additional information. In fact, if you weren't at the zoo, your feelings of terror might have saved your life.

I think it's interesting that, in the Bible, God doesn't tell us how to feel without telling us what truth to believe. He gives us the context in which to feel our emotions. He never just tells us about the bear without telling us where it is.

When there is a command to be joyful, have hope, or love one another, there is also a corresponding truth. Jesus taught that putting his truth at the center of our lives is what will bring lasting freedom and joy to our souls. "Jesus said to the people who believed in him, 'You are truly my disciples if you remain faithful to my teachings. And you will know the truth, and the truth will set you free.'"[4]

Many people want to feel the joy of the Lord, but they do not *know* how God says they can attain it. They have not discovered the information from God's Word that leads to joy.

Like me, my father grew up in a Christian home and has been a Christian since childhood. In order to discover things God has given him that he takes for granted, he will often ask someone who became a Christian as an adult, "What is the biggest difference Christ has made in your life?"

He once asked this of an African friend, Femi Adedayo. Femi said, "My grandmother was a witch doctor. When I was a boy, she had masks hanging on the wall of her hut. She would carry on conversations with these masks, or rather with the spirits that manifested themselves in them. I learned to fear the spirits. If something bad would happen to a person, people in my village would ask 'Who cursed him?' The biggest difference Christ has made in my life is a freedom from fear."

Femi did not need to be afraid of the evil powers he had seen as a child, he did not need to fear being cursed, and he did not need to fear death. Christ had freed him from the power of evil. The knowledge that Christ defeated the powers of our enemy once and for all at the Cross gave Femi a freedom from his emotion of fear.

Jesus Christ brings to each of us a new set of information about the world around us. Without him, we have reason to fear and worry. With him, our emotions have a whole new context. Jesus' words ring true: "You will know the truth, and the truth will set you free."[5]

Value

We get the most emotional about the things that mean the most to us.

Nobody gets upset when somebody runs over their newspaper with a blue Ford pickup, but if the same blue truck bumped over their cat, Fluffy, that is another issue entirely. The newspaper has very little *value;* Fluffy is practically a member of the family.

The relative importance of value is obvious, perhaps, but it's a lesson we rarely learn when it comes to emotions. Our emotions are a reflection of our priorities, what's really important to us.

I can't say I was a fan of *The Apprentice,* but I have flipped the channel to the show and watched a bit. You probably know the format: Candidates compete for a job with Donald Trump, the billionaire. Everything Mr. Trump does is the biggest, the best, and the most expensive. His private plane is not some small corporate eight-passenger jet; it is a full-size airliner with every luxury you can imagine. The rooms of his New York penthouse are covered with marble and gold leaf, like something straight out of the great French palace of Versailles.

If one of the candidates wins one of the business games Trump set up to test their ability to make money, they get to do something Trump style. In one episode, the winners got on Trump's jet to fly to the most expensive country club in California (which he happens to own) and got a full spa treatment.

The values of the show portray that the ultimate happiness is to live life Trump style. The show is built around the idea that everybody—if they could—would live their life like Donald Trump.

To Trump, value is really all about who has the most toys, the most extravagant lifestyle, and the ability to make the most money.

Of course, Jesus taught something totally different.

The apostle Paul had a radical change in his values when he met Jesus face-to-face. He had been on a mission to be the best religious zealot he could be. He had put everything into it. He was a persecutor of Christians, a perfect adherent to Jewish law, a Pharisee of Pharisees, religious leader extraordinaire—bar none.

After his encounter with Jesus, his life got turned upside down. In an instant his priorities changed, and what now mattered to Paul was getting to know Jesus. Paul puts it this way: "Yes, everything else is worthless when compared with the infinite value of knowing Christ Jesus my Lord. For his sake I have discarded everything else, counting it all as garbage, so that I could gain Christ."[6] To attain happiness and significance in this life, we must be willing to lay down the value of being perfect, the value of doing our duty, the value of our Trump-like priorities, and just long with all our hearts to get to know Jesus.

That is *infinite* value.

The *Value* tool is about asking ourselves what our emotions are telling us about what's really important to us. Where does this or that fall on our priority scales? Ultimately, we need to align our values with what God says is valuable. That's what will transform us.

Believe

Our emotions reflect how we understand the world to work. These *beliefs* are our assumptions about life.

At a funeral, some may cry, even sob, at the loss of a loved one. Yet others have a joy in their hearts and even laugh. What's the difference?

Some who cry may do so because they believe that their loved one's life has just ended, that there is nothing after death and no eternity. Those who smile or laugh do so out of a deep belief that there is an eternal life, and this loved one is now with God. We all will be reunited eventually.

Emotions reflect what we believe and reveal our assumptions about how the world works.

Emotions may also reflect mistaken beliefs.

I work from an office in my home, something I really enjoy. Because of this, Laura and I only need one car. If I have an appointment at the same time that Laura has to take the kids to soccer practice, I can borrow a car, or there is an Enterprise car rental place just a few blocks from our house. Most of the time, it works well for us to have only one car, and it keeps us on budget.

But hypothetically, let's say that Laura knew I had an appointment and needed the car by 2:00 p.m. But it's now 2:30, and she's not home or answering her cell. I'm feeling a little bothered. Is she so neglectful of me that she forgot I needed to leave to meet this person at 2:00? I make phone calls postponing my meeting by a half hour, and then another half hour. My anger builds. By 3:30, I am really mad. Laura has totally disregarded my appointment.

But then I get a phone call saying there has been an accident. (And I thank God this is just hypothetical!) My wife and kids are in the emergency room. They have cuts, bruises, and one of the boys has a potentially serious injury. (Let me tell you, I can get choked up right now just thinking of such a thing.)

What happens to my emotion? Immediately, my anger is gone, and now I'm worried sick about the well-being of my wife and children.

What was the difference? At first, my emotion was based on the belief that my wife had neglected my schedule. She just was inconsiderate. For two hours, I believed she really didn't value me or my needs as she should have. I jumped to a wrong conclusion.

But then the facts came in and changed everything.

Again, my emotions weren't wrong—they reflected something I believed about Laura. It might be said that my belief regarding her should have been different, that I should have maintained faith that she would never stand me up that way. I should have believed what I know to be true of her.

So many times in life, we are hurt or angry because what we believe about God, other people, or our circumstances does not line up with the way we understand the world to work. Then a new understanding comes that changes everything. I think the *Believe* tool is most helpful in understanding what our emotions tell us about our relationship with God.

Just like Jonah, we often expect God to work a certain way, and when we don't see that he is, we become frustrated, even angry at him. Our emotions are real, valid—and they honestly reflect our beliefs about God. But maybe they're not well enough informed about how God actually works. Maybe we don't really know God as well as we should, just as I didn't really know Laura as well as I should have in that hypothetical situation.

The *Believe* tool is something we need to use, especially in times of suffering.

How can we endure great hardships? It comes down to what we truly believe in situations. What do you *believe* about ultimate reality? Do you really *believe* what the Bible has to say about your salvation, about God working all things together for good, and that someday you will be with him?

The *Believe* tool is about examining our emotions to determine what we truly believe about how the world works, how people in our lives act, and how God moves in our lives.

⟨⟨⟩⟩

I spoke of Dianne and Bob and how they put this toolbox to work in their lives. It really changed how they live.

Dianne's struggle with anger in her life came to a resolution when she examined it using the techniques we are talking about. Dianne has learned to treat emotions as indicators that are useful to help her become more spiritual, more godly. She explained the process to me:

> I think through what I want and examine my heart with the Lord. Either through prayer, journaling or whatever. Then, if it is a godly desire or a selfish desire, it becomes pretty clear. I submit my desires to the Lord and trust his timing. Stopping to think about the *why* behind what I feel has been amazing. It has led to greater joy and freedom in Christ—I can replace wrong thinking with the truths of Scripture. I can submit wrong desires to God and ask him to change my desires (James 4:7). I can ask him to fulfill the desires of my heart in his time. I can surrender to his lordship, because I know exactly what I have to surrender![7]

Using this process, Dianne realized what she was really angry about was that God was not fitting into her box, was not doing for her what she expected. When she realized her ideas about how God loved her were messed up and replaced them with the truth, the anger dissolved. In the process, Dianne developed a fuller and better understanding of God's love for her and grew spiritually.

And you remember Bob and his son Karl?

Bob took Karl inside and, in the context of the toolbox, asked him about his feelings. *Focus*: Why was he angry? Karl said it was because he always lost to Alex; he could never measure up. It was *always* the same. No matter what, he never won. *Know*: They talked about the facts and

Karl's expectation of the results of battling a twelve-year-old almost twice his size. They talked about the fact that it had nothing to do with Karl's ability at sword fighting; it had nothing to do with who was better or faster. *Value*: Bob explained to Karl that he did not have twelve-year-old expectations for his beloved eight-year-old son, and neither should Karl have those expectations for himself. *Believe*: To battle Alex should be for fun, but Karl could not go into it expecting victory. His worth as a young man was not based on winning against his brother, but on being the best Karl he could be and seeing that this was a time to just have fun.

Bob's conversation with Karl became a mini lesson in the toolbox of *Focus, Know, Value,* and *Believe.*

<<>>

Because of our culture, secular philosophy, and the rational age we live in, we are inexperienced when it comes to this business of experiencing our emotions in daily life. Mere novices. Through emotions, God enriches our lives with feeling and response, but we have set emotions aside. In the process, we have lost the art and life skills of understanding emotional experience.

God wants us to be emotionally mature with emotionally full lives. Becoming emotionally mature is not, as many teach, about becoming emotionally controlled. It is about becoming emotionally adept, emotionally wise, and emotionally skilled. It is about having lives that are chock-full of wonder and feeling—and then having the ability and practiced skill to live well and wisely in a richly emotional world.

The cost of getting to this good place is working through a process of development and training. It is a long road, a journey that takes a lifetime. There are no magic pills or five-step plans to grow you to emotional maturity. It is about allowing yourself to feel and learning to understand what your feelings are and what they mean.

To get the best out of life, we must be on a journey toward the sanctification of our emotions. Is your love greater this year than it was last year for that person in your life who is hard to understand or just rubs you the wrong way? Are you less prone to let your child have it for no good reason? Are you less likely than before to feel jealousy over a colleague's promotion, even though you thought it was rightfully yours? Is your joy in worship at your church increasing as the years go by?

Has our spiritual growth made a difference in how we *feel*? If not, we must ask ourselves if we are really growing at all.

Jeffrey Schwartz is a guy who loves to study the brain. He has found that the brain rewires itself when we do mental work. In one study of those with severe phobias, obsessions, and compulsions, he says, "When . . . sufferers used the power of their minds to redirect regularly their focus of attention in wholesome ways, they literally rewired their own brains. . . . It was clearly demonstrated that they could systematically change the response of the brain to these situations and so cease being frightened, stressed, or sexually aroused, whatever the case may be."[8]

By changing our thinking, we can rewire our emotions! God knows this; it's how he built us. By listening carefully to what God has to say and feeding our minds on his teachings, we can transform how we feel.

We all know this is true if we take just a moment to think about it. No normal thirty-year-old has the emotions of a two-year-old. Or, better said, a thirty-year-old experiences the same emotions as a two-year-old, but has the greater wisdom and skill to know what they are and how to respond to them and others.

If this were not true—if the skills of emotions were not developed and trained over a lifetime—what a crazy world it would be! You'd have a boss throwing a screaming fit every time a colleague did not let her borrow a pen, or a spouse breaking down in tears every time he was served baked potatoes when he wanted mashed. But come to think of it, a crazy world is what we have—and such things do occur. We make the mistake of looking at these situations as examples of people who can't keep their emotions in check, under control, or in a box, when in truth the issue is not the emotions themselves but the lack of emotional maturity. Just from what we've learned briefly in this chapter—our toolbox of *Focus, Know, Value,* and *Believe*—we know that the boss is not scream-ing because of a pen, and the spouse's tears are really not about a baked potato. Other things are going on.

We can learn to have mature and appropriate emotional responses that glorify God and bless the people around us. We can handle setbacks and tragedies with grace, dignity, and joy. That is the power of God active in us. When others see how we respond to what the world throws at us, they will know that what we have in Christ is truly worth having beyond all else. When they see us giving glory to a good God even in our tears, they will be amazed and say to themselves, "Whatever they have, I've got to get that."

Because we are authentic followers of Jesus, we will become really good at celebrating, enjoying good friends, and living with joyful hearts.

⟨⟨⟩⟩

The game of Parcheesi was for a long time a favorite of our boys. I was the gold camels, Laura was the green buffalo, Jackson chose the maroon tigers, and our youngest son, Evan, had the blue elephants.

I remember one particular game very well.

Evan was creaming us. He had gotten three of four elephants from his start all the way around the board and safely home beyond all harm. The camels, buffalo, and tigers were far behind. It seemed like just a matter of time until Evan won. He was desperate to win, trying any strategy, including offering the pact of "I will not get you if you do not get me" with anyone who would listen. You see, in Parcheesi another player can send you all the way back to start if they land on the space where you are.

Evan's last blue elephant was sent back to start two times when it was getting close to home. We were all gunning for him, as we knew it was our only chance to catch up. Each time, Evan, who was six at the time, cried and felt so discouraged.

Meanwhile, Jackson was having about the worst game on record. He was far behind all of us. I thought back to the way he used to play the game—which was much like Evan played now—emotionally desperate to win. In a game a year earlier, after Jackson had been sent back to start, he had picked up his piece and thrown it across the room in utter frustration. I had told him to go upstairs to his room, telling him he was done with the game. But Evan interceded for him and suggested that he just lose a turn and continue playing. Thanks to his brother's big heart, Jackson finished the game and learned a lesson about grace. Now in this game, looking over at Jackson, I was so proud of him. Even though he was clearly in last place, he played with a big smile. He was even making fun of himself as he fell farther and farther behind. How far he had come in knowing how to deal with the feelings of losing!

Well, it was my turn to roll, and I needed a nine to send Evan back to start. One die was a five, and the other landed askew on the corner of Jackson's cowboy lasso, which just happened to be adjoining the Parcheesi board on the table. I rolled again and it was a four, giving me the dreaded nine. I wrestled with myself—my dad's heart wanting my son to get the win and feel encouraged, yet also not wanting Evan to go through this without learning an important lesson about sportsmanship. In the end, I thought of Jackson's change in attitude a year earlier and knew that Evan must learn the same hard lessons about winning and losing. With a heavy heart, I sent the blue elephant back to start.

More tears and pacing around the room with a crushed spirit followed. (For Evan, not me.) Laura was going to win now; it seemed like a foregone conclusion.

But hope sprang fresh when Evan rolled the necessary five on his first roll and came out of the start. He was off and running again. Meanwhile, Laura had all the green buffalo in her safety zone and close to home. In Parcheesi, you have to roll the exact number to get home, so Evan had a slim chance if Laura did not roll the numbers she needed. He was just a quarter of the way around the board with his elephant. It was a long shot, but on they raced.

Laura rolled and could not get in. Evan was now halfway around the board. On his next roll, he struck gold. Doubles. For doubles, you get both sides of the dice, a total of fourteen, plus another roll. Not only did he get doubles, but he was able to send Jackson back to start and get twenty bonus spaces. Now he had thirty-four and another roll. Evan was into his safety zone.

Now it was Laura's turn again, and again she did not get the three and two she needed to get home.

On Evan's next turn, he rolled the perfect number and won. He had achieved a great come-from-behind victory.

Jumping up and down and hugging his three-year-old sister, he could not contain his joy. Cailin called out while in his pogo-stick embrace, "I am so proud of you, Evan! I knew you could do it."

I was glad that I had sent him home and hadn't taken the easy way out, letting him win. Glory and a life lesson were achieved.

After the game, we were able to sit down and talk with Evan about the lessons he had learned. How when it feels like the end, it isn't always the end. How winning is even sweeter when you have to work hard to achieve it. How he can have fun with his family even when he is sent back to start.

As a dad, I am hoping that next time I send him back to start, I will see a good-natured smile instead of tears.

God is in the business of teaching us through the game of life. Life is hard; we get our pieces all the way around the board only to be sent back to start time and time again. And I wonder how often God feels like I did as a father, rolling that nine and cringing that I would see my precious son discouraged once again.

Through childhood, all of us develop some skills in understanding our emotions and dealing with them. We gradually learn what they are attached to, what they are truly focused on, and what they mean in the context of other things. The question is whether in adulthood we continue to develop in emotional skills and wisdom and grow the emotional maturity that God wants us to have.

BLOG 08: TRUTH

STEPHEN]·····[This chapter has definitely shed a bit more light on how emotions often seem to be all over the place. It is encouraging to be reminded that I was once a kid who threw a screwdriver at my brother because he said something I didn't like (hitting his guitar in the process . . . not wise!), and now to see that as an adult I have a greater ability to analyze, understand, and control my anger.

The Focus, Know, Value, Believe steps have put into words what has already been happening in various areas of my life to some extent.

It is also good to clarify that at times emotions are wrong (i.e., when they don't have the info right), and so shouldn't just be blindly followed. Not seeing emotion as the enemy that needs to be repressed is truly liberating, and maybe even confirms what I already do in my life but have always tried to fight against or have chosen never really to think much about!

ANDREW]·····[I have been there; when I am "just tired and weary and can't handle things." Yet, at those times, I wonder if my emotions are more real—I am too tired to maintain the barriers of emotional "control." I have been thinking about your principles: Focus, Know, Value, Believe. You make it sound so easy . . . but it's not! What is behind this way I am feeling? I don't know. I am just frustrated. I find it interesting that your second principle in analyzing the emotions is Know. I assume that, in some way, logic/ knowledge and emotions maintain each other in a checks and balances system where one cannot rule without the regulation of the other.

By the way, you didn't fool me with the "heavy heart" line. Admit it. You were out to destroy your son Evan in Parcheesi. Still, I appreciate the lesson Evan learned, a lesson I am learning on the Parcheesi board of life.

MARIAN]·····[Emotions need training. Mine, raw and ragged at one time, as they were when let out of the box, could be unruly and undisciplined. My natural reaction to an uncomfortable emotion has been to shut it down—push it back into the hidden place. I guess it has been easy to think that I shouldn't "feel" that way, and go into rational mode. But God doesn't do that, does He? He asks questions, does not judge. How good it is to have tools to use to challenge those emotions. That is all about confidence building and I need that to be able to really accept my emotions as a vital and integral part of me. They might actually be there for a good purpose. I will ask the why and seek to discover what is behind each emotion. To check out the facts, see what is really important to me, and to go on drinking in God's revelation that I may base my life on His truth.

TODD]·····[One paragraph really grabbed me: "We can learn to have mature and appropriate emotional responses that glorify God and bless the people around us. We can handle setbacks and tragedies with grace, dignity, and joy. That is the power of God active in us. When others see how we respond to what the world throws at us, they will know that what we have in Christ is truly worth having beyond all else. When they see us giving glory to a good God even in our tears, they will be amazed and say to themselves, 'Whatever they have, I've got to get that.'"

One of my neighbors lost her life a few weeks ago after battling hard against cancer. Her cheerful attitude so dominated her suffering that I never caught on to how sick she was. At her memorial service, her husband shared how much she had ministered and witnessed daily to anyone in her path. As he spoke, it was plain to see that this horrible tragedy would not deter him from glorifying God and blessing everyone around him. Everything the man was saying was so appropriate and inclusive. He was sharing Christ and seeking to draw his non-Christian neighbors into God's eternal kingdom. He was challenging believers, too. This paragraph in the book describes this man's mature emotional responses perfectly.

BOB]·····[Maybe my favorite quote so far, because it rings so true: "Without a worn Bible, we will never get through the troubles of life with a glad heart." And one of the most helpful observations so far: "Becoming emotionally mature is not, as many teach, about becoming emotionally controlled. It is about becoming emotionally adept, emotionally wise, emotionally skilled." Truth really is in large measure known and lived—or not—through the emotions.

JULIE]·····[This chapter was wonderful with unveiling the entire concept that I've got a very long way to go before I'm emotionally mature. By suppressing my emotions, sweeping them under the rug, and not even addressing them most of the time, it's going to take me a while to figure out how to use the toolbox of resources correctly and apply it to my life and teach my children how to do this same thing. It will be so worth the time and energy, though, because I long to live a life where I'm good at celebrating, enjoying friends and living with a joyful heart!

TOM]·····[I'm amazed at the friends I run into who say they don't need to read the Bible again because they read it once, or they have already heard that particular story "a million times." Or it's just obvious they don't have much of a commitment to it. I fall into this trap myself—thinking I don't need it because I know it. How arrogant. It seems to me that I am either growing closer to or moving away from God—I'm not standing still. What I'm feeding my mind and heart with determines my direction—how I'm going to react to the challenges in life that I face. Life is challenge enough. How much more so when I am not prepared. That's a recipe for a hard heart. Unfortunately, from experience, I know that the more I ignore the Spirit's leading in this area, the softer his voice becomes. I don't want to ignore it anymore.

My sixth grade teacher made us memorize Psalm 139. A whole chapter! Each of us had to stand up in front of the entire class and recite it. I remember our teacher said that she hoped our Bibles would automatically fall open to that chapter by the end of the school year. At the time, what initially seemed like just a lot of work was actually preparing us for the future. As many of you know, this chapter is all about how God knew us before we were born, had ordained our days in advance, knows the number of hairs on our head, and about how we can never get away from his love. What a perfect chapter to hide in our hearts as we moved into adolescence, experienced peer pressure, began to understand how the "world" cheapens life through rationalizations such as abortion, and as we prepared to serve God as adults. That's powerful stuff. And you know what? My Bible automatically opened to Psalm 139 by the end of the school year.

Enter the discussion at www.faithfulfeelings.com.

MY BLOG

_____

_____

_____

_____

_____

_____

_____

_____

_____

_____

_____

09 Grow

When the dancers took to the promenade
Well my heart leapt high
And I was unafraid
Of the feeling I'd stifled for so many years
Tell me how do you
How do you feel
Well the band took their places and got all in tune

And then the caller's voice
Well it rang out beneath the moon
And then the boys took their girls and they started to reel
And they were singin' how do you, how do you feel
And then the people in the town said that they'd call the police
If we didn't keep down all this disturbin' their peace
And Officer Black, you know he answered their pleas
And he ran up on the hill just to see
Well he hid in the bushes just a stone's throw away
And then we all saw this change comin' over his face
But he was bouncin' to the beat and started hoppin' on his heels
Singin', how do you, how do you feel
And then the townspeople asked him if he'd make some arrests
Could they find peace and quiet so they could go back to bed
He said if it's peace that you want, you're gonna find it on the hill
But the silence that you keep is the silence that kills[1]

This is one of my favorite songs,"Promenade," from one of my favorite artists, Rich Mullins, now deceased. I've always been inspired by the honesty and simplicity of his music. And I've sometimes been surprised at the complex depth of his lyrics.

I'd listened to this song many times before I really realized it was about the very subject I was studying. Mullins speaks of the "feeling I'd stifled for so many years" and how his "heart leapt high." And there's that haunting question and call: "How do you, how do you feel?"

I believe God wants you to feel. He wants you to dance, even if the church tells you not to and sends out a grumpy policeman to stop you.

Online, I found the lyrics to "Promenade" paired with these words from the lips of Jesus:

You are the salt of the earth. But what good is salt if it has lost its flavor? Can you make it salty again? It will be thrown out and trampled underfoot as worthless. You are the light of the world—like a city on a hilltop that cannot be hidden. No one lights a lamp and then puts it under a basket. Instead, a lamp is placed on a stand, where it gives light to everyone in the house. In the same way, let your good deeds shine out for all to see, so that everyone will praise your heavenly Father.[2]

A changed heart is salt and light to the world around you. That is what makes our lives vibrant and alive and draws people to Jesus. Of course, *salt* and *light* here are metaphors for what is inside us, the distinctive qualities the world tastes and sees in us. Salt and light aren't referring to our ideas or our belief systems or our theology, but rather to the love and joy and hope that are inside us and shock the world with their presence.

God wants these emotions to grow in us, to become distinctive qualities so powerful and magnetic that others take notice and say, "I've got to have what she has." That is the kind of person Jesus was talking about.

As the world sees emotions flourish in us, it sees God.

〈〉〉

As I mentioned, some time ago I decided to read through the Bible and categorize every verse on emotion according to how it viewed the emotion. It was an amazing experience. And it led me to a couple of new understandings.

First, God has intentions for our emotions. What I see in Scripture is a three-part model of emotions that helps develop our character and make us more like Jesus. The Bible indicates that some emotions are ones we should *grow* and develop. Others we are encouraged to *keep,* cherish, or allow ourselves to feel. And then some emotions we should eliminate from our lives and *be done with.*

I've come to think of emotions as a garden that we are to tend and cultivate all our lives. And these three categories of emotions—*grow, keep,* and *done*—are like flowers and plants: Some we grow from seeds, some are unplanned and surprise us but we keep them, and some are destructive weeds that we must root out and be done with.

The next three chapters will look at these three categories of emotions in this garden model for developing our Christian character and becoming more like Jesus.

The second understanding I came to is that some emotions are in all three categories. It's not that the Bible simplistically says that an emotion is always one we should grow or always one we should get rid of. The Bible seems to assume what we've been saying here—that emotions depend on their objects. So, in some cases, the Bible calls us to hate (we are to hate sin, for example), and in other cases we are called to eliminate our hatred (say, of another person) and be done with it.

To me, this is most interesting. At the time the New Testament was written, there was a lot of talk about the emotions. Stoics and Epicureans saw emotion as a disease, something we were to be cured of by using the power of reason. Later Stoics, following Plato, looked at the emotions as irrational forces to be defeated. As we've seen, their model, and their solution to emotional problems, was tragically wrong. And yet, the New Testament, coming out of the same time and place, takes a very different view and adopts a totally different model—one that scientists and psychologists today are embracing. The Bible brings emotion and reason together into the unified "heart."

I believe this three-part garden of emotions—*Grow, Keep, Done*—along with the gardener's toolbox we've already put together—*Focus, Know, Value,* and *Believe*—can significantly help us if we are struggling in our emotional lives. It can also be a guide to help us develop the Christlike character God wants in us.

〈〈〉〉

The Bible specifically indicates four emotions that God wants us to *grow*:

Love for neighbors, God, and goodness
Joy in God, good relationships, and the good things in life
Hope in our eternal destiny, in God's supreme power, and in his promises
Hatred of evil[3]

Each of these emotions is not just hanging out there by itself. It is very important to remember that every emotion is connected to an *object*. It is tied to what we think, know, value, and believe about something. Determining the place that a particular emotion should have in our lives involves understanding *why* we feel it and the nature of its focus on a particular object—a person, idea, or thing.

Love

The Bible speaks extensively and broadly about the subject of love and how we are to grow love in our lives. And much is said about the difference between *genuine* love and the mere *appearance* of love.

We can't forget the familiar verse from 1 Corinthians 13: "If I could speak all the languages of earth and of angels, but didn't love others, I would only be a noisy gong or a clanging cymbal."[4] Some of Jesus' most pointed teachings on love chide the Pharisees for being so preoccupied with following their rules and duties that they fail to truly love individual people. Their lives are a sham, Jesus says.

The Bible says time and again that God wants to grow love in us that's real, personal, and genuine, not love that's prompted and forced by obligations and duties.

Laura was in competitive piano performance through high school. Her teacher's students often went on to Julliard, the top music school in the United States. However, for Laura it was all duty—a stringent, four-hour-a-day practice regimen imposed on her. She became a good pianist because duty will usually accomplish something, although at great cost to one's soul. Duty can even appear to be love of something, or devotion, but it really isn't. Duty will never take you where love will—to the level of a great pianist whose passion achieves excellence. When Laura's duty was done, she wanted nothing to do with piano for the next ten years.

What is the difference between love and duty? Why is love a higher goal? One answer: because duty never motivated anybody to do anything great.

Now when Laura plays the piano, she is looking to redeem the love she lost in pursuit of fulfilling her duty.

I had the privilege of working alongside George Verwer for a year as his personal assistant. George birthed Operation Mobilization (OM), which now employs more than three thousand workers and has trained tens of thousands of young Christians through short-term missions programs. Perhaps you've heard of OM's oceangoing ships, the *Doulos* and the *Logos Hope*. Throughout the year, thousands of people in the world's poorest cities visit these floating bookstores and training centers and have the opportunity to hear of God's love.

OM was birthed out of extravagant love. A love for people.

When George was a student with my father at Moody Bible Institute, he organized missions trips to Mexico. My dad went on one of these trips, and their basic diet consisted of chocolate sandwich cookies — imagine, *days* of living on cookies. You see, the group had received a large donation of cookies, and George decided that if they lived off the cookies, they could use their food money to buy more Christian literature to distribute.

George cared so much about the people that he really thought it was no big deal to subsist on cookies.

On his honeymoon, which was another missions trip to Mexico, George offered wedding cake at every gas station in exchange for gas. Nobody would take him up on it until he neared the border of Mexico. They got free gas for the journey and had more funds for the work.

These days, George says he is not as proud of some of the crazy things he did in the early days of OM — and one of his favorite preaching topics today is living a balanced life!

George Verwer's extreme actions came out of his extravagant love. God used this man's love for people to birth one of the greatest modern world movements of young people. OM is an organization that goes to the most difficult places in the world to minister to people's physical needs and share the Good News of Jesus Christ. What would compel so many thousands of young people to give up their comforts and live in very tough places—and get by on chocolate cookies? *Extravagant love.*

On the one hand, love that comes out of a deep-hearted passion is costly and sacrificial. Yet those who have it don't mind the cost, the sacrifice—or the chocolate cookies.

On the other hand, love that's an act of the will, an obedience, or an obligation demands so little of us, because we typically invest only enough to accomplish our duty. This "dutiful love" robs the church of its influence and power, and it's something that others see through very quickly. This is one reason why so much of the world is cynical about Christianity.

God rejects this thinking. His demand is for extravagant love, passion coming from the heart.

Do you remember the account in the Bible when Mary takes some expensive perfume and pours it on Jesus' feet? It must have been really strong stuff because the whole house was filled with the sweet scent! Then Judas gets really out of sorts. "This stuff costs what somebody would earn in a year! How could she do that?" he rants. "We could have given the money to the poor."[5] Little did the other disciples know at the time that, as the group's treasurer, Judas was stealing from the moneybag and was totally motivated by greed.

But Jesus replies, "Leave her alone. She did this in preparation for my burial. You will always have the poor among you, but you will not always have me."[6]

Mary poured out her extravagant love for Jesus. Are you a Judas or a Mary? And what does that mean in your life?

For me, it wasn't perfume, but shampoo . . .

I am a "save the best for last" kind of person. From the time I was little, I ate first what I liked least to get it over with. In my sock drawer, I usually pick the socks to wear that are most likely to give out first. If at the end of the day there is a significant hole, I can enjoy ripping into it and turning it into a good rag. I can use it next time I wax my car. When I go into my closet, I often wear the oldest thing first in order to save what is nice for a special occasion.

(I know some reading this will find me weird, but let me tell you, there are plenty of others reading this who are just like me! *You know who you are . . .*)

I was taking a shower one day when I noticed something amiss. I have some shampoo I received for Christmas last year—probably the most expensive shampoo I have ever owned.

Actually, I bought it for myself and told Laura to give it to me. Usually, I buy whatever shampoo seems the best deal in bulk from our local warehouse club. However, this was salon bought and was like instant menthol invigoration for the hair. I call it Ben-Gay for the hair. It's like getting a scalp massage at your local spa. Your scalp tingles . . . even burns a bit; your eyes can feel it, your nose smells it. I love it.

But being me, I used the bargain-basement shampoo most days and left this special stuff for a special time. I used it once in a while, but mostly, as usual, I was "saving the best for last."

Well, I began to notice one week that my shampoo was going down very fast for using it only once a week. And then I discovered that my wife was using it every day. (It really is a great shampoo!)

Now, let it be said that Laura has all kinds of lotions, creams, fragrances, scents, and special bath oils of her own.

I have Bargain Hair Suds.

This special shampoo was something extra, something special, something way beyond Bargain Hair Suds. It was my treasured possession. All my discipline in saving it was doing no good at all!

Now, I didn't want to seem petty (which, of course, I was), so I never mentioned it, but every time I looked at that bottle and saw a little less remaining, it really bothered me.

Then came the day when I looked at that shampoo and saw it was almost gone. And somehow, for some reason, I thought, *I do not want to use that. I will save it for Laura because I know she really enjoys it.*

Almost immediately I thought, *Where did that come from?*

My begrudging and silent "allowance" of Laura to use my prized shampoo was perhaps a duty-driven act of love. My spontaneous desire to have her use the last drops was a more genuine outpouring of love.

Somehow, God had converted my little duty-driven pity party into a spontaneous act of real love.

It was a little thing, but I think God wanted to get me past "love from duty" and grow me into "love from passion."

〈〈 〉〉

The Bible also teaches that true love is *up close and personal.* True love is about people you can touch.

Jesus was God incarnate, yet he loved up close. He could have invented radio and gotten his message to the whole world with one broadcast. Would that have worked? Not really. The gospel message isn't something contained in words or theologies that could be broadcast to everyone. The message is *Jesus.* And Jesus is the medium for that message. Indeed, in Marshall McLuhan's famous words, "The medium is the message."[7]

I think God wants us to know that love is not about what we tell people or give to people. Love is us. *We* are love to people. Up close and personal.

Have you ever thought about the fact that Jesus had best friends? He had twelve disciples. Then he had three special disciples: Peter, James, and John. And from those, he had the disciple "that he loved," John. He also had some kind of special relationship with Mary, Martha, and Lazarus. Jesus saw things he liked in particular people, and he loved them in special, individual ways.

The gospel exploded across the world as each Christian, following Jesus' example, loved those they knew personally.

The same principle is alive today in the church, the body of Christ. The New Testament teaches that there is a special bond of love between believers, a bond as strong as family.

In *Sex God,* Rob Bell talks about sexuality, spirituality, and worship. And he paints a picture that all three are together in community. Sexuality is spiritual and it is worship. Ultimately, Bell is saying that God created people to *be connected* to one another. Worship is one part of connectedness, spirituality is a part of connectedness, and sex between a husband and wife is a part of connectedness.

Up-close love demands an intimate connection. Duty-driven love is too easy to do from far off. You write a check, and you don't have to get your hands dirty alongside others to help a cause. You make a phone call, and you don't have to go outside your house to visit someone face-to-face. You schedule a meeting, and your "love" can fit your busy life.

God says that real love demands the sacrifice of ourselves to someone else. It requires that we get close, find out about the other person's hurts and dreams, smell the alcohol on the breath, hear the pain of the unwed mother, visit the poor person on the other side of the tracks. It means rearranging your schedule to take care of a child, take someone dinner, or visit someone in the hospital.

The love that God wants us to grow is a love connected to others, in touch with others. Love must be up close and personal.

〈〈〉〉

Sometimes from Christian teaching, you get the idea that God really loves you for no good reason. That it's just in his nature to love you. That he just loves you because he *is* love.

That is not just an impression I have. There was this German guy named Nygren who wrote a book about it in 1953. His ideas have had a lot of influence. They have made their way down to pastors and teachers, including some like Rob Bell, who writes

Agape [love] doesn't love somebody because they're worthy.
Agape makes them worthy by the strength and power of its love . . .
There is a love *because,* love *in order to,* love *for the purpose of,* and then there is love, period.
Agape doesn't need a reason.[8]

I buy into the first line, big time. That is unconditional love. We do not deserve it, but we are loved anyway. All of us fit into the unworthy category.

The last part—about love having no reason—sounds so spiritual at first. But think about it for a minute . . .

God knows all about you; he created you, he sent his Son to die for you, but wait . . . he cannot find any specific, personal reasons why he loves you? How does that make you feel?

It makes me feel really empty and unloved. I want to be loved for really good reasons. For things that make me special.

The problem is that people do not understand that "unconditional love" and "love because" are not opposed to one another. These two things can and do exist side by side in true biblical love.

When we were first married, Laura used to ask me, "Why do you love me?" I used to never want to answer that question. I felt I didn't need to qualify my love. But I have come to understand that giving people real reasons for why we specifically and specially love them increases their understanding of our love for them. After all, we chose our mate for the *why* behind our love.

I have no interest in Laura loving me "in general" or "just because." I want her to love me because she takes great pleasure in who I am. Me, specifically.

The truth is that God loves us *specifically.*

Psalm 139:13-14 reads

> You made all the delicate, inner parts of my body
> and knit me together in my mother's womb.
> Thank you for making me so wonderfully complex!
> Your workmanship is marvelous—
> how well I know it.

Read the entire psalm and you will see even more.

God put time into thinking how he was going to make us, the special abilities he would give each one of us, the family he would put us into, and what purpose we would play in his world. We are his special creation. He created us in his image, knew us from our conception, and knows every detail about us. Just as we love our own children, God cannot help himself. He crafted each one of our unique looks, talents, and abilities, and he sees good things. He places great value on us! The greatest value, in fact—he sent his precious Son to die for our sins.

This appeared in the *Charlotte Observer*:

> Charles Jonathan James Paddock was only minutes old, and he was in my arms. . . . I could not stop looking at my son, the child I had long dreamed about and prayed for. He had no idea of his significance, no understanding of what was happening. He simply stared back. . . . But as I was sitting there falling in love with my boy, I was stirred by thoughts of a greater love—the love of God, who calls himself my father. I had known about God's love for as long as I could remember, but for the first time I understood in my soul why God said he loves us like a father. Sheer delight. . . .
>
> Words of God quoted by the prophet Isaiah came to my mind: "I have called you by name. You are mine." . . . Merit had nothing to do with it. Charlie had done nothing—he could do nothing—to earn my love.[9]

God loves each of us specifically, not generically. We are his special creation, the work of his hands. And he wants us to love others specifically too. This is the love he wants to grow in us.

⟨⟨⟩⟩

So *how* do we grow the love God wants in us?

I think this may not be all that complicated.

I think we get detached from people somehow, and over time whatever passion we had fades. It's because we've become detached, separated, disconnected. Becoming up close and personal with someone tends to grow love in us.

So, here's a thought: Do one thing. Just one thing. Spend time with one person in need. Take some real time with that one person. Ask God to grow love in you for this person. Give yourself to one person in need.

And then see what God does in you.

It's a beginning.

Joy

Many times throughout Scripture, we are told to rejoice and be filled with joy. It's clear that God wants to grow joy inside of us.

Many theologians and teachers suggest that the Christian's joy comes from God and is not dependent on our circumstances. Fair enough. But then they suggest that because of this, biblical joy is not really an emotion. Calvin Miller, in his book *The Taste of Joy,* writes, "Many Christians confuse happiness with joy, as I did. Happiness is about a buoyant emotion that results from the momentary plateaus of well-being that characterize our lives. Joy is bedrock stuff, on the other hand. Joy is confidence that operates irrespective of our moods. Joy is the certainty that all is well, however we feel."[10]

Well, you already know how I feel about this. If joy is not an emotion, what's the point? If God is not talking about a feeling of true joy, what makes the Christian life worth living?

I believe what God has in mind, and what the Bible really says, is that joy is a real emotion. God commands us to feel happy, feel joy, feel good. To feel the real emotions of joy. Not all the time, of course, not in every season or at every moment—God is not interested in plastic Christians. But somehow, the good feeling of joy should be something that defines who we are. We should be people who live in this place of real, emotional joy.

What God has in mind is not a redefinition of joy, but a redefinition of *us.*

Shouldn't knowing Jesus change your happiness level in a totally radical way? Didn't Jesus himself say that he came to give us abundant life? So, is this abundant life real or not?

I think one of the keys to experiencing this abundant life is keeping focused on God as our source of joy. Our circumstances change from day to day, life sometimes is difficult, events can even be tragic, but when we focus on God himself and his love for us, it brings real joy—regardless of circumstances.

I fall short of this so often. I am often a prisoner of my circumstances. I am too often discouraged when daily things are hard; and more times than I would like to admit, I miss the joy God provides in the situation. When playing with my precious kids, I sometimes worry about their uncertain future—a dangerous world, threatening current events—and before I know it, I've been so caught up in my worry that I miss the joy of hearing my sons' laughter or seeing Cailin's ballet.

I think we're like this with God, too—becoming so worried about the events of today and tomorrow and focusing so closely on circumstances that we miss the smile on God's face and forget his remarkable salvation and provision.

I think this is what God wants to change—*us,* and our outlooks on life. I don't think God is suggesting that we redefine joy, turning it into a mental exercise.

<<>>

In the Bible, the joy God gives is always *because* of something:

Because of something God has done
Because of a blessing God has given
Because Paul has seen a good friend
Because God has been faithful in history
Because someday we will be in a better place
Because of what Jesus did on the cross to free us from sin

Think back on our key words: *Focus, Value, Know,* and *Believe.* These are all "because" words, aren't they? Joy *because* our focus is on our ultimate future, not on our immediate future. Joy *because* we value our salvation more than that missed promotion at work. Joy *because* we believe that our sins are paid for in full. Joy *because* we know what good things God has done for us in the past.

Why do we lack happiness? It's because our joy is based on the wrong "because." It's because we've based our happiness on objects that cannot bring joy for more than a short time. The things that lie behind Christian joy are a deep and wide ocean—we can never get to the end of the joy they can produce.

Joy also is sweeter when it is hard won, when it comes after times of hardship.

A specific kind of psalm, called a *lament,* shows this clearly. In psalms of lament, things start off bad. The author is brutally honest with God and catalogs his discouragement, trouble, and bad circumstances. (There's a practical tip in this for us: To set the stage for newfound realizations of joy, we need to recall where we've been, what we've endured, and the hardships we've gone through.)

Consider Psalm 77:

I cry out to God; yes, I shout.
Oh, that God would listen to me!
When I was in deep trouble,
I searched for the Lord.
All night long I prayed, with hands lifted toward heaven,
but my soul was not comforted.
I think of God, and I moan,
overwhelmed with longing for his help.

You don't let me sleep.
I am too distressed even to pray!
I think of the good old days, long since ended,
when my nights were filled with joyful songs.
I search my soul and ponder the difference now.
Has the Lord rejected me forever?
Will he never again be kind to me?
Is his unfailing love gone forever?
Have his promises permanently failed?
Has God forgotten to be gracious?
Has he slammed the door on his compassion?
And I said, "This is my fate;
the Most High has turned his hand against me."

Then comes the switch, the conscious and deliberate change of focus,
transforming despair into joy:

I recall all you have done, O LORD;
I remember your wonderful deeds of long ago.
They are constantly in my thoughts.
I cannot stop thinking about your mighty works.
O God, your ways are holy.
Is there any god as mighty as you?

You are the God of great wonders!
You demonstrate your awesome power among the nations.
By your strong arm, you redeemed your people,
the descendants of Jacob and Joseph.

INTERLUDE

When the Red Sea saw you, O God,
its waters looked and trembled!
The sea quaked to its very depths.
The clouds poured down rain;
the thunder rumbled in the sky.
Your arrows of lightning flashed.
Your thunder roared from the whirlwind;
the lightning lit up the world!
The earth trembled and shook.
Your road led through the sea,
your pathway through the mighty waters—
a pathway no one knew was there!
You led your people along that road like a flock of sheep,
with Moses and Aaron as their shepherds.

These last verses are full of "because." It is all there: God's power, God's provision, his control over everything, his faithful work in history for his people, his care for his people.

I like to put these verses in the form of *Focus, Know, Value, Believe*:

Focus: "I recall all you have done, O Lord. . . . They are constantly in my thoughts. I cannot stop thinking about your mighty works."
Know: "By your strong arm, you have redeemed your people."
Believe: "You are the God of great wonders!"

Where is *Value*? It's contained in the form of the poem, the switch from despair to joy. It is like the parable in Matthew 13 where Jesus says, "Again, the Kingdom of Heaven is like a merchant on the lookout for choice pearls. When he discovered a pearl of great value, he sold everything he owned and bought it!"[11] Making the switch, giving up the values of this world for the values of the Kingdom, is the fuel of our joy.

In Acts 16, we are told the story of Paul and Silas singing in prison. Severely beaten, perhaps with rods, their feet twisted into stocks that were probably positioned to add torment to their already damaged bodies, here are these two guys singing hymns and songs to God.

How could Paul and Silas sing in prison, having joy in the midst of suffering? That dark night, in the power of the Holy Spirit, somehow they emptied their souls of their own suffering and found joy. How?

Because.

Because they focused on the good things of God and how they had been counted worthy to suffer for their Lord Jesus.

If they can have joy "because," why not you?

‹ ◊ ›

The life of Olympic gold medalist Eric Liddell is a true-life story of the even-in-hard-times joy the Bible talks about. You may remember seeing Liddell's story dramatized in the movie *Chariots of Fire*.

Soon after winning an Olympic gold medal at the 1924 Games and setting a new world record in the four hundred meters, instead of cashing in as a national hero, Eric left as a missionary for China, where he had grown up. After he had been back in China for more than a decade, some as a rural bicycle evangelist, the smell of war was in the air. And after the Japanese invaded China in 1937, life became more dangerous. Eventually, Eric sent his wife and two precious kids to safety in Canada, just a few weeks before the attack on Pearl Harbor. Eric stayed on in China to continue his missionary work.

Before he was due to leave for Canada to join his family in 1943, the Japanese rounded up all the foreign nationals in his area and threw them into camps. At the age of forty-one, the Olympic champion was suddenly a prisoner of war.

Eric Liddell lived the rest of his days in confinement, dying of a brain tumor just months before the camp was liberated.

David Mitchell, a fellow prisoner, writes of Liddell during those days in the camp:

> Eric Liddell stood out among the 1800 people packed into our camp that measured only 150 by 200 yards. He was in charge of the building where we younger children had already been away from our parents for four years because of the war, lived with our teachers. . . . His gentle face and warm smile, even as he taught us games with the limited equipment available, showed us how much he loved children, missing his own so very much. . . .
>
> Not only did Eric Liddell organize sports and recreation, throughout his time in the internment camp he helped many people through teaching and tutoring. He gave special care to the older people, the weak, and the ill, to whom the conditions of the camp were very trying. . . . Despite the squalor of the open cesspools, rats, flies, and disease in the crowded camp, life took on a very normal routine, though without the faithful and cheerful support of Eric Liddell, many people would never have been able to manage. . . .
>
> None of us will ever forget this man who was totally committed to putting God first, a man whose humble life combined muscular Christianity with radiant goodness. What was his secret? He unreservedly committed his life to Jesus Christ as his Savior and Lord. That friendship meant everything to him. By the flickering light of peanut-oil lamp early each morning he and a roommate in the men's cramped dormitory studied the Bible and talked with God for an hour every day.[12]

Isn't that what we all long for, to be the same joyful person either in Olympic glory or prison camp squalor? To have joy and hope that are built on such incredible bedrock that nothing can take them away? That is the kind of joy our God offers to us if we will only embrace him, love him, and learn all we can about him.

Writing this now, I see a unifying factor in all the stories I have told about joy in hard times. Maybe it's what's missing in my life.

Perhaps I do not need God *enough.*

Am I really passionately pursuing regular communion with God? Do I look for those "because" reasons for joy in any circumstance? Do I say with the psalmist that I remember God's deeds, and "I cannot stop thinking about your mighty works"? Do I spend time in study and prayer with God as Eric Liddell did in the concentration camp?

Our joy grows as our need and desire for God grows.

If we don't have joy in our lives, perhaps we do not need God enough.

‹ ◊ ›

I think it is hard to find joy in hard times if we do not practice it during the good days. Let me explain that a little bit. Joy in hard times comes when we know good stuff about God and his plans for the future so intimately that these truths can break through our discouragement and doubt.

If we do not learn to really worship God for who he is and what he has done, from a deep, authentic part of us on good Sundays, we will not know how to have authentic, God-based joy on hard Thursdays. If we build joy during the good times only on things like having fun on our days off, buying a new item to wear that we think is really cool, or kicking back with friends, that joy will disappear when the object of our joy changes or the fun times end. When the pain of this broken world intrudes on our good times and something really bad happens, all the "stuff" we took joy in—the "because" we were depending on—will not be there.

So let's practice the right *because,* the solid joy-in-the-Lord stuff, all the time. I'm not suggesting that we dispense with the other things—we can rejoice in them as well. But we must find our greatest joy in God, even on the good days. Concentrate on what he has done, fill your mind with how he loves you, memorize his good promises. Put on some good worship music on your way to the grocery store and sing at the top of your lungs. Embrace the truth of those words in such a way that you just have to sing really, really loud.

Be known for how you take joy in what really matters.

Hope

Evan has been living with great expectation over the last couple of weeks. Qui-gon Jinn, famed *Star Wars* Jedi Master, fashioned in Lego, is coming in the mail.

Lego sets come and go, with one figure included one year and another the next. A few weeks ago, we went to a Lego Club extravaganza at our town's history center, and they gave us the address of a Web page where you can find rare or discontinued Lego figures.

So Qui-gon Jinn is on his way here.

Evan was crazy to get right to work in locating some of his favorite *Star Wars* figures from past sets. Anything Lego and anything *Star Wars* is of particular interest these days at our house. Put them together and you have a recipe for a complete entertainment package—hours of fun in a confined space.

Evan spent his own money, sent via Mom's check to a man in California who claims to have the one-inch-tall Jedi Master in his possession. The wait has been excruciating. Every day after school, Evan's immediate focus has been to check the mail, something he had never really cared about before. He is hoping so much to get that crazy Lego *Star Wars* figure in the mail he can hardly stand it.

Evan is living in great hope that any day will be the day.

〈〈〉〉

Why don't we have this same childlike hope in our spiritual lives?

I think one answer is that too many times we have been taught that hope is a noun, whereas God means it to be a verb.

Modern theologians have been very emphatic in their emphasis that hope is a noun, not a verb. As a result, we really don't know what to do about hope or what to do with it. As a noun, it's an abstraction, distant and vague in our minds. An *idea,* not an experience. We work so hard to keep the plate of hope spinning in our minds, all the while losing the real expectation of hope in our daily lives. We've lost the wide-eyed reality of hope that Evan knows as he anticipates the imminent arrival of Qui-gon Jinn—who, by the way, is in the mail and might, just might, arrive today!

Life-transforming hope is not merely an idea or concept; it is the real expectation that *God will happen to us today.*

A few summers ago, I went to the Christian Booksellers Association convention. Authors were there to sell books to retailers; musicians were there to present their new songs. A general session might feature a prayer by Chuck Colson, followed by a musical performance by Selah, followed by the Gaithers to lead a worship segment, followed by Rick Warren to give the message, with a closing song sung by Jars of Clay. This particular year, a few well-known authors had been asked to give a short talk on the basics of the Christian faith. One talked about love, another talked about faith, and a third talked about joy.

But for all these remarkable speakers and musicians, I will always remember Joni Eareckson Tada, who rolled up to the microphone in her wheelchair.

You may already know the life and ministry of this incredible woman of God—how as an athletic teenager, she broke her neck in a diving accident and lost the use of her body. She has been paralyzed ever since from the shoulders down. Her story of moving from despair to hope is told in her book *Joni.*

That night, Joni talked about *hope.*

The power of that moment was not so much in *what* she said, but in the tone of her voice and the power of her conviction. You could tell that hope was where she lived her life. You could tell that, for Joni, hope was not a nebulous noun; it was a very active *verb.*

She spoke about her accident as a gift. And her gift is in giving others hope. She told us that the hope of heaven was a hope of being able to get up out of that confining chair; but that was just a side thing—a small part of it. Her disability had made her really understand that our hope is totally in Christ. There have not been many times in my life when I could say a person's face *literally* glowed. This was one of the few, and we all saw real Jesus hope that day. There was no doubt.

Hope is the faithful emotion that is our companion (our friend) for difficult times and tragedies.

〈〈〉〉

Three months ago, we wrote a check to support Dan, the son of one of the members of our small group, who was going on a spring-break missions trip to Mexico. Three weeks ago, we organized meals for Dan's family in the aftermath of an awful tragedy.

I had received a surprise call from Mexico, from Dan's dad, asking for help and prayer. While having fun with his friends, Dan had fallen on his neck. These days, he cannot feel anything below his neck and is not able to eat solids or breathe on his own. Many of the hopes he had for his earthly life have been dashed. Last week, he was hoping he'd be able to swallow a few slices of banana on his own.

In a very real way, hope means so much more to Dan now than ever before. In saying that, I don't mean to diminish the difficulty of his life now, but I know that it's through hardship and tragedy that hope becomes a verb. When we realize we can't set our hope on the shallow things we did before, our ultimate hope becomes God himself.

We live in a world filled with despair. People we rub shoulders with every day go on hoping for some kind of better tomorrow. The little things of life take over our hope so easily—our team winning the big game, a new car, a good result on a medical test. But life is too fragile to make these things the object of most of our emotions. These are not to be the object of our everyday hopes and dreams. Jesus is. We never know what is going to happen to those we love or to ourselves.

<<>>

Evan Elliott, proud owner of a Lego Qui-gon Jinn, also has severe
allergies to dogs, cats, and dust mites, among other things. In the hope
that he can get over having these strong allergic reactions that trigger
asthma attacks, he gets allergy shots. The first time he got his shots after
Qui-gon Jinn arrived in the mail, he told Laura, "Mom, that shot did not
even hurt when I held Qui-gon Jinn in my hand." The next week it was a
different story; it was back to pain as usual. Evan said to Laura, "I guess
I got used to having Qui-gon Jinn."

Hope that is not based on the things of God is only a temporary fix.

What we have is the hope of God in our lives, of someday being in a
better place, whatever our circumstances. What we have is life-giving
hope through the Holy Spirit.

And what we have is the hopeful expectation of Jesus coming.

Probably not in the mail. But perhaps tomorrow.

<<>>

Of all the emotions we want to grow, hope is the hardest one to remember as a verb. It is easy to think of hope in terms of beliefs or expectations we have of the future. But what infuses hope with its emotional
vigor is the value and excitement we attach to our beliefs and expectations. As Paul writes, "I pray that God, the source of hope, will fill you
completely with *joy* and *peace* because you trust in him. Then you will
overflow with confident hope through the power of the Holy Spirit."[13] We
so often miss the *peaceful overflowing* part of hope. Because hope is
about believing, we need God's help and the power of the Holy Spirit to
accomplish it in our lives. But we can certainly enlarge our hope as we
place our belief squarely in what he promises.

How much standing-on-tiptoes, butterflies-in-the-stomach, latch-onto-it-
like-a-vise-grip hope do you have for the things God says are in your
future? Does it feel like the hope that your true love will marry you? Like
you are planning the wedding in your mind? Looking forward to the day?
Thinking about how your life will change?

Here's just one promise to consider: "He will wipe every tear from their eyes, and there will be no more death or sorrow or crying or pain. All these things are gone forever."[14] Now go out and shout *that* from the rooftops! Better yet, live out your hope before everyone, and live your life in light of the coming triumph of hope and joy and love over death and sorrow and pain. You are a member of the kingdom of hope!

Take that, you evil world!

Take that, death!

Take that, war and terrorism!

Take that, cancer and AIDS and typhoid and malaria!

Take that, volcanoes and earthquakes and hurricanes!

Take that, sin and sorrow and selfishness in my own heart!

It is only a matter of time before you all will be gone forever.

I encourage you—challenge you—to build hope into your life. Find a way to remind yourself that hope is a living, active emotion. Maybe it's a simple phrase like "It's gonna be better someday" or "All this sorrow and pain is going to end" or "It's only a matter of time until Jesus returns." Remind yourself throughout the day that your real home is in the new heavens and new earth. Use your catchphrase to bring to mind all the best things you are looking forward to, all the good things we have been talking about. When the small things of life flare up—the annoyances, the disappoint-ments, the people who let you down—go to this "hope place" for just a moment. A brief reminder in your spirit is all it will take. That can be a first step in building an *overflowing* hope into your life.

Hate

It's surprising to think that the Bible calls us to grow the emotion of *hate*. But it makes sense: God hates sin and evil, and so should we.

For me, this understanding began with a verse in Jude. Jude, in its only chapter, talks about evil and disobedient people that have crept into a struggling congregation in one of the first-century churches:

> Some ungodly people have wormed their way into your churches, saying that God's marvelous grace allows us to live immoral lives. The condemnation of such people was recorded long ago, for they have denied our only Master and Lord, Jesus Christ. . . . And don't forget Sodom and Gomorrah and their neighboring towns, which were filled with immorality and every kind of sexual perversion. Those cities were destroyed by fire and serve as a warning of the eternal fire of God's judgment. . . . Like unthinking animals, they do whatever their instincts tell them, and so they bring about their own destruction. What sorrow awaits them![15]

After another litany of woe and destruction, Jude turns his attention to how we are to live amid such dire and vile circumstances. One verse in particular had a lot to do with my quest to discover the role that emotions are to play in the Christian life: "Be merciful to those who doubt; snatch others from the fire and save them; to others show mercy, mixed with fear—hating even the clothing stained by corrupted flesh."[16] In our response to evil, we're to show mercy to other people and to snatch them away from the fire so they don't get burned; and we're to *hate* anything that has *even been touched* by the corruption of evil.

We read this, nod to it—and yet we can watch or read or listen to almost any form of movie or TV or book or online site without *feeling anything*. We even *enjoy* these things without the slightest revulsion or righteous hatred of evil rising up in our souls.

I once got a violent bout of the flu after eating a McDonald's McRib sandwich. Now, whenever I see ads for it, I feel sick. It brings back immediate and strong memories of the taste of a McRib sandwich— and worse, the vile sickness coming up from my stomach. (Just writing about a McRib sandwich is literally turning my stomach right now.) I cannot stand to look at one, smell one, or even think about one.

I hate McRib sandwiches.

So why doesn't *sin* turn my stomach all the more?

Watching evil that is promoted and glorified as good should nauseate us, just like watching one of those reality shows where people have to eat raw sheep intestines or live roaches to reach the next level of the game. Why aren't we disgusted by the evil we see and hear and read?

Are we developing a biblical hatred toward the pornographic images in our society? Are we developing a deep revulsion for gossip and criticism and slander of others? Are we deeply offended by the sins of our culture and our age—the proliferation of violence, and abortion, and the cheapening of human life? Jude's brief epistle has just twenty-five verses, fifteen of which deal with the dire consequences of evil. He *hated* it.

(It occurred to me that, someday, you and I may meet Jude in heaven. He may ask us what we did with his little book. Did we listen? Did we learn from him to hate sin, seeing evil's eternally destructive results rather than its temporal pleasure?)

It shows the depth of our moral corruption when we do not hate the things we should hate.

As we grow closer to God, we will have a growing hatred of all that offends his holiness. Let us cry out that we would have what Psalm 97:10 says: "You who love the LORD, hate evil!"

And in our media-saturated world, we must reclaim the words of Psalm 101 as our own:

> I will refuse to look at
> anything vile and vulgar.
> I hate all who deal crookedly;
> I will have nothing to do with them.
> I will reject perverse ideas
> and stay away from every evil.[17]

<<>>

We all have trouble living the reality I'm talking about. Love, joy, hope, and hatred of evil do not fill us like they should. How are we to make progress toward emotional wholeness? What is the method for turning nouns into verbs in our lives?

The first thing, I think, is to realize that there's something more—a more *passionate* love, a more *exuberant* joy, a more *fervent* hope that we're missing out on.

And then let's decide that we're going to get it! Let's get really intense about figuring out what we need to be feeling.

By searching God's Word, with our eyes peeled for "emotional content," we can understand something of what God wants us to *feel.* Then we need to build those emotional understandings into our lives until they become a kind of holy obsession. Also, getting to know God and embracing his values is going to transform our emotions. But we have to spend time putting God's Word into our lives on a daily basis. It will change how we think—and how we feel. Memorizing Scripture that speaks to an area of need or digging into a good book on a particular area of struggle will help us focus on God's perspective. Attending a Bible study, or beginning to fill our minds with praise and worship may also be key. We need to get our minds set on the right stuff. We need to get really serious about changing our minds and focusing on what God says is true.

Understanding how emotions work will help you grow the right ones in the garden of your life. Using the gardener's tools of *Focus, Know, Value, and Believe* can help you understand what changes you need to make in your garden. Be very honest with where you are now and what you need to change to become emotionally whole. Don't settle for less than God intends for you. He's a fully emotional person, and he wants that for you, too.

This thing of growing our emotions is a Holy Spirit-led, interactive process. It does not all depend on you; it's not all about your ability to change old thinking and bad habits. Laura used to really strive to grow spiritually—doing the list. I know it might be easy to read a book like this and then just make a new list.

That's not the point.

One day, I just told Laura, "You don't have to struggle to grow. That's God's job—kind of like he does with the flowers in the garden. He will make sure you get the water you need, the sunshine, the nutrients. What you need to do is respond to him." That is still true. God will do this. He is able to transform your mind and emotions as you submit to his leading and what he brings into your life. Just be willing to let him do whatever it takes to grow his garden in you.

BLOG 09: GROW

ANDREW]······[God's desire for love, joy, hope, and hatred is a demand. When you put it that way, I begin to understand the importance of what this book is talking about. It isn't about my choosing to love the unlovable. It is about my loving the unlovely because my heart is overflowing with a passion for the things of God (the unlovely being one of them). Hope is becoming a "real expectation" for my wife and me. We can't wait to see how God will show himself again today. Every day is exciting! Lord, grow my love, joy, hope, and hatred.

MEDINE]······[Growing in God-filled emotions is a blessing. During the war, I lost hope, I have never been so hopeless in my life. I found courage from my dad's words: "Look to the Lord, do not despair, hope." My dad was the weakest and sickest of us all; in fact we had to carry him in a wheelbarrow. He helped us to grow in our trust and hope in Jesus and that hope kept us going.

BOB]······[Previous chapters have been like that big bird that runs across the water, flapping its wings, gaining momentum to fly. Every chapter has been a step, gaining momentum. This chapter takes off. It speaks of "the unified heart" in the Bible, emotion and reason, testifying to the divine nature of Scripture. It nails the problem of "duty" only: "Duty never motivated anybody to do anything great." I think of that stringent and noble qualification of Medal of Honor winners—"above and beyond the call of duty." And I think of how many Medal winners (read the commendations) got their prize because they loved their fellow soldiers so much they fell on a grenade, just in time. "Greater love than this has no one: that they lay down their life for another."

Or: "Love is not about what we tell people or give to people. Love is us. We are love to people. Up close and personal."

Or the Eric Liddell story, with the conclusion: "If we don't have joy in our lives, perhaps we do not need God enough."

I keep thinking of people I want to give this book to. But that's because I need its message so bad myself.

"Life-transforming hope . . . is the real expectation that God will happen to us today."

Exactly.

And the part about hating sin is as important as anything in the book so far.

ANA]·····[I really liked this chapter. It is biblically solid and practical, yet always keeps that edge of faith in the forefront. This is something that requires our involvement, but will include a miraculous intervention of God.

I could relate to the "hope" section and the suggestion to create a simple phrase to focus on the reality of our hope. When I lived with a group of young women, there were days where one or more of us would be very discouraged. We would spend hours listening to one another and supporting one another. On those occasions when we didn't have time for a long talk, we'd encourage one another with the phrase, "Remember—we're gonna win." We were confident of the end game with Jesus, so we could endure the present trials.

I was deeply challenged by the "hate" section. It's so easy to get lulled into the world's standards. I remember one of my girlfriends used to tell me that, whenever a new fashion came out that she hated, she would remind herself that within a year she'd get used to it and be wearing it herself. I think this applies as well to hating evil and what we see on commercials or ads. Things that shocked me in the beginning start to seem "normal" after I'm bombarded with them day after day. This was an excellent section for me to apply to my own life.

TOM]·····[Something happened early in my college days. It couldn't have been much because I cannot even remember what it was. But it seemed like a big deal at the time. For some reason, I remember thinking, "Two weeks from now, this won't even matter." I don't know how I came up with two weeks. Anyway, how true that was. I hate to admit it, but what seemed like such a big deal was just a surface issue of no lasting significance. Since then, I've had to deal with some real big issues: my son developed Type 1 diabetes (no cure as of yet); my birth mom contacted me, and some family feelings seem permanently bruised as a result; my once very healthy mother has developed several significant health issues that threaten her life. As my mom and I have discussed, we are not people without hope. And it is a great comfort that "it's gonna be better someday."

Enter the discussion at www.faithfulfeelings.com.

MY BLOG

_____

_____

_____

_____

_____

_____

_____

_____

_____

_____

_____

_____

_____

_____

10 Keep

Even though I believed somewhere down in my gut that it was coming, it still hit both Laura and me hard.

I had cancer.

The story started in early 2006 when I felt a nudging in my spirit that I needed to go to the doctor for a checkup. There was no specific reason, but the thought kept nagging that I needed to get to the doctor. I had not had a physical for probably five years. So I made an appointment. Because our doctor is usually booked months in advance, I made an appointment, didn't think that much more about it, and went on the appointed day. Everything looked good—my heart sounded strong, my cholesterol was fine, my blood pressure was right on target, and my weight was okay.

He caught just one thing: a large lump in my neck.

Our doctor is an ace when it comes to diagnosis. The first time he saw our son Jackson, he discovered a heart condition that needed immediate surgery—something that other doctors who had seen Jackson had missed. It may have saved his life. We felt that our doctor genuinely cared about our family. Now he suspected something was up with my thyroid and was sending me for immediate blood work and an ultrasound of my neck.

I have always disliked needles and medical procedures. Medical shows are not my thing—well, except for *House*. But even then, it sometimes becomes necessary to flip to another channel or leave the room at certain times. I've never been in the hospital other than to get a cast on a broken arm or some stitches. So I especially did not like all the poking and prodding around my neck. It made me feel so vulnerable to lay my head back and have somebody pushing and sticking things into my neck.

White as a sheet, I really felt faint when I saw the great big needle coming in for a biopsy of whatever it was that was growing on my thyroid.

The biopsy was inconclusive; it was either cancer or the kind of thing that could turn into cancer. So they prepared to operate.

Sometime during that experience, I remember being alone in the house and getting down on my knees next to the couch in our living room and just crying before God, praying that he would preserve my life. I told him that I loved my wife and family so much, and I wanted to see my kids grow up. I pleaded that I did not want to go through this ordeal, that I had so much left I wanted to do for God on this earth and so many dreams that had not yet been realized.

I had down days. Laura and I had some honest days of wondering why all this was happening. Yet we turned to God, concentrating on what he was trying to teach us and realizing how dependent we were on him.

Let me tell you, I gained a lot of compassion for other people who are sick.

When the analysis from the first operation came back, it was confirmed: a large cancerous mass. One whole side of my thyroid had been completely overgrown with the bulgy tumor.

Yet somehow, Laura and I never lost a good night's rest, even the day before surgery. The peace of God was with us. Overwhelmingly, we felt so thankful to God that I'd had that prompting to go to the doctor. We felt thankful that all I needed was two surgeries—tough, yes, but no radiation, no chemo. We felt thankful that a world-renowned expert who sees people from all over the country would take me as his patient.

Sure it was hard, but God was also good. As I'm finalizing my work on this book, I have just completed my second surgery and have been declared cancer free!

During this life experience, there was a time for grieving, a time for wondering about the future, a time for some heart-wrenching crying out to God. But there was also a time for focusing on the goodness of God, on what we were learning, on the promises he had given us.

All of this was part of the process. We *kept* the emotions that naturally flowed from the hard situation. They had to be *felt* and *worked through*. At the same time, we worked hard not to let the negative feelings overflow the banks and envelop us in a flood of doubt, sadness, or self-pity.

Soon after my surgery, a good friend sent me a list written by John Piper to his church on the eve of his own cancer surgery. It was titled "Don't Waste Your Cancer." Wow! Look at all the good reasons I had to get through this test with peace and strength:

» You will waste your cancer if you do not believe it is designed for you by God.
» You will waste your cancer if you believe it is a curse and not a gift.
» You will waste your cancer if you seek comfort from your odds rather than from God.

» You will waste your cancer if you refuse to think about death.
» You will waste your cancer if you think that "beating" cancer means staying
   alive rather than cherishing Christ.
» You will waste your cancer if you spend too much time reading about cancer
   and not enough time reading about God.
» You will waste your cancer if you let it drive you into solitude instead of deepen
   your relationships with manifest affection.
» You will waste your cancer if you grieve as those who have no hope.
» You will waste your cancer if you treat sin as casually as before.
» You will waste your cancer if you fail to use it as a means of witness to the
   truth and glory of Christ.[1]

One of the things I learned from my experience with cancer, echoed here
by John Piper, is the value of the emotions that come from unexpected
experiences and hardships.

〈〈〉〉

Just as there are beautiful emotions that we nurture and water and grow
like flowers, there are emotions that spring up unexpectedly in the most
unlikely places at the most unlikely times—emotions we must keep and
sometimes nurture. Gardeners will tell you how they can design the
"perfect garden"—even to the point of diagramming the garden layout
on paper or on a computer—so that plants and flowers bloom at just the
right times in a perfect balance of cycles year-round.

But experienced gardeners will also tell you that there are always
surprises—plants or flowers that poke through the ground in corners,
from under rocks, at the edges—that were never diagrammed or planned.
They might throw the garden "off-balance" because they aren't what the
gardener had in mind.

Some gardeners will weed out these surprises, banishing them to the
compost pile to preserve the perfect-garden symmetry they're striving to
maintain. But other gardeners follow the natural approach, taking what
the ground gives them, keeping and nurturing these surprises to see what
special beauty they might bring.

God wants us to *keep* the unexpected emotions he brings into our lives.

These are feelings we need to keep for a time—not deny. Not ban them from our gardens. It's in the experience of these things that we come to understand more about ourselves and God. These emotions yield a special beauty and purpose.

The list of *Keep* emotions is long. And endlessly surprising. Some *Keep* emotions are like beautiful annuals, with small but colorful petals that pop into our lives for a short while with brief pleasures:

Love of baseball, mountains, or Ben and Jerry's Coffee Heath Bar Crunch ice cream

Renewed hope for a good and successful future for yourself or others

A joyful celebration over an engagement or the birth of a child

Some *Keep* emotions are strange:

Anger that communicates truth or corrects injustice

Jealousy for God and his righteousness

And some *Keep* emotions come from the difficult, rocky parts of our gardens, the hardships of our lives:

Sorrow in repentance

Sadness or grief over loss

These are all emotions we need to keep, nurture, cultivate—at least for a time. Through them, God helps us understand him better and know more deeply what he is doing in our lives.

At the same time, as we shall see, many *Keep* emotions need to be managed so that they don't start to take over the garden. Sorrow or

righteous anger, for example, can spread unchecked and begin
to destroy the better, more beautiful things in our lives.

Unfortunately, I must admit, that also applies to loving Ben and Jerry's
Coffee Heath Bar Crunch ice cream.

‹‹›

One of the more difficult emotions to keep is *grief.* Too often, we identify
grief as being the same as our loss—and we stuff it, repress it. This
creates bad stuff underground and creates problems later.

When loss hits us in life, God wants us to feel the loss, to embrace
our grief.

My friend Phil and his wife have known a devastating sorrow. Wanting to
get pregnant for a very long time, they finally had success through the
wonders of modern technology. Phil kept us informed, and both Laura
and I were thrilled for them: They were not only pregnant, but with twins!

But then Phil sent a heartbreaking e-mail:

Dear Matthew,

I'm sorry to have to start the new year with sad news, but I do need to let
you know that our little daughters, whom we named Zoe and Alethea, were
born prematurely (23 weeks) and lost through miscarriage, on December
19th. One of the twins' water had broken a week before, and it finally became
clear, once infection had set in, that they both had to be delivered. We buried
them on the 29th. Jennie was home from the hospital in time for Christmas,
and we spent some time with the wider family. We can testify to God's presence and peace during the hours leading up to the delivery, but of course we
are still numb with shock, grief, and disbelief. We fall into God's hand in our
weakness. . . .

Yours in Christ,

Phil

I replied, really feeling my brother's grief:

Oh Phil,

Laura's and my heart just broke when we read this, and we shared a teary hug. I am so very sorry, may you find God's grace and peace sufficient at this hard time.

Matthew

A few months later, Phil sent me a list of Scriptures that had been his comfort and strength:

"My times are in your hands."[2]
"The LORD gave and the LORD has taken away; may the name of the LORD be praised."[3]
"The LORD remembers us and will bless us."[4]
"May the God of hope fill you with all joy and peace as you trust in him."[5]

The process of godly grief takes time. First, there are times of intense feelings. We share our pain with others, expressing, grieving with the body of Christ. Others can help by walking beside us, quietly listening and being there for us. Later on, we can begin to work toward restoration and comfort by dwelling on, embracing, and believing in the promises and love of God.

Phil's story reminds me of a horrible tragedy that grabbed the headlines several years ago in my home state of Illinois.

Pastor Scott Willis and his wife, Janet, were driving behind a semitruck with their six young children when a piece of metal fell off the truck and punctured their minivan's gas tank. The ensuing explosion left the two devoted Christian parents with six little bodies to bury. Can you imagine the horror of seeing your children killed in such a way?

"The depth of pain is indescribable," Scott said. "We're ordinary people."

Scott and Janet did not deny their overwhelming grief. They cried, wept, and felt the deep pain of overwhelming loss. They *kept* their feelings of grief and lived in those painful moments.

Scott later told a group of journalists, "God knows all of history and time from its beginning to its end. What happened to us wasn't an accident. God is never taken by surprise. God had a purpose for it, probably many purposes."[6]

Scott was right, although it took years to understand some snippets of the why behind the tragedy.

It turned out the driver of the truck had never earned his license from the State of Illinois. He had received it by paying a bribe or campaign contribution to the man who would later become Illinois governor, George Ryan. (After leaving office, Ryan was tried and convicted on federal corruption charges. The Willis accident was part of what set off the chain of events that led to Ryan's conviction.)

Recounting the tragedy, Janet wrote to the judge in the Ryan case, "I am sharing these facts only because I believe if justice rules, wrongdoing will be deterred. . . . All of us have waited patiently for justice."[7] (That actually is another area where Scripture is clear. There is some consolation in knowing that, in the end, God will do justice to all evil.)

In Scott's words to the judge about his children, "We love them. We miss them. We do not despair. We live with a God-promised hope in Jesus Christ. . . . My wife and I have a strong desire to forgive Governor Ryan, but it must be on an honest basis: sorrow and admission. Even a six-year-old boy knows when he's done wrong he needs to be truly sorry, and admit it. Then forgiveness and mercy can be graciously offered. That would be our joy."[8] In time, Scott and Janet moved on, "refusing to dwell there." Today, they focus on the joys of their three remaining children, some twenty-four grandchildren, and a future home-going where there will be a great reunion. I think all heaven is anxiously awaiting that day as well.

Recently, I was with Bob Buford, author of the book *Halftime,* which challenges people to get out of their comfort zones after having success in business and put their time and abilities to work building God's Kingdom.

When my time with Bob was finished, I asked him if we could pray together.

He began praying about seeing his son someday in heaven. As you may know, and as I knew, Bob lost his son in a tragic swimming accident twenty years ago. His son was in his twenties when he died.

This reference to his son was not part of our conversation, not a focus of our hour together, but there it still was—some twenty years later—at the forefront of his mind. Multimillionaire, successful business owner, Christian author, a guy who has motivated thousands to get serious about changing their world for good.

Father of a dead son.

In the midst of all the amazing success he has enjoyed, first on his mind was his great ache, his awful, still-tender scar—a scar that will last until Bob sees his son again in heaven.

Bob Buford will be the first to tell you, as he writes in his book, that without the tragedy of losing his son, an only child, God might never have gotten such a powerful hold on his life to use it in such an amazing way. And after more than two decades, after all the good it has done in his life, he is still known by those scars.

Bob Buford has *kept* the emotion of grief in his life. And it has deepened him, enriched him, and matured him in his relationship with God.

<⟨⟩>

Anger is an emotion that we as Christians tend to get all wrong.

Anger should never just be stuffed back inside. Even sinful and destructive anger cannot be healed without dealing with the feelings head-on.

It would be really hard to be a good parent without anger. It is how we communicate the difference between wrong and right, and what is valuable to us. You should be angry with your child if he or she hits another child with a brick or steals a candy bar. In a sinful world, anger is a needed corrective force in response to wrong actions. And it is through anger that we respond rightly to the wrongs and sin and evil in the world. The way we show others the difference between someone taking our stapler and someone abusing our child is measured by how angry we become.

Anger also serves to protect us and those we love. We're supposed to get angry when someone tries to hurt us or a loved one. It helps us to react quickly and do something to counteract the evil. We are at the height of alert and strength, ready to act in defense. Imagine that a big, 258-pound carpenter walks up to a two-by-four with a hammer, rears back with all his might, and swings at a nail—he is just doing his job, right? Now imagine he rears back with his hammer—and aims it toward a child. Our reactions would be totally different, wouldn't it? Acts of wrongdoing, sin, and evil deserve an immediate and appropriate response of righteous anger and action.

I had a good friend in college who was a pacifist. I once asked her, "Are you telling me that if a man got into your house with a knife and started after your sleeping children you would do nothing?" Alexis said, "I do not know if I could do it, but that is what I believe. I would do nothing." I did not believe her then, and after studying emotion for ten years, I really do not believe her now. She was too fine a person. Her anger would have forced her to change her mind, and I believe that she would have done all in her power to stop the man before he struck her children. Anger, as God planned it, is a weapon against injustice. We use it to protect the innocent and stand up against evil. Anger is essential in a sinful world. There is evil in the world, and we should be angry about it.

You know, God gets angry too. He gets angry with you and me when we sin. Our disobedience offends him. That's why in order to satisfy justice, which our sin necessitated, he sacrificed his Son for us. Look up *anger* or *wrath* in your Bible concordance and read just a few of the many, many verses on God's anger. And don't let anybody tell you that God's anger is not fierce emotion. God takes evil very personally; it destroys all he loves.[9]

Some anger pops up like weeds in our lives, and this can be hugely destructive. We will discuss this type of anger in the next chapter. But there are times when injustice strikes, wrongs are done, sin abounds, evil flourishes—and God wants us to feel righteous anger and act to stop the tide of evil.

⟨⟨⟩⟩

Jealousy is an emotion that we are taught to be afraid of. But did you know that the Bible speaks of *good* jealousy?

"Good jealousy" has been blacklisted in our English Bibles by replacing it with the word *zeal*. In the original Greek, there is only one word for "jealous," and it sounds like our English *zealous*. Our translations have taken this one word and translated it in two ways—mostly using *jealous* when it is bad and *zealous* when it is good, as if the underlying word had two totally different meanings. I do not believe it does.[10]

The most basic meaning of the word translated *jealous* is the same in every instance: the defending of an object's rightful or perceived rightful place in your life. The emotion is neither wholly positive nor wholly negative. The object we are jealous of is considered valuable and good; it is the action of trying to take it that is considered wrong. If we look at every time the word is used in the New Testament—even in its positive uses, where it is translated "zealous"—we can see the same basic meaning.

Paul writes to the Corinthians, "I am jealous for you with the jealousy of God himself. I promised you as a pure bride to one husband— Christ."[11] Some of the Corinthians were behaving as if they were not the bride of Christ, and Paul is jealous that they give Christ the devotion he is legitimately due. Jealousy for your wife, if she is being pursued by another man, is a legitimate and right emotion. She's your wife! Jealousy for your neighbor's brand-new red BMW convertible? Well, that's another matter. It's your neighbor's car!

Jealousy, when felt for the right reasons, can result in some of our most spiritual and sacred moments. It can even prove our love and devotion.

An illustration of this appears in Numbers 25. When the Israelites were traveling around in the wilderness for forty years, they found themselves camped close to the nation of Moab. Some of the men felt bored around camp with the same old manna every day, same old tent, same old desert, same old routine: Who could blame them?

So when some Moabite women asked them to come to a festival, they said, "You bet."

"So the Israelites feasted with them and worshiped the gods of Moab. In this way, Israel joined in the worship of Baal of Peor, causing the LORD's anger to blaze against his people."[12]

God's anger against his people had an immediate result. People started dying. Some twenty-four thousand people died in just a short time.

God told Moses he had better round up all the men who were leading the Israelites into these pagan orgies and kill them before things really got bad. The righteous were already gathering at the entrance to the temple, crying and weeping and asking God to stop the plague. The situation was serious; all Israel was in danger of being wiped out.

Then something happened that took the people one step further toward total annihilation. One of the men brought a woman from Moab into his own tent to sleep with her. Not only that, but he did it in front of Moses and all the weeping people of Israel, amid the executions that may have already been going on.

Here's what happened next:

When Phinehas son of Eleazar and grandson of Aaron the priest saw this, he jumped up and left the assembly. He took a spear and rushed after the man into his tent. Phinehas thrust the spear all the way through the man's body and into the woman's stomach. So the plague against the Israelites was stopped. . . .

Then the LORD said to Moses, "Phinehas son of Eleazar and grandson of Aaron the priest has turned my anger away from the Israelites by being as zealous [jealous] among them as I was."[13]

In some way, maybe we all were saved by what Phinehas did. Were it not for his jealousy and righteous anger, we would be in danger of losing the nation through which God would eventually send our Savior, Jesus Christ.

This word *zeal* is the same word as *jealousy*. Can you imagine a stronger emotion than one that would motivate Phinehas's violent action? There was no trial, no oral argument, and no jury. One man, armed with righteous jealousy for God's honor, went out and administered justice.

Now, I'm not advocating vigilante justice and going outside the legal system. This story, what the Bible says, reflects how things were done in a different age and culture, but it carries for us an important lesson: Jealousy is something God calls us to feel sometimes.

When we see the name of Christ defamed, when we see the gospel trampled, when we see Hollywood and music producers pouring out garbage to steal the minds of our kids, when we see the poor exploited by corrupt leaders—sometimes it's our obligation to feel righteous jealousy and act on it appropriately.

〈〈〉〉

Gardeners will tell you that sometimes a garden will bear a plant or flower that they had forgotten about or neglected. Likewise, there are some emotions we have ignored or too easily forgotten.

One of these is genuine *sorrow* over sin.

One of the greatest books on emotion ever written, which I mentioned previously, is *Religious Affections* by Jonathan Edwards. He wrote in defense of the great Puritan revivals, one of the greatest turnings to God in the history of our nation. Critics at the time disparaged the emotional displays of sorrow and repentance that were part of what God was doing. Edwards's response was this great book, defending the expression of emotion in the Christian life.

A sign of great revival in the church is when people become overwhelmed with sorrow over their sin. God responds to genuine sorrow in amazing ways. He responds with grace and restoration. There was this king in the

Old Testament called Ahab, who was the prototype of the evil king. When I say "prototype," I really mean it. Through the entire history of the Jews, the name *Ahab* was used as a synonym of disobedience and rebellion against God.

A reputation like this is not built in a day—you needed to be one really bad dude. Listen to what the Bible says: "No one else so completely sold himself to what was evil in the LORD's sight as Ahab did."[14]

Soon after this, however, a different Ahab emerges.

Elijah the great prophet of the Lord—the same guy who never died and was taken up to heaven in a fiery chariot—comes to Ahab and tells him that his whole family is going to die and be eaten by dogs and vultures. The king finally gets the point and rips off his royal clothes and starts going around in rags and old sacks. He even slept in the terribly scratchy and uncomfortable stuff. We are told that he "went about in deep mourning."[15] And it must have been genuine, because phony repentance does not fool God.

God is really touched by this change of heart and tells Ahab that he is not going to destroy his family when Ahab is living—he will wait until after he is dead to bring the terrible judgment. This is an amazing story to me. That God would respond in that way to heartfelt repentance from such a bad guy is astounding and encouraging to a sinner like me. So you have to ask yourself, *Why did God respond that way?* It was Ahab's genuine, heartfelt sorrow over what he had done. His *sorrow* over sin.

If emotion tells us something about the truth of what we value and think and believe, then true, gritty, intense, emotional sorrow shows a genuine change of heart. That is why it is so important to God. If we say we're sorry without feeling bad about it, we show that we don't really believe that what we have done is all that bad. It is only when we realize the depth of the hurt we have caused, or the evil we have done, that we feel real gut-wrenching sorrow.

Sorrow over sin is just one kind of sorrow that we need to express to God and to others.

There's also sorrow for those who do not yet know Christ, another
emotion we have too easily neglected.

One of the most incredible sermons I have heard was given by Bill Hybels
about his "Popeye moment." You know Popeye, the cartoon character
who gets all muscle-bound when he eats his spinach. When Popeye gets
to the absolute end of himself, when he cannot stand the evil injustice
that is going on around him, he says, "I can'ts stands no more." Then he
eats his spinach and saves the day.

Hybels, founder of Willow Creek Community Church and prophet of the
seeker-sensitive church movement, had his Popeye moment about
churches that were no longer relevant to unchurched and hurting people.
He talked in his sermon about driving four hours to the little church he'd
attended while growing up. Its doors were closed, its life ended.

He sat in the parking lot and wept for the dead church that did not reach
lost people.

Hybels still cultivates that godly sorrow in his life—it drives him to get
out and minister to people. Hundreds of thousands of people have been
touched because of Bill Hybels's sorrow and anger over a church that did
not meet the needs of hurting people.

Sorrow—over sin and for those who have not found Jesus—are emotions
we need to cultivate and keep.

〈〈〉〉

The emotions of grief, sorrow, anger, jealousy, and others—what many
call *negative* emotions—are difficult to understand and deal with. It's
where I think we, as Christians, are most confused. Because we identify
them as negative, we want to repress them.

I saw a psychologist interviewed about the crazed killer in Lancaster,
Pennsylvania, who shot children in an Amish one-room schoolhouse.
He said, "These kinds of people have no emotional immune system."

Emotion is there to keep us from doing others harm; it is like an immune
system against doing the wrong thing—a part of our conscience. Serial

killers, the worst kinds of murderers, do not feel compassion for their victims, and they are not able to feel the pain of another—they have dulled and dried up their feelings. That is why they can do what they do in such senseless acts of violence.

The absence, or death, of emotions is bad. Having no grief over loss, no sorrow over pain, no anger at injustice, would lead us to be very warped people. So we dare not think that negative emotions are to be controlled, denied, and cut back. The truth is, they enrich us, give us fuller balance in our lives, and create in us an emotional fullness—despite the hard reality of the feelings themselves.

If we declare war on our negative emotions, we are in just as much trouble as if we reject joy and love. Of course, legitimate anger, jealousy, and sorrow can all rage beyond the boundaries that should contain them. Some of us struggle with this more than others. Yet we cannot let the occasional flash flood convince us that all anger must be banished. Instead, we need to use the flood times as a chance to make changes in ourselves and how we relate to others. With practice, we can learn to harness the power of negative emotions, as Jesus did when he used his anger to drive the money changers out of the courts of the Temple.

Many of us will need help from our friends and small groups to get our feelings out in the open. As counselor and psychologist Henry Cloud writes in his book *Rescue Your Love Life*: "Stop acting in ways that cover up what you are really feeling. If you have any doubts about what those are, common ones include silence, withdrawal, overactivity, anger, argumentativeness, indirectness, sarcasm, nitpicking, blaming, mean-ness, bitterness, and jealousy. Ask your mate to tell you the ways you hide your true feelings and the ways your defenses get in the way of being known."[16]

From our understanding of emotion (based on what we focus on, know, value, and believe), we can agree with Dr. Cloud that "most of the time, a problem that involves feelings can't be fixed until the feelings are heard and understood."[17] That goes for our marriages, relationships with our kids, situations at work, and interactions with God's people and God himself. If we continue to cover up our true feelings, we will stay stuck in our spiritual journeys.

Marcia Reynolds, an expert on the workings of the brain, puts it like this in her article "Outsmart Your Brain":

We physically cannot suppress emotions. We instead attempt to suppress feelings. The emotional reactions are still occurring, causing stress and illness in the body and raging at inappropriate times, usually in our cars or at home with those we love.

In fact, we become so adept at suppression that over time, we condition our brains to disconnect from our emotional responses, which in turn, inactivate our ability to express our feelings and our capacity to understand the emotions of others. The neural pathways to the middle brain actually shrink in size, or never fully develop, limiting our abilities to feel and empathize.

Therefore, the more we teach self-control and the suppression of feelings, the more we impede the positive feelings, including happiness and passion, restricting instead of increasing our mental abilities.[18]

Most of us are better at hiding our feelings than we are at bringing them out into the open. Honest expressions of feelings make us uncomfortable, or show that we're too involved, and we don't know what to say in response.

Remember my friends Bob and Dianne? One day, Dianne was sitting at the Sunday dinner table with her extended family, and she was talking about the fact that her neighbor, a beloved friend, was moving away. She started to cry, tears slipping down her cheeks. The immediate and strong response from around the table was that she should not get emotional, that it was more spiritual to be calm and reserved.

They were wrong.

Dianne was being real with those she loved. And she was also living in the emotional fullness and health that God intended.

‹ ‹ › ›

We have an extraordinary white flowering crabapple tree in our backyard.

The extraordinary thing is where it is and what it does. You see, it is just at the corner of our deck, and it has grown up and over our picnic-table area like a living arbor. It has been an unexpected and beautiful serendipity in our lives, one we have kept and cultivated.

Every year, it has to be pruned so that we do not have branches hanging in our faces when we eat outside, but it is a painful job to cut back this perfect, unordered painting of green. One branch perfectly follows the railing of the deck all the way to the steps that lead to the backyard. Last year, I had to trim it back so we could get out. It was a family decision on how and where to lop off a piece so as not to lose the wonderful, whimsical wildness, while at the same time making it possible to walk easily into the backyard.

In spring it is in full bloom. White flower petals fall like rain in the warm breezes. To eat outside, first we have to sweep off the deck, and if we have drinking glasses out there for more than ten minutes, we will have petals in our water. There is typically a flower trail through the back door and into the kitchen from six little feet coming in from play.

I was outside one spring with Cailin, who was four at the time. She said, "Daddy, I do not like that tree." I asked her why, and I began to go into all the reasons I loved its beauty.

She said, "Because soon it will lose all its flowers, and it will be just green again; it will not be so beautiful anymore."

Emotions are sometimes like that tree, and we sometimes respond like Cailin. Instead of just experiencing the beauty of the moment, we become afraid of the pain of the future when the beauty will end and life will be less than extraordinary again.

We need to fully experience the emotions God brings into our lives—both the good and the "negative." We cannot afford to prune back those emotions or banish them from the gardens of our lives. It is how God deepens and enriches us, through joy and pain.

BLOG 10: KEEP

STEPHEN]·····[I sometimes feel like such a half-person, I often feel like I live a lie, I live dishonestly with myself. Switching off parts of myself depending on where I am and who I'm with. I feel like I'm only real on my own, and that only God really understands what's going on. I think this chapter has shown me a scary glimpse of the solution . . . but I am scared to death to think that the solution is to allow others in! Can't I just stay in my own comfortable shrinking existence? . . . I want to get out, but I first need to be willing to make the necessary moves.

I love playing drums . . . going crazy when people aren't in the room I really let rip and try new things. I remember starting to play in church and feeling very pressurized by my own thinking and the glares every time I did something different. After a while, I became a small drum player who never experimented . . . having joined a band at university, I have re-found an ability to express myself through drums and am starting to grow as a drum player again.

JAN]·····[I too have had cancer, and then my mother, to whom I had been close all my life, died. I have been struggling with grief, depression and disappointment with God. I had believed Psalm 91 and now it had "come near me." After reading John Piper's list, and the reaction of Pastor Scott Willis to the loss of his six children, I feel entirely different. I can accept that these things are part of God's plan for us and He is good.

REBECCA]·····[I am reminded when reading this passage about a verse that says, "The sovereign Lord has given me his words of wisdom, so that I know what to say to all these weary ones. Morning by morning he wakens me and opens my understanding to His will." I think that so often I live by circumstances, whether good or bad, and allow them to get the best of me. But one of the biggest lessons I learned was from my friend about a year ago. Her brother was tragically killed in a car crash. But while she wondered why this had happened, she said to me, "We don't know why. But I do know that he was a wonderful brother. We can't change what has happened, so we must grieve his loss, pray that others will come to know God during this hard time as our lives are a testament to them, and then move on." That was so powerful. Here, in the midst of one of the most awful losses in a person's life, she could grieve the loss and still see her life as a testament of God's will to all those who didn't know Christ.

The other thing she said to me was this: "We never know why God does the things He does. But I do know this—He always has a plan. This summer I had to come home early from my camping trip because I was so sick, and little did I know that God brought me home to spend the last few months with my brother. That was a miracle in and of itself.

And even though my dream after graduating college was to hike the Appalachian trails, God knew that my brother's time was limited and therefore brought me home. The night before my brother died, we were talking about what it would be like to be in Heaven someday. Little did we know that God would take him so soon after that. But again, God does have a divine plan, and while we may be sad for a while, we must continue to see His goodness and pray for His peace while we are suffering this great loss."

JAMES]·····[I like this chapter. Something about it made me feel that I can relax, sit back, and learn what God is wanting to teach me through the variety of emotions that come my way during the course of any given week. Somehow, the chapter was reassuring and comforting.

MARIAN]·····[I realize yet again the privilege of being an emotional being. Like a garden, I can cultivate some emotions while weeding out others. God has given me the freedom to have a beautiful, fruitful garden or a barren patch of ground. Tears came to my eyes as I read of the pain of Phil and Jennie in their loss—perhaps because I too had two miscarriages. I haven't thought about my own loss for some considerable time. Maybe that is part of my heart needing to recapture and keep something of grief that will reach out in compassion to others. And anger that I know is buried deep within, over the injustice of my own childhood—being hated simply because mine was the wrong face at the wrong time. Yes, I choose to keep righteous anger, but please give me wisdom to prune it, Lord, so it does not run amok in my garden. Keeping and cultivating—they go together. I keep what is appropriate, and give them space and room to grow, and tend them in the process. May my emotional garden be even more beautiful for You, Lord.

TODD]·····[I cannot imagine what a parent feels when they lose a child, or how a sister feels when she loses a brother. My best friend from high school died in a car accident when he was 18. I thank God for the person who entered my room, quietly closed the door, got me to talk about my friend's death, and led me to prayer. I understand why most people would not want to touch the subject with a 10-foot pole, but this good neighbor modeled Jesus and really helped me put a finger on my grief. Embracing grief then (a lifetime ago), and keeping it now, has improved the way I relate to God and others. Without dwelling too much in the past, it still serves as a good wake-up call to me in present moments, and pushes me forward into our positively bright future.

JARED]·····[I feel like I can truly connect with this idea of keeping those emotions in us that maintain our humanity. I know that I have a tendency to avoid conflict, and in turn to suppress certain emotions. Several times in my schooling or continuing education, I have ended up taking some form of a personality test. This particular conflict resolution test reminded me that I would lean toward avoidance and internalize those "negative" emotions. While growing up, I was taught that emotions would just get me into trouble and get me nowhere. Yet, when I did not have the opportunity to fully express my doubts and hurt, I could not begin to feel genuine repentance when I was told to apologize. These often-shunned emotions can be critical to developing our hearts toward a holistic view of others and ourselves.

Enter the discussion at www.faithfulfeelings.com.

MY BLOG

_____

_____

_____

_____

_____

_____

_____

_____

_____

_____

_____

_____

_____

11 Done

You may be asking, "But there *are* bad emotions, aren't there? Are you saying that all emotions are good?"

Not at all. But remember, emotions always have an object. Sometimes the object of an emotion is a good and proper thing; sometimes it's a bad thing. Anger can be justified when we are angry at something evil, but it's wrong when our anger destroys someone or kills a relationship.

Some emotions fall into all three categories—those we should *grow,* those we should *keep,* and those we need to *be done with* or get rid of.

It is not biblical to say that a particular emotion is always bad or always good—it depends on the object.

But clearly, some emotions, depending on the object, can be bad for us. God speaks harshly of these emotions, commanding us to banish them from our lives.

Again, let's think of *Done* emotions in terms of the garden. There are plants and flowers that spread like wildfire in a garden. Sometimes, they can even be quite beautiful—at least superficially. But they choke out all other life, rob the soil of needed nutrients, and throw the ecosystem of the garden out of balance. Likewise, emotional weeds can throw our lives out of balance, damaging us—sometimes before we even know it—in ways we don't necessarily recognize until it's too late.

We need to weed out the *Done* emotions from our lives. The Bible tells us to literally kill them. And yet we need to be careful to understand and distinguish between what's a weed and what's not a weed. Gardeners will tell you they get nervous when a novice pokes around in their garden— it's too easy to pull out a *Grow* or a *Keep* emotion—roots and all— thinking it's a weed.

Consider this chapter a guide to the weeds in your life. . . .

〈〈〉〉

The Bible includes what theologians call *vice lists*—verses that itemize or list various damaging attitudes or destructive actions.

This happened to be a literary device popular with philosophers around the time of Jesus. The concept was simple: You put down in writing a list of all the stuff you think is really, really bad. Philosophers could then argue over their lists and try to figure out what things were the worst, what things the other guys had on their lists that should not be there, what things they were missing, and what basic bad stuff was at the root of all the other bad stuff. (This is the kind of thing we pay our philosophy professors to argue about to this day.)

The writers of the New Testament, especially Paul, picked up on this device and used it here and there in the books they wrote. They used these lists to show us what characterizes a bad person and what things to look for in identifying people who do not honor God.

Plenty of emotions show up in these lists.

Three good lists to read are in Romans 1, 2 Timothy 3, and Ephesians 4:

> Their lives became full of every kind of wickedness, sin, greed, *hate*, *envy*, murder, quarreling, deception, malicious behavior, and gossip. They are back-stabbers, *haters of God*, insolent, proud, and boastful. They invent new ways of sinning, and they disobey their parents. They refuse to understand, break their promises, are heartless, and have no mercy.[1]

> For people will *love* only themselves and their money. They will be boastful and proud, scoffing at God, disobedient to their parents, and *ungrateful*. They will consider nothing sacred. They will be *unloving* and unforgiving; they will slander others and have no self-control. They will be cruel and *hate* what is good. They will betray their friends, be reckless, be puffed up with pride, and *love* pleasure rather than God. They will act religious, but they will reject the power that could make them godly. Stay away from people like that![2]

> Get rid of all bitterness, *rage*, *anger*, harsh words, and slander, as well as all types of evil behavior.[3]

Let me quickly point out several things about these vice lists in the Bible:

» There's no question that the Bible identifies emotions that can become sin in our lives. Evil has corrupted our emotional lives, and it is a lot worse than we could have imagined. So, yes, there are *bad* emotions that need to be dealt with.

» The phrase "all types of malicious behavior" suggests an object that is not right, a reason that is not appropriate. In other words, these emotions are bad because they connect to an *object* that is not worthy, or they have the intent of hurting God and others. In the second passage, we see the repeated use of the word *love*, which is a great emotion to feel for God, friends, and family (*Grow*); or even chocolate bars and swimming (*Keep*); but here it is an evil love because it has the wrong object; the ones who hate what is good "love only themselves and their money," and "love pleasure rather than God."

» The phrase "get rid of" contradicts popular Christian teaching on the subject of negative emotions. I think Christians tend to teach the myth that emotions should be *controlled*. But that's not biblical when it comes to *Grow* emotions and *Keep* emotions, which are to be cultivated and encouraged. And when it comes to *Done* emotions—controlling them really doesn't work. The Bible makes it clear that these emotions need to be *eliminated*. "Get rid of" them, the Bible says.

I contend that *Done* emotions need to be eliminated, weeded out, and banished from the garden.

One more thing: It's interesting to me that listed right alongside *murder* are such emotions as jealousy, anger, loving pleasure more than God, being ungrateful, and even "harsh words." Wow. This makes me sit right up in my chair and pay attention! I don't know about you, but I consider myself pretty okay on the murder rap, but when it comes to harsh words . . .

The Bible indicates that our charge is not only to stop doing wickedness, but to get rid of such things as jealousy, destructive anger, pride, hating good stuff and loving bad stuff, and being unforgiving and heartless (no love and compassion). We, along with the *really bad* people who do things like murder, are to weed these things out of our lives. (Wait, maybe *we* are sometimes the *really bad* people; all these things are on the same list.) God calls us to totally root out destructive emotions in our lives, especially sinful emotional patterns that tear up relationships.

‹ ‹ › ›

I'm still learning this.

When we lived in Aberdeen, Laura and I bought our first television, after five years of marriage. As newlyweds, we had always enjoyed not having a TV. We read books, took walks, and talked. Then we found a ten-inch, black-and-white TV at a garage sale for £5 (about $8 U.S.). Just right for a student budget.

The first benefit of owning a TV in Scotland was that we could watch the NBA championship. My home team, the Chicago Bulls, was in the finals; it was the Michael Jordan era. It was on at two in the morning, but I could watch my Bulls win the championship.

However, we soon found that standards for TV were really different in Scotland. They could show just about *anything.*

One night, I found that the movie *9 1/2 Weeks* was on. I didn't know much about the movie, except that it was rather sexually explicit even though it was considered a mainstream movie. I had never seen anything like it, and quite honestly, I was curious about it.

That night, Laura had already gone to bed, and I had complete freedom to stay up and do whatever I wanted.

I was tempted. I really wanted to see what a movie like *9 1/2 Weeks* would be like, to have my sexual senses aroused and titillated.

But I told myself no and went to bed. I considered that a moral victory in my life. I avoided sin, did the right thing.

But later, when I read Jesus' words in the Sermon on the Mount, I understood something that made me realize that this and other similar "victories" were far short of what Jesus expected.

Jesus says in Matthew 5, "But I warn you—unless your righteousness is better than the righteousness of the teachers of religious law and the Pharisees, you will never enter the Kingdom of Heaven!"[4]

I got to thinking about the way Dr. J. Julius Scott, one of my favorite Bible teachers at Wheaton Graduate School, said that the Pharisees

looked at the law. Dr. Scott's specialty was in Jewish backgrounds—
he studied the culture and religious beliefs of the Jews from the close
of the Old Testament to the coming of Jesus. And he said that the
Pharisees made a *fence* around the laws of God—something that was
always further out, surrounding and protecting the law itself. They made
the issue of distance a virtue.

For example, if the law said you could walk one mile on the Sabbath, they
said you could only walk three-quarters of a mile. If the law said a man
could not trim the edge of his beard, they would ban you from ever using
a pair of scissors.

I thought about that as I read and reread the words of Jesus: "Unless
your righteousness is better than the righteousness of the teachers of
religious law and the Pharisees, you will never enter the Kingdom of
Heaven." And after Jesus said this, he immediately started talking about
how if you are angry at somebody, it is as if you have murdered them;
if you lust, it is as if you've committed adultery.

I had always struggled with this teaching. What is Jesus' point?

It seems as if Jesus is *contrasting* his own teaching with the law lists
of the Pharisees, their virtue fences around the law.

It fit into place, and I gained new insight.

I think most of us were taught in church that this passage is about a
longer list: do not murder, do not commit adultery, do not lust, do not get
angry—lots of "do nots." We interpret this as if Jesus is creating a vice
list, building a virtue fence, and multiplying two laws to make four.

But Jesus wasn't into fences. He wasn't about the list. He didn't agree
with the Pharisees about all that.

So what *is* he saying?

It occurred to me that Jesus' point is that we should no longer even
desire to do the wrong thing. He wants us *to have hearts that love and
long to do the right thing.*

It isn't that Jesus is saying that murder is the *same* as anger. Clearly, it isn't true that lust is the *same* as adultery. What I think Jesus is saying is that regardless of whether it's murder or anger or lust or adultery, what matters is that the desire for sin is still there and *the desire for God is not.*

So, for someone to build a fence around bad things and call it a virtue isn't enough.

The murderer and the lustful man are the same, in that neither desires God deeply or fully enough.

That night in our Aberdeen apartment, I thought I had won a victory by not watching *9 1/2 Weeks.* But I had simply created a fence and mistakenly thought that, by not climbing over it, I had triumphed.

But Jesus says he wants me to lose my lustful desires altogether. He wants to bless me with a new heart, not have me take satisfaction in a shallow victory.

Instead of feeling good about not watching a movie that would dishonor my wife and feed the desire to have some illicit sexual encounter, I needed to cry out to God for a heart that does not even desire to watch such a thing anymore.

Now I understand a little better how jealousy, hatred, loving money, being heartless, and destructive anger made it onto the vice lists. Yes, these are things I need to weed out of my life, just like any of the other vile stuff we find on those lists. But in Christ's view, it's not about one sin being above or below another.

It's that they *all* keep us from desiring God.

〈〈〉〉

We each have to figure out what bad things we really love.

Our sin problem really stems from one thing: In the moment we fall to temptation, we love that thing, we desire it, we delight in it. In desiring it, we are replacing our desire for God.

Jesus evaluates the failed religious leaders of his day by talking about what they love: "Everything they do is for show. On their arms they wear extra wide prayer boxes with Scripture verses inside, and they wear robes with extra long tassels. And they love to sit at the head table at banquets and in the seats of honor in the synagogues. They love to receive respectful greetings as they walk in the marketplaces, and to be called 'Rabbi.'"[5] They loved the attention, the image of righteousness, the show.

The apostle Paul, when talking about some of the experiences of the nation of Israel, said this: "These things happened as a warning to us, so that we would not crave evil things as they did."[6] We've seen that when telling Timothy what it will be like in the last days, the first thing Paul thinks of is how people will love the wrong things: "For people will love only themselves and their money. They will be boastful and proud, scoffing at God, disobedient to their parents, and ungrateful. They will consider nothing sacred."[7]

Sin is about the bad things we love.

The apostle John puts it like this: "Do not love this world nor the things it offers you, for when you love the world, you do not have the love of the Father in you. For the world offers only a craving for physical pleasure, a craving for everything we see, and pride in our achievements and possessions. These are not from the Father, but are from this world."[8]

The deep battle with sin is not only a struggle to overcome the temptation to do something bad now and again, but it's a recognition of a darker terror that lies within each of us: We are born lovers of evil.

Love for evil things demands our attention and often directs our actions. We act on the objects of our desire and submit ourselves to their dangers and their consequences.

Sin is sin because it's bad for us. Sin is sin because it's a desire for something other than God.

It replaces God in our lives.

⟨⟨⟩⟩

If you want to conquer a besetting sin, you need to stop loving it.

Our pastor told a story that illustrated this point so powerfully to me. One day, a man came up to him after church and asked if he could share a personal experience. The man said that he had been addicted to pornography.

He had been a Christian leader, respected in his church. Although he was ashamed of his double life, he could not seem to stop.

We've all had these strongholds at times in our lives, haven't we? Places of deep darkness that are filled with things that we love to do because they bring pleasure or fill some deep need that we don't know how to fill any other way. The man was surfing the Internet one day, looking at terrible and unspeakable things, a video feed featuring multiple participants. Suddenly, one of the young men in the video looked up right into the camera.

The Christian leader saw that it was the face of his own son.

The jolt was unbearable. In that one instant, he became completely broken. All the sorrow he needed for true repentance was upon him in a great wave.

Immediately, he knew he would do whatever it took to be free. He went from a lover of porn to a hater of porn in one glance. Years of duplicity were wiped away, and he could no longer stomach his addiction. It now made him terribly sick.

The love for this evil thing was utterly and completely broken in his life. He could no longer derive any pleasure from it. All he could see was the destruction it had wreaked in the life of his son.

The desire is now gone from his life. Banished. Weeded out. His love of evil was turned to a hatred for evil.

The redemptive postscript to the story is that the man's son had also experienced a life transformation. He is now a missionary in Asia. Within days, or even hours, the broken dad was on a plane to the other side of the world to seek forgiveness and reconciliation with his son. He has not looked at pornography since.

We certainly must battle temptation with willpower when it comes upon us. Of course. I would never suggest that we shouldn't resist temptation. The Bible tells us to.

But I think ultimately that isn't the full answer. Not in the long run. Will-power alone will never conquer a besetting sin; only by turning love to hate will we win a lasting victory. The ultimate answer is ridding ourselves of the love of evil and replacing it with revulsion of evil.

How do we do that? Not easy, I know, barring a traumatic experience that shocks the evil out. But there are other things we can do.

For some of us, it's like cracking a combination lock to get to freedom. We need to be like those guys in the movies with a stethoscope against a safe's lock, listening to the click, click, click, click of the tumblers as they fall into place.

Focus, Know, Value, Believe.

Listen to what your emotions, your desires, your loves, are telling you.

What is behind the particular love of something bad in my life? Why do I love these things? What does God say I should think about them? What are the consequences, the damage? What does this love do to my family, my friends? What harm do they cause to those involved in them? How do they keep me bound in guilt?

Click, click, click, click as you get another number to open the lock to freedom.

The process may be long, but if you understand that the answer is in finding why you love these things and teaching yourself to despise them, you've made the start you need.

〈〉〉

You're probably aware of the bad emotions you hold dear in your life, but in case you're at a loss, the Bible gives some very specific suggestions as to what they might be.

The Bible speaks of many emotions that we need to weed out of the gardens of our lives, but here are a few I want to focus on:

» Anger that destroys relationships
» Love of money
» Jealousy of others or stuff or position
» Fear and worry about future things

Which of these are weeds in your garden?

‹ ‹ › ›

I've talked about anger as an emotion that God sometimes wants us to nurture and grow and keep (when it has the right object). God himself is angry toward sin and evil.

But any reading of the Bible tells us that a lot of our anger is sin. A careful study points to these three insights about anger:

» Anger is sinful when it is destructive to relationships.
» Rarely, if ever, are we justified to get angry for a personal offense
      against us.
» Anger is always to be short lived and quickly covered by grace, longsuffering,
      and forgiveness.

Anger that divides, tears others down, and destroys relationships is selfish and ungodly. In the vice lists, anger is almost always cited in the greater context of relationships. This is the anger that comes from pushing our own agendas, building ourselves up, and taking offense at things done against us personally.

Anger against sin and injustice, if heeded, will bring people back into relationship, as forgiveness and healing are offered by the one who is angry. Of course, there are those times when an offense against us is totally evil, and the other person will not repent. But even then, I think of Jesus at the cross showing mercy and forgiveness toward those inflicting pain on him. Even while on the cross he said, "Father, forgive them, for they don't know what they are doing."[9]

When we get angry at personal offenses against us, we lose a chance for others to be amazed at the forgiveness Christ offers, and we lose the chance to suffer graciously, as our beloved Jesus did for us.

We lose a chance to demonstrate to others the power of God's grace. That is "salt" and "light" to the world around us.

On the other hand, when we are angry about injustice on behalf of someone else, for their good and protection, we are in that very act being salt and light. We are standing up for the powerless.

And for all types of anger, there is no way to get around this command: "Don't let the sun go down while you are still angry."[10] Anger is to be resolved quickly in grace, forgiveness, and a spirit of moving on. We are never justified to hold on to our anger or nurse it, feeding it with our thoughts and memories.

Destructive anger must be weeded out and banished from the garden. Often it is when we have cause for anger but do not get angry that God can best work through us in others' lives.

〈〈〉〉

The love of money is something worth mentioning in our prosperous times and affluent society. We have so much. We want so much more.

We know that this love leads to all kinds of trouble in our lives. "For the love of money is the root of all kinds of evil. And some people, craving money, have wandered from the true faith and pierced themselves with many sorrows. But you, Timothy, are a man of God; so run from all these evil things. Pursue righteousness and a godly life, along with faith, love, perseverance, and gentleness."[11]

It's all about *stuff.*

It seems the richer our countries become, the more dysfunctional they are, and the more psychologists and counselors we need to hire. I think as we get more stuff, we see that it doesn't satisfy us, so we either look to get even more stuff, or we start to look to other, darker things to satisfy our lusts.

Your emotions will point you toward the truth. *Focus. Know. Value. Believe.*

You can take an honest look at yourself and figure out pretty quickly how much you love money. For example, compare how buying a new car turns you on compared to giving money to people who need it, spending time with your family, or serving in the youth group ministry. If money is too high on your list, you are in for long-term trouble.

Just as Paul counseled Timothy, pursue loving more important things than money.

〈〈〉〉

I remember the walk clearly.

I was struggling with some financial difficulty in our ministry, and I was thinking of some other ministries I know. One has a great big mailing list in multiple countries, which they can use to raise funds for literature projects in Africa.

How I longed for that. I believed what we were doing was every bit as important.

One local ministry I had recently visited had fantastic offices, with big glass windows, gorgeous office furniture, and a new state-of-the-art telephone system. I work on a butcher-block slab we bought at Ikea. My trash can cost five bucks; a stereo stand from high school serves as my printer and paper stand. My prayers echoed my despair: "We do not waste your money like that, Lord, so why do we struggle? Why am I worrying about one-hundred-dollar decisions?"

Thoughts like that were going around in my head, and this was not the first time.

On that walk (I think I could even show you the place), the finger of the Holy Spirit extended down and touched my heart, convicting me.

This was jealousy. "This is what God has given to them, not you," the Spirit said. "Haven't I provided all *your* needs?"

I knew right then that my self-righteous attitude was simple jealousy, and it was hurting me. It was stealing my joy and vitality, turning thankfulness to bitterness and envy. Right then, I began to repent of my jealousy of other ministries. I began to thank God that he had blessed them, and I looked to God to bless us with what we needed.

Yes, there are some righteous kinds of jealousy, as we saw in the section on *Keep.* Unfortunately for us, most often we are jealous of what we do not have, of what is not rightfully ours—the bad kind of jealousy.

Another weed in the garden to root out.

⟨⟨⟩⟩

The emotions of fear, worry, and anxiety can be thorny ones to deal with. Yes, often they must be rooted out, but we first need to make sure we aren't novice gardeners weeding out the wrong plants.

It's like what my son Evan said after spending the night in the ER with a severe asthma attack. He came home, and the first thing he said to his beloved older brother, Jackson, was, "Were you worried about me, Jackson?" Jackson gave him a great big hug and said, "Of course, I was." Our anxiety over the state of those we love shows how we love them. Their health issues and tragedies mean something to us.

We see the same attitude of concern among the saints of the Bible. Paul despaired of his health and life on more than one occasion; he wrote about his anxiety of missing far-off friends or seeing dear friends sick. He really was concerned about them. Should we consider Paul's anxiety a sin? I don't think so.

God also intended for fear to play a protective role in our lives. It's good that we fear rattlesnakes. We teach children to fear running into busy streets. God wants us to fear the consequences of doing wrong. The "fear of God" keeps us from harm.

When we are commanded not to fear and not to worry in the Bible, it is always said in a gentle voice. It is the voice of a father comforting his children. The command "Fear not" in the Bible has an entirely different tone than the commands not to be angry or not to be jealous of your neighbor's house. They are the tones of a warm bath, a cup of tea, or a good night's sleep. God is saying, "Relax, I'm here."

But there is a type of fear, worry, and anxiety that God tells us we are not to allow in our lives.

It is fear of the future, fear for our eternal destiny.

The Bible indicates that we are to live in two times. One time is today. The other is eternity. We are to set our minds on doing what we can before God today and to contemplate what it is going to be like to be with him in paradise someday. But the time between those two points— between now and then—we can do nothing about; we have no control over it. Therefore, we must leave that time to God.

That time—the unknown future—is where most of our worry and fear dwells, isn't it? The unknown tomorrow is where God wants us to let go and trust him.

When I was diagnosed with the tumor in my neck, I could do nothing about the "what ifs." What if it's cancer? What if I need surgery? What if the surgeon slips and nicks the nerve that controls my breathing? What if I lose my voice permanently—an ever-present danger with thyroid surgery? I couldn't dwell there. I had to dwell in the fact that God had given me all I needed for this day and that he had promised to take care of my tomorrows.

I remembered well how God had gently come alongside me to dispel worry at another fearful time in my life.

Some years ago, I was on a ferry across the Mediterranean Sea on my way to North Africa. I felt totally alone and afraid. Not exactly what you'd expect of a Christian on a missions trip. As I looked around me, I thought again and again, *This is so stupid. How did I get myself into this?*

My boss had sent me to visit a friend and coworker in North Africa. As I left the base in Spain, I had smiled and tried to behave as if it were no big deal as I scribbled down the phone number on a scrap of paper. They knew what they were doing, right?

Yet, as I sat on the ferry crossing the Mediterranean, the incongruity of my situation struck me. I had a suitcase, a little money, and a phone number. That was it. I did not have an address. No one knew I was coming. I had nobody to meet me. I had no idea what to do once I stepped off that boat. I would need to exchange some money and figure out how to use a Moroccan phone—but what if nobody answered at that phone number?

Having traveled before in the majority world—nations where most people live in severe poverty—I knew what was awaiting me at the port. An army of "helpful" people were about to descend on my six-foot-five, white, American frame: My figure stood out like a lone tall tree in a cornfield. They would want to help carry my bag, they would want to get me a ride, they would offer to find me a hotel, and all with an eye on the tips I might give. How was I to know who would be honest and who would be setting me up to steal my belongings? How was I to even find someone who could speak English well enough to be understood?

This situation was compounded because the Christians I was going to visit were all undercover workers in a country that was hostile to the gospel. They lived so as not to bring attention to themselves. The man I was visiting did not have a phone. The number I had was for a friend of his, someone not even associated with the mission I belonged to. I do not remember exactly what was in my bag, but they had given me things to hand carry that could not be sent through the mail. The police, who went through the mail, might find literature or Bibles. If they did, they could show up at the door of the addressees and take them in for an interrogation or throw them out of the country. I could not just walk up to a friendly police officer and ask for help to find my friend. If he started questioning what I was doing, the contents of my bag could condemn me to an unknown future.

No wonder I was filled with anxiety, my emotions in a turmoil larger than the passing waves. Even seventeen years later, I get a lump in my throat when I think about what happened next.

As I walked around the deck of the ferry, worried sick and praying about my situation, I walked past Nancy and her daughter.

They were long-time, close family friends from my home church in Wheaton, Illinois.

We stared at each other in amazement. I could not believe my eyes. What do you think happened to my emotions as I thought of what this meant for me? You see, Nancy's husband, Wendell, had been my dad's coworker for many years at a major Christian publisher. I had followed their kids through school. They had been in our home many times. Wendell was to serve as my sponsor a few years later for my ordination.

So just as I was about to enter a strange country halfway around the world, worrying about my situation and immediate future, these precious friends of the family appeared right next to me.

That was God's way of providing for my encouragement in that situation. I responded with great relief and joy.

But the situation was not quite what it seemed. After we hugged and greeted one another, I learned that they were en route to visit a very secret Bible translation project. They could not be seen with me after we left the ship, they could not give me any help, and they could not tell me where they were going.

So when they left me a few minutes later, I was alone again. The situation was exactly the same. I was back at square one. I had nothing more than the phone number I started with.

Yet now everything was different. My fear and anxiety had left. My situation had not changed, but my perspective, my thinking had changed—God was going to take care of me!—and that made all the difference. My emotions changed.

Anxiety, worry, and fear were banished from my garden. I could depend on a God who would arrange such a meeting.

He had sent me on this trip, and he would not allow anything to happen that was not in his plan. As I concentrated on what God had done to reassure my fearful heart, I knew that I could trust him to care for me. Now, instead of fear at the center of my thoughts, I was overwhelmed with gratitude to a kind and generous God, a God who goes out of his way to whisper love and comfort to his children.

I walked off the boat with confidence and soon heard a strong voice on the other end of the telephone line saying that he would arrive at the ferry terminal in a few minutes to pick me up.

I sometimes think back to that situation when I am filled with worry. As a result of the God-arranged meeting on a ferryboat in the middle of the Mediterranean Sea, I understood more about trusting God. A change in what I believed, what I thought, had transformed my worry *in an instant*. I went from thinking of myself as totally alone, more alone than I had ever been, to understanding that God was there watching over my every step.

And that can be your experience as well.

Our worry doesn't always change as easily as mine did that day on the ferry. But the firm and gentle voice of Jesus can always be heard in Scripture, reassuring us:

> Look at the birds. They don't plant or harvest or store food in barns, for your heavenly Father feeds them. And aren't you far more valuable to him than they are? Can all your worries add a single moment to your life?
> And why worry about your clothing? Look at the lilies of the field and how they grow. They don't work or make their clothing, yet Solomon in all his glory was not dressed as beautifully as they are. And if God cares so wonderfully

for wildflowers that are here today and thrown into the fire tomorrow, he will
certainly care for you. Why do you have so little faith?

So don't worry about these things, saying, "What will we eat? What will
we drink? What will we wear?" These things dominate the thoughts of unbe-
lievers, but your heavenly Father already knows all your needs. Seek the Kingdom of God above all else, and live righteously, and he will give you everything
you need.

So don't worry about tomorrow, for tomorrow will bring its own worries.
Today's trouble is enough for today.[12]

If your life is filled with far too much worry, fear, and anxiety, chances are
you are living in God's time—the time between today and eternity. Look
closely at the Scriptures that tell us not to fear and worry, and each time
you will find reassuring promises from God, take-it-to-the-bank reasons
why you do not need to live with fear, anxiety, and worry anymore.

⟨⟨⟩⟩

How do we weed out the *Done* emotions from the gardens of our lives?

Laura had a time in her life when she struggled with anger. Here's how
she dealt with her *Done* emotion:

Sometimes I would get really angry for a good reason and let it all out in
a way that hurt people I love. Other times, I would get angry about something minor that really didn't matter that much, but it would allow me to
release stress.

I realized anger was controlling me. It was taking over my life.

I realized rather early on that my way of handling anger was taking me
nowhere good, clearly not where I wanted to be in my relationships or in my
spiritual life. It was leading me away from godliness.

I had no idea how to fight my problem, because it had been a deeply
rooted part of my life for so long. I couldn't figure out the difference between
being angry or stressed. I couldn't discern the big deals from the little ones.
Everything turned into a big, emotionally messy response.

So I started small.

Initially, when I got angry, I would stop and ask myself a series of questions:

What am I upset about?
Am I really angry about this or just stressed about something else?
Is this something I should be angry about?
Is this a big deal or a little one?
Can I let this slide?
Is this worth the destruction it might cause?
How can I see this from the other person's point of view?
Could the other person be right?
How can I handle this well?
Can I build up the other person through this conversation?

As I stood there steaming, upset, angry, I was running through this list of questions. Frankly, I despaired of this long process. I felt so frustrated by the need to do this. It was hard work and required so much self-discipline.

Often, I blew through it and still handled it badly. I wish I could tell you that it only took a year, but it ended up taking far more time than that.

At first, I lost the battle more than I won. I lost daily. Eventually, I began to lose my battle with destructive anger once a week. At some point, it was once a month. Then only once every two or three months.

Now, fifteen years later, destructive anger still takes over, but very rarely. Praise God, I am a peaceful woman. Our home is a happy place. And I continue to guard my heart. I am never going back there again.

My proudest moment was when, a few months ago, a friend of mine and her daughter told me how much they love for me to call because I am so joyous. They said that just the sound of my voice puts them in a good mood. I was shocked down to my socks.

God has changed my emotional life so that instead of being known as an angry woman, I am known now as a joyous one.

I am living proof that anyone can overcome their struggle against harmful emotions. It's hard work, but worth every step.

When faced with this dilemma, Laura instinctively turned to the toolbox. Her questions brought her to *Focus, Know, Value,* and *Believe*—maybe not in so many words, but she had the inner sense to evaluate her emotions in similar ways. *Done* emotions represent our lifelong struggle with sin. They are weeded out of the gardens of our lives by focusing on how they hurt us and others; by knowing how God feels about them; by determining what they tell us about what's really important to us in a particular moment; and by comparing them to what we should believe about God and ourselves.

<<>>

Perhaps for you this has been a hard chapter to read. It was certainly hard for me to write. We think we are doing pretty well—we have our virtue fences erected and in place—but when we understand that God's standards also apply to what we desire and how we feel, it reveals how far we are from where we need to be.

Does it seem to be too much? Good. *Keep* that feeling for just a moment. Grieve over your sin. But soon you will find, as I have, that these are the moments when God's love is the most pronounced, tangible, and powerful.

If you do not know that kind of no-matter-what, no-matter-how-bad, no-matter-how-many-times-you've-fallen forgiveness in your life, you need it.

It has to be experienced to be believed.

BLOG 11: DONE

ANDREW]·····[Boy, did the light bulb come on for me in reading this chapter. I have so many fences in my spiritual life—good fences that protect me (from myself). The realization is that I am not victorious just because I didn't cross the fence. True victory comes only when my desire for those "greener pastures" is overcome by my desire to please God. The heart is the key. So why do I still measure spirituality by how many things I do (read my Bible, go to church, tithe, etc.)? Not only am I done with the weeds in my garden, I'm done with superficial measurements of spirituality. The better measurement is "do I desire God more today than yesterday?"

JAN]·····[This has been the most useful and helpful chapter. It coincides with my pastor's preaching on "sufficient unto the day is the evil thereof"—taking one day at a time.

I am a dog walker now, having been a teacher. My income is very low compared with what it was. I have been overdrawn at the bank a lot. This chapter has shown me that I'm jealous of the lifestyle of my clients. I'm angry with their cavalier way of treating me and my services, and I'm worrying about future finances instead of trusting the Lord. Last night, I had only one dog booked for today. I prayed about the Lord providing daily, and a lady rang for me to take her three dogs, so I had four today! My whole attitude toward the emotions in my life has changed today. I can see that I've got these weeds that need removing. I seem to have all the ones mentioned, and now I can do something about removing them.

The example about resisting the sexy film was really good. To be so full of God that you don't even want to do those sinful things—like getting furious, envying your neighbour's lifestyle, or worrying about whether God will provide or not—is just what I want. I've always wondered how some people seem so full of the Lord in every way. That's how. They want what He wants. They are so full that when they are pushed and overflow what comes out is Jesus, not a lot of sinful negatives. I want to be like that.

JAMES]·····[Now I see more clearly than ever why I have to be constantly learning from God's Word. How else can I know which emotions I am to cultivate, which emotions I am to keep, and which emotions I am to root out of my life? I suspect that the list of emotions to be rid of that are discussed in this chapter is only the beginning of a much longer list.

MARIAN]·····[This is hard, because so much of this has hit home! How easily I can justify and excuse myself. These things are not only destroying my own heart, but wounding God Himself. I see a smug complacency within me, which has condoned sin—like the virtue fence. If I desire a passion for God Himself, then my heart needs to be purged of the other desires that war against His will. I see my anger as being so destructive—having wounded so many close to me. And the accumulation of so much "stuff," what does that reveal about me? My heart is full of sadness as I see the way sin has crept in and the weeds have been allowed to spread in my garden.

My only hope right now is in the Cross. My old, sinful nature was nailed there with Jesus (Romans 6:6). His Spirit is one with my spirit, which means He is working with me on the inside to root out these things. Keep me focused, please, Lord, as we weed my garden together.

BOB]·····["Sin is about the bad things we love."

When it comes to the emotions that we should be "done" with, "the ultimate answer is ridding ourselves of the love of evil and replacing it with a revulsion of evil."

In other words, the response to a bad emotion is not "self-control!" or "no emotion," but the emotion God gives, and that God has, toward the object that causes our emotion to be bad. He despises it.

There is great power in despising what God himself rejects and loathes. This is the path to fellowship with him in that area.

And in fellowship with God, nothing evil can touch us.

JULIE]·····[This most definitely is a chapter I will need to go back to time and time again. I really need to sit and digest what I just read, because it really hit home to where I am right now. I know, for me, the emotions listed to "be done with" that I struggle with often are anger and fear and worry about future things.

In fact, I was pretty convicted as I was reading the chapter, because I've been holding onto anger and stuffing it inside, and it's been causing havoc in my life and in my relationship with my spouse. This anger, although suppressed inside, is coming out in all kinds of messy ways, and it's a very miserable place to be. It's obvious that my way of dealing with certain emotions is just not working.

It also never occurred to me that every time I am fearful or anxious, chances are I'm living in God's time—the time between today and eternity. That's for the Lord to handle, not me, because I'm not God. It really put things in perspective for me!

Enter the discussion at www.faithfulfeelings.com.

MY BLOG

_____

_____

_____

_____

_____

12 Heart

God made us emotional beings because he is an emotional being. His love for us is a passionate verb, and it grieves him when we love him back with a lifeless noun. He wants our hearts and his heart to be together.

We are called to live in the heart of God.

⟨⟩⟩

Love is at the center.

It is at the center of God's heart and actions.

> For God loved the world so much that he gave his one and only Son, so that everyone who believes in him will not perish but have eternal life.[1]

It is at the center of our relationship with God and other people.

> "Teacher, which is the most important commandment in the law of Moses?"
> Jesus replied, "'You must love the LORD your God with all your heart, all your soul, and all your mind.' This is the first and greatest commandment. A second is equally important: 'Love your neighbor as yourself.'"[2]

It is at the center of why we are to do what we do.

> Three things will last forever—faith, hope, and love—and the greatest of these is love.[3]

Living out of the heart of God is living in genuine relational love with God and other people.

I like the Bible verse in which Paul, the mentor, writes to his protégé Timothy, "The purpose of my instruction is that all believers would be filled with love that comes from a pure heart, a clear conscience, and genuine faith."[4] Paul is grooming Timothy to be one of the new leaders of the church, and he is about to give him advice for the job. He wants Timothy to know the goal. The goal is to have love spring from the truth of who you are, from what you value and believe—a pure heart, a clear conscience, and a sincere faith.

We regard Paul as a great thinker, a theologian extraordinaire. Maybe we should think of him more as one who knew God's redeeming love and was a great lover of people. Just look at the introductions and endings to his letters to see how he passionately talks about people— those he loves.

Love is at the center. It informs every other emotion we experience, and it must be informed by God's great love for us.

As Henry Scougal, a seventeenth-century Puritan pastor, writes

> Love is that powerful and prevalent passion, by which all the faculties and inclinations of the soul are determined, and on which both its perfection and happiness depend. The worth and excellency of a soul is to be measured by the object of its love. He who loveth mean and sordid things, doth thereby become base and vile; but a noble and well-placed affection, doth advance and improve the spirit into a conformity with the perfections which it loves.[5]

<‹›>

We are conditioned to think that if we *believe* love, whether we really *feel* love does not really matter. We are taught that what matters is reason, theology, factual truth. But God has so much more for us than theology in a box.

What we feel—our loves—reveals what we really believe and becomes the motivation for how we live.

The apostle John makes it clear that if we are not *feeling* love, we do not really believe the truth.

> Dear friends, let us continue to love one another, for love comes from God. Anyone who loves is a child of God and knows God. But anyone who does not love does not know God, for God is love. God showed how much he loved us by sending his one and only Son into the world so that we might have eternal life through him. This is real love—not that we loved God, but that he loved us and sent his Son as a sacrifice to take away our sins. Dear friends, since God loved us that much, we surely ought to love each other. No one has ever

seen God. But if we love each other, God lives in us, and his love is brought to full expression in us.[6]

John is saying, "Look to your emotions. Look to your love. Take counsel from them and see the truth about yourself. If you really know God, you will feel this great love toward God and other people."

Living in the heart of God is living a life driven by genuine love and affection.

<<>>

There is a fascinating story in one of Paul's last letters, the one to Philemon. Paul comes to really love and care about a runaway slave named Onesimus. He figures out that Philemon, Onesimus's owner, is also one of Paul's converts. This master has every right to execute Onesimus for running away. Paul longs to see Philemon treat Onesimus as the Christian brother he now is and free him. He greatly appeals to Philemon's heart and love, saying, "I didn't want to do anything without your consent. I wanted you to help because you were willing, not because you were forced."[7]

Living in the heart of God means our actions must flow from holy passion, just as God's actions do.

God wants us to do things for him *because we want to.*

We think if we force ourselves to do the right stuff, control our reactions, grit our teeth, and do our duty, it is godly. But it isn't. That kind of "will-power living" and control of our emotions is far from godliness. What can look like spiritual maturity to many is really just emotional repression—our deluded efforts to look good, assuming a form of godliness, without the truth being in us.

Living by a list of dos and don'ts won't get us where we want to be. Of all people, John Calvin said, "Duties, however, are not fulfilled by the mere discharge of them, though none be omitted, unless it is done from a pure feeling of love."[8]

‹‹›

Laura gave me a copy of *Blink: The Power of Thinking without Thinking* for Christmas. She thought it might have some connection to my research on emotion. Boy, was she right!

In *Blink,* Malcolm Gladwell does not make a specific connection to our emotions. But the book is all about how emotions guide our daily lives and how informed, instantaneous emotions and impressions are often even more trustworthy than our conscious, well-thought-out reasoning. It is also about the fact that we can educate our emotions so that they become an increasingly reliable guide for decision making and behavior.

I believe that is how God made us.

Gladwell tells this story at the start of his book: In 1983, the J. Paul Getty Museum was approached by an art dealer with a wonderfully preserved Greek statue. The asking price was almost $10 million. It was an extraordinary find. If authentic, it could put the museum on the map. It would be the centerpiece of the entire collection. The museum lined up scientists to run tests and found the statue to be above reproach. Core samples and intense surface scans seemed to prove its authenticity. All the tests indicated it was authentic. They were thrilled!

Its unveiling was a front-page story in the *New York Times,* and the museum is in California!

But then some of the greatest archeologists and experts on Greek statues were called in at the last minute to look at the piece, and they *immediately* felt dismay. None of them could pinpoint exactly why, but they knew it to be a fake instantly. Their instincts said that it wasn't quite right; their gut feelings told them that something about it wasn't consistent. Factually, they couldn't prove anything, but emotionally they knew the truth. They believed it to be a fake.

And they were right. The debate raged for some time until they slowly traced the story of the forgery. It truly was a fake.

The Getty Museum invested months of high-tech research and investigation to get the scientific facts to make their decision, yet these world experts dismissed the statue as a fake in seconds.

The art experts' emotional reactions had told them the truth and trumped the factual knowledge of the team of scientists. They had knowledge that was beyond tests, technology, and rational investigation. These guys had immersed themselves in the subject for years, had lived with the real deal so much, they *sensed* a fake when they saw it.

That is what we should be like as Christians. Our emotions, as they are informed by immersing ourselves in, studying, and loving the things of God, can lead the way in understanding and right living. This natural and powerful part of spirituality is not about lists or creeds or being a Calvinist or an Armenian. It is about really knowing and breathing and pursuing God with everything in us.

Living in the heart of God means knowing him so well and believing him so much that we can live out and understand the truth through our emotions.

Yes, what we know about God is based in part on what the facts tell us— what theology tells us. But it's also based on what we know personally, relationally, and emotionally, because of how we have immersed ourselves in him. Our hearts can hold truth about God.

Living in the heart of God also means giving ourselves fully—hearts and minds—to what we know is true about God, what we believe.

In some sense, our Christian lives and our growth in Christ are all about this deep knowledge of God. It is loving him with mind *and* heart.

That is what true "belief" is, and that brings us right into the center of the heart of God.

In the words of John Wesley, a man who knew a thing or two about awakening and reviving God's people, "Feelings are the divine consolations of the Holy Ghost shed abroad in the heart of him that truly believes. And wherever faith is, and wherever Christ is, there are these blessed frames and feelings. If they are not in us, it is a sure sign that, though the wilderness became a pool, the pool is become a wilderness again."[9]

Living in the heart of God is about immersing ourselves in this deep, personal heart knowledge of him. Our hearts inside of his heart.

This is what you want. This is what he wants.

〈〈〉〉

Let me tell you about our friend Denise, a divorced working mom of four. Denise has a quick smile and loves to laugh. She is someone who is passionate about her relationship with the Lord and authentically lives out her faith every day.

But Denise has had it hard. She got married at twenty-one. Within a few years, she and her husband had their dream house—he had a good job with a good salary.

She was a nominal Christian, living a life to please her husband and make him happy. They went to church when dating, but after a few years of that, the church thing was over for him.

He became increasingly controlling and violent. Soon their walls had punching holes from these episodes. Sometimes when he was angry, he took it out on Denise and hit her, too. Eventually, he began an affair with another woman. Leaving Denise and their four children, he moved in with his girlfriend. He stopped paying the mortgage on their house, and the bank was soon to foreclose.

Denise was destitute, with four children, separated, and empty. For two years she lived in a three-bedroom house with her parents and four kids, an hour's drive from her kids' school. To try to maintain some normalcy, she drove them back and forth each day. Can you imagine?

Her husband, meanwhile, took Denise to court for every imaginable reason, leaving her thousands of dollars in debt. He quit his healthy six-figure job so he did not have to pay child support, and he lived off his girlfriend.

Denise was left with nothing.

But in the midst of all this, her relationship with God came to life, its passion restored.

She told me, "I had happy moments in my marriage, but no joy; I was not focusing on the Lord. Isn't it weird that I have so much more joy now when the circumstances are so much worse? Quite often, I find myself singing the song 'The Joy of the Lord Is My Strength.' My former husband asks me, 'How can you be so happy?' and I tell him, 'Because I have the Lord.'"

The times when she has been totally alone have been especially hard. She remembers sitting in the living room with her Bible on her lap just sobbing. She started a thank-you list to write out what she could thank God for. It started out with very simple things such as "I am still breathing." Later it expanded to things such as "I am his child," "This is only temporary," and "knowing who I am in Christ."

She began to live in the heart of God.

The Psalms became very important in her life, especially Psalm 150. The Psalms spoke to her honestly about heartache and difficulty.

She consciously worked on changing her *focus*, praying, "Lord, please help me focus on you and what is pleasing to you." She told me she has learned to focus on God, not on her circumstances, because all her circumstances stink. These words flow out of her easily with a few tears: "I will trust in God with my whole heart. I know whatever happens in all this, he is there. God is my rock. I know whatever happens is for a reason. I know whatever happens is for my best."

As I was writing this, my kids walked in with the mail. In it was Denise's Christmas card.

She made it by hand, and it's beautiful. Four smiling kids with bright eyes are glued to a fun border on a Christmas-red card with a snowflake ribbon and snowflake medallion. Inside, there is a bordered text that has been pasted in, with several tasteful snowflake stamps. It reads:

May your heart be lifted in praise this
Christmas for the wonderful gift of
Jesus and the Joy He brings to our lives.
Have a wonderful Christmas and a
blessed New Year!

I know why she made her Christmas cards with her own hands. She
wanted to express to us the great celebration that is going on in her
heart—straight from the heart of her Lord and Savior.

Living in the heart of God means knowing that we have a new heart
in Christ that is alive and able to shine in any circumstance.

How can it be that I, with a great marriage, a wonderful house, and a
good job, find myself wondering if I can celebrate as Denise celebrates—
this divorced mother of four who owns almost nothing?

That is the wonder of following Jesus with all your heart. Having everything taken away reveals that God really is all we need, and in that
realization is the greatest joy.

God, active and present in our lives.

Followers of Jesus deciding that, no matter what seems true in this world,
they will base their hearts on what God says is valuable, what God says
is true.

They will believe.

God has made a powerful promise to everyone who puts their trust in
Christ: "I will give you a new heart, and I will put a new spirit in you. I will
take out your stony, stubborn heart and give you a tender, responsive
heart."[10]

Some people with new hearts from God are in my life: Ed, Jim, Denise,
Bob and Dianne, George, Ben, and many more. That heart is waiting for
me and for you.

It is my great desire that we become ever more real and alive Christ followers, with good works flowing out of transformed hearts.

BLOG 12: HEART

STEPHEN]·····[Lord, may I be willing to take the risk of trusting in you. To allow myself to stand out in this world. To value the things you value; to love the things you love, and hate what you hate. To be so madly in love with you that I would willingly give all I have for your sake and the sake of others. . . . Flip me, I'm gonna need help!!

REBECCA]·····[As I read this chapter, I remembered being on a missions trip one summer and learning such a great lesson from a child. As I looked around the place I was, there was a sadness that came over me. In spite of what we were doing there, I saw so much pain, suffering, and poverty. But toward the end of our trip, this one little boy came up to me and said, "Miss J, why are you so sad?" I told him that I was sad because I was think-ing about how much I had and how they had so little. I also told him that I wished I could give his community more, not just financially but also with serving them. He said, "But Miss J, we are so happy with what little we have, and are thankful for how much you all have done for us. Plus, God has given us friends and family—and most of all, we are surrounded by so much love. Just because you have a lot and we have so little doesn't mean we can't be happy. Sure, there are times when we wish we had more, or that we had more resources to help others, but we learned that it's not what we have but what's in our hearts that matters." I was awestruck by this child. I again was reminded that our hearts and our actions are what matter to God, not the stuff or the material possessions. In other words, do we live to serve and love God, or do we live our lives centered on ourselves?

MARIAN]·····[My heart is warmed and encouraged. Love is powerful. It melted my own heart of stone. It enabled me to open my emotional box. To face the past, to celebrate the future, and to live each day with God's help. He will complete what He began, I have His promise on that, a heart filled with joy, and a heart focused on Him. I recall the words that I have written in the front of my Bible by Jeanne Guyon, an 18th century French nun who suffered so much for Jesus: "The Lord is at the centre of my being; therefore, He must become the Centre of my being."

Yes, Lord. I choose the way of love with Your help.

TODD]·····[My favorite bit of this chapter follows 1 Timothy 1:5. "The goal is to have love spring from the truth of who you are, from what you value and believe—'a pure heart, a clear conscience, and sincere faith.'"

Other points helpful to me:

"The worth and exceliency of a soul is to be measured by the object of its love."

"Take counsel from them [your emotions] and see the truth about yourself."

"What we feel—our loves—reveals what we really believe, and becomes the motivation for how we live."

"Focus on God, . . . not circumstances."

Love God more than anything. Love what God loves. Live in the heart of God.

SARAH]·····[I long to know the heart of God better. I believe that as I search and begin to understand Him, with my finite mind, I will better understand my heart. Oh, to know the heart of God, and to become more like Him.

JULIE]·····[I agree that our growth in Christ is about loving Him with our mind and heart. So often, we hear folks who give their testimonies of how they came to Christ talk about having a bunch of knowledge about Christ in their minds, but they didn't have Him in their hearts. I think this is what they are referring to. They finally understood His amazing love for them, and embraced Him as their Savior, and started loving Him back (not just knowing a bunch of stuff about Him). They started a love relationship with Him, complete with feelings and emotions.

It seems such a waste of time to do things out of duty, for the sake of trying to keep a certain image, without passion and vibrancy. My prayer is that God would stir up His passions in my heart, and that I would be all about what He has for me. That I would love the things He loves, see people through His eyes, and live with more passion for the things of God!!!

JARED]·····[I was also struck by the fascinating words of Malcolm Gladwell. How often we have flashes of opinion, or senses about things and people, that we are basically taught to repress. We must be fair, careful, rational, or relative. But God also wants us to follow our hearts. He wants these hearts to be beating and active and flowing with emotions of love toward Him and His kingdom, present and future. We need to Blink with Love.

Enter the discussion at www.faithfulfeelings.com.

MY BLOG

_____

_____

The greatest spiritual struggle I had in writing this book may surprise you.

I can say it in one word: *me.*

I have worked hard to find the truth in these things, yet in understanding God's plan for my emotional life more deeply, I see how I fall so very short. I still worry too much, and I don't overflow with joy like I desire to. My love for my neighbor is often so shallow and superficial. I do not feel it deep down.

I don't laugh with my kids enough, and on hard days I'm not quick to cling to my hope in God's promises. I don't give enough warm and genuine hugs to my family at church. How long has it been since I wept with somebody and felt their pain as my own?

I am an emotional struggler, and I suppose I will be until I'm home with Jesus. But I want those things more than ever, and I believe I can—and will—do better.

If you ever meet me and I let you down, please forgive me. Here I have all this expertise in the study of human emotion, but I'm not some off-the-charts loving joy machine. You might find me a little awkward socially—but I hope not after we've had the chance to sit down for a cup of coffee together.

Writing this book has been part of the journey for me, and I have learned a lot along the way. God's grace is big enough to cover me with all my insecurities, emotional problems, and challenges. God knows me, loves me, and has made me who I am. He is remaking me day by day!

I see more clearly now what he created me to be and what he desires me to *feel*.

I hope I get to meet you someday. It may not be in this world; we may have to wait for a better place, where we will both be emotionally whole and able to look into each other's eyes with the feelings of love and enjoyment that God has planned for us. Until then, keep working, learning, and growing.

God will be faithful to both of us.

Notes

O1 : Feel

1. A. W. Tozer, *That Incredible Christian* (Harrisburg, PA: Christian Publications, 1964), 50–52.

O2: Discovery

1. See René Descartes, *The Passions of the Soul,* trans. Stephen Voss (Hackett, 1989).
2. David Hume, *A Treatise of Human Nature* (1739). The full text of *A Treatise of Human Nature* can be found online at http://oll.libertyfund.org//files/342/Hume_0213.pdf.
3. Erwin Lutzer, *Managing Your Emotions* (Chappaqua, NY: Christian Herald, 1981), 38.
4. Kay Arthur, *A Marriage without Regrets* (Eugene, OR: Harvest House, 2000), 64.
5. James MacDonald, *I Really Want to Change . . . So, Help Me God* (Chicago: Moody, 2000), 189.
6. D. A. Hagner, *Matthew 1-13* (Dallas: Word, 1993), 136.
7. Markus N. A. Bockmuehl, *The Epistle to the Philippians* (Peabody, MA: Hendrickson, 1998), 59.
8. Joyce Meyer, *Managing Your Emotions: Instead of Your Emotions Managing You* (New York: FaithWords, 2003), 13–14.
9. Romans 12:9-16

O3: Breathe

1. E. P. Sanders, *Judaism: Practices and Beliefs* (London: SCM Press, 1992), 128.
2. C. S. Lewis, *Letters to Malcolm: Chiefly on Prayer* (New York: Harcourt, Brace and World, 1963), 92–93.
3. Luke 10:41-42
4. Isaiah 40:31
5. Galatians 2:20
6. Luke 18:18
7. Luke 18:19-23
8. Matthew 26:38
9. Luke 19:9-10
10. Ezekiel 11:19

O4: Bound

1. Michael Sniffen, "Moussaoui Scornful of Victims," Associated Press article published April 14, 2006, in the *Pittsburgh Tribune-Review.* Article can be found online at www.pittsburghlive.com/x/pittsburghtrib/search/s_443673.html.
2. "September 11 Horror Relived at Moussaoui Trial," Yahoo! Asia News, April 7, 2006. Article can be found online at http://asia.news.yahoo.com/060407/afp/060407052535int.html.
3. Jeff Temple, "Feelings or Faith?" *BCC Bulletin,* vol. 6, no. 8. (August 2005).
4. 1 Kings 3:12
5. Quotes in this section are taken from 1 Kings 3:20-26.
6. Charles Darwin, *The Expression of Emotions in Man and Animals* (New York: D. Appleton, 1920).

7. J. J. Campos and K. C. Barrett, "Toward a New Understanding of Emotions and their Development," in *Emotions, Cognition, and Behavior,* eds. Carroll E. Izard, Jerome Kagan, and Robert B.
Zajonc (Cambridge: Cambridge University Press, 1984), 230.

8. Ronald Koteskey, "Toward the Development of a Christian Psychology: Emotion," in the *Journal
of Psychology and Theology* (1980): 303.

9. Antonio Damasio, *The Feeling of What Happens* (New York: Harcourt Brace, 1999), 64–67.

10. Antonio Damasio, *Descartes' Error: Emotion, Reason, and the Human Brain* (New York: Avon,
1994), 34–51.

11. Ibid., 53–54.

12. Robert C. Solomon, "The Logic of Emotion," *Noûs,* 11:1 (March 1977): 45, 49.

13. *Star Trek II: The Wrath of Khan,* screenplay by Jack B. Sowards, story by Harve Bennett and
Jack B. Sowards. Revised final draft, May 24, 1982. Script may be found online at www.
godamongdirectors.com/scripts/khan.shtml.

14. John Eldredge, *Waking the Dead* (Nashville: Nelson, 2003), 42. Italics in the original.

15. See Hebrews 12:2.

16. See Matthew 26:53.

17. John Calvin, *Institutes of the Christian Religion,* vol. 1, trans. Ford Lewis Battles et. al.,
in *The Library of Christian Classics,* ed. John T. McNeill, (Philadelphia: Westminster, 1960),
589.

O5: Release

1. 2 Samuel 18:33–19:4

O6: Power

1. Jim Collins, *Good to Great* (New York: HarperBusiness, 2001), 128.

2. Psalm 34:1-8, italics added

3. Ed Aulie told his story to the author in a conversation on June 14, 2006.

4. James 1:2-4

5. 2 Timothy 3:5, NIV

6. WMBI interview on "Mornings," December 7, 2005, 5:45 AM.

7. Psalm 119:20, 47

8. 2 Chronicles 20:12

9. 2 Chronicles 20:15

10. 2 Chronicles 20:21-22

O7: Friend

1. William Lyons, *Emotion* (Cambridge: Cambridge University Press, 1980), 58–59. M. B. Arnold, a
pioneer in modern studies on emotion, writes, "It is the sequence *perception–appraisal–emotion*
that will alone explain the conditions necessary for arousing emotion." (M. B. Arnold, *Emotion
and Personality,* vol. 1 [New York: Columbia University Press, 1960], 182.)

2. Plato, *Republic* X 604a10-606d7, *The Republic of Plato: Edited with Critical Notes, Commentary,
and Appendices,* trans. Paul Shorey, ed. James Adam, 2 vols. (Cambridge: Cambridge University

Press, 1902). See also, Plato, *Laws*. I 645-646, trans. A. E. Taylor, *The Collected Dialogue of Plato Including the Letters*, trans. Lane Cooper, et. al., eds. Edith Hamilton and Huntington Cairns (New York: Pantheon, 1961).

3. Euripides, *Medea*, trans. Edward P. Coleridge (1891). The full text of Coleridge's translation of *Medea* can be found online at http://classics.mit.edu/Euripides/medea.html.

4. William James, "What is an Emotion?" in *Mind*, 9: 34 (April 1884): 189–190. Emphasis in the original. The full text of James's article can be read online at http://perso.orange.fr/pascal.ludwig/home/emotions/james.pdf.

5. Jonathan Edwards, *Religious Affections*, ed. James M. Houston (Portland: Multnomah, 1984), 6–7.

6. Emotion can act like our other senses to perceive reality. See, for example, Rick Ellrod, "Emotion and the Good in Moral Development," in *Foundations of Morality, Human Rights, and the Human Sciences*, eds. Anna-Teresa Tymieniecka and Calvin O. Schrag, vol. 15 of *Analecta Husserliana* (Boston: D. Reidel, 1983).

7. Philippians 4:4

8. NIV

9. Edwards, *Religious Affections*, 26.

O8: Truth

1. Quotes in this section are from Jonah 3:8–4:11.
2. Deuteronomy 11:18-22
3. Philippians 4:8
4. John 8:31-32
5. John 8:32, NIV
6. Philippians 3:8
7. E-mail to the author from Dianne, June 20, 2007.
8. Jeffrey Schwartz, "Mind Transcending Matter" *World*, April 3, 2004. See also Jeffrey Schwartz and Sharon Begley, *The Mind and the Brain* (New York: Regan, 2002).

O9: Grow

1. "Promenade," by Rich Mullins. Copyright © 1995 by Edward Grant, Inc. Used by permission.
2. Matthew 5:13-16
3. Two things to note about this list: First, it would be right and good to include the fear of God. However, because this is such a complex and misunderstood topic, it seemed it would add a layer of theological difficulty and make everything more cumbersome. For a discussion of the fear of God, please see my book *Faithful Feelings: Rethinking Emotion in the New Testament* (Kregel, 2006). Second, notice what is not listed in the category of *love*: love of self. It is a popular notion in our day that before one can be healthy you must learn to love yourself. The Bible does not seem to recognize the idea of growing a love of oneself; rather, it assumes that we all naturally love ourselves. In other words, a lack of self-love is not generally a problem for us; our problem is a lack of love for God and others. For a discussion debunking some of the myths around the concept of self-love, please see *Faithful Feelings*.

4. 1 Corinthians 13:1

5. John 12:5, author's paraphrase.

6. John 12:7-8 (quotation). Entire account is found in John 12: 3-8.

7. Marshall McLuhan, *Understanding Media: The Extensions of Man* (New York: McGraw-Hill, 1964), 7.

8. Rob Bell, *Sex God: Exploring the Endless Connections Between Sexuality and Spirituality* (Grand Rapids: Zondervan, 2007), 120.

9. Craig Paddock, "Father's Love," *Charlotte Observer,* June 19, 2004.

10. Calvin Miller, *The Taste of Joy* (Downers Grove, IL: InterVarsity, 1983), 10–11.

11. Matthew 13:45-46

12. David Mitchell, "I Remember Eric Liddell: Olympic Athlete of 'Chariots of Fire,'" Overseas Missionary Fellowship, Bromley, UK.

13. Romans 15:13, italics added

14. Revelation 21:4

15. Jude 1:4, 7, 10-11

16. Jude 1:22-23, NIV

17. Psalm 101:3-4

1 ◯: Keep

1. John Piper, "Don't Waste Your Cancer," www.desiringgod.org/ResourceLibrary/TasteAndSee/ByDate/2006/1776_Dont_Waste_Your_Cancer.

2. Psalm 31:15, NIV

3. Job 1:21, NIV

4. Psalm 115:12, NIV

5. Romans 15:13, NIV

6. Marvin Olasky, "Corruption and Providence," *World* (September 23, 2006): 44.

7. "Corruption and Providence: The Willis Letters," *World* magazine Web Extra, September 14, 2006. Article can be found online at www.worldmag.com/webextra/12246.

8. Ibid.

9. For a discussion of God's anger in the Bible, see my book *Faithful Feelings* (Kregel, 2006), pages 105–113, 223–229.

10. I document the roots and failings of this separation between *jealous* and *zealous* in *Faithful Feelings.*

11. 2 Corinthians 11: 2

12. Numbers 25:2-3

13. Numbers 25:7-8, 10-11

14. 1 Kings 21:25

15. 1 Kings 21:27

16. Henry Cloud and John Townsend, *Rescue Your Love Life* (Nashville: Integrity, 2005), 147.

17. Ibid., 163.

18. Marcia Reynolds, "Outsmart Your Brain," www.outsmartyourbrain.com.

11 : Done
1. Romans 1:29-31, italics added
2. 2 Timothy 3:2-5, italics added
3. Ephesians 4:31, italics added
4. Matthew 5:20
5. Matthew 23:5-7
6. 1 Corinthians 10:6
7. 2 Timothy 3:2
8. 1 John 2:15-16
9. Luke 23:34
10. Ephesians 4:26
11. 1 Timothy 6:10-11
12. Matthew 6:26-34

12: Heart
1. John 3:16
2. Matthew 22:36-37
3. 1 Corinthians 13:13
4. 1 Timothy 1:5
5. Henry Scougal, *The Life of God in the Soul of Man* (Boston: Nichols and Noyes, 1868), 40. The Nichols and Noyes edition may be found online at http://books.google.com/books?id= BncAAAAAMAAJ&pg=PA40&vq=doth+advance#PPR1,M1.
6. 1 John 4:7-12
7. Philemon 1:14, italics added
8. John Calvin, *Institutes of the Christian Religion,* trans. Henry Beveridge (Grand Rapids: Eerdmans, 1989), 3.7.7.
9. In *Explanatory Notes Upon the New Testament* (London: Epworth, 1976).
10. Ezekiel 36:26

STEPHEN is a fifth-year mechanical engineering student, studying in Edinburgh. He is single and enjoys traveling, amazing science and ingenious inventions, wildlife documentaries, anime films, cycling, and all sorts of books. He was brought up in a Christian home, and God has always been a reality in his life. He made a commitment to Christ at a young age, but only really got serious about his faith from the age of eighteen. He is currently wrestling with uncertainty about what God is calling him to do regarding vocation, marital status, and service to the church and others. He appreciates time to himself, but loves nothing better than camping and hiking with friends.

DREW is a pastor in suburban Chicago. He and his wife, Sarah, invest a lot of time caring for the people in their church. Drew grew up as a pastor's kid and learned a lot from the godly example of his parents. He also learned to *control* his feelings and was strongly influenced by the regimented standards of his conservative church. Today, he still struggles with understanding the balance between passion and temperance. But through this, God is teaching Drew what it means to "love God with all your heart."

JAN has been a Christian since 1973. She comes from a non-Christian background where emotions ran high. She has had problems with self-image for most of her life. She has been a teacher for many years, but now has her own dog-walking business. She is single and has shared a house with another Christian woman for many years.

Early in her career, **ANA** was a special-education teacher, creating and operating a program in a locked unit for severely emotionally challenged children. After she married, she and her husband moved to the Arab world and were thrown headfirst into Arabic study and cultural adjustment. Their career path in the Middle East and Africa has included founding a language school; founding a social-development foundation that serves street-based children; directing a housing development organization; and founding an international development foundation to support social entrepreneurs. Ana does personal training as a hobby. She calls the Middle East "my home." She and her husband have been married for twenty years and have "nine children waiting in heaven, but none to hold here on earth."

JIM is a retired professor now living on a farm in the Midwest. The slower pace of retired life is gradually restoring some of the depletions that a busy academic life seemed to create. Living closer to nature, watching glorious sunrises, weeding, cutting firewood, and enjoying a large vegetable garden are all doing wonders to quicken and enliven Jim's spiritual joy and wonder.

SARAH is a pastor's wife, staying home to support him in his ministry role. She became a Christian at the age of eight, and has followed the Lord ever since. Growing up in a fundamentalist church influenced her greatly during the early part of her life. God has recently shown her the freedom of Christ in every aspect of her faith walk. She looks forward to growing more in her freedom in Christ and not being held captive to traditions and the fear of man.

MARIAN and her husband are from Surrey, UK, and have just celebrated their fortieth wedding anniversary. They both enjoy cricket, bird-watching, and walking in the countryside. They have a grown son and daughter and also care for Marian's elderly mother, who lives nearby. Marian's childhood experiences in a dysfunctional family, which broke up when she was eleven, left her emotionally shut down. The Lord has been healing her wounds and setting her free since she became a Christian thirty-five years ago. She is part of the ministry team in her church and prays with confidence that the Lord will do for others what he has done for her. She knows there is still more to do to bring her fully alive, and she is cooperating with God on the healing and releasing of her heart.

MEDINE was a war refugee for eighteen months in the Republic of Congo. By God's grace, she and her family survived hunger, disease, bombing, and other calamities. She now lives with her husband and son in Pennsylvania.

Last year, **REBECCA** was a third-grade Spanish bilingual teacher until major spinal cord surgery sidelined her and kept her from returning. It has been almost a year since Rebecca has been able to work or do any sort of physical activity, but she hopes to return to teaching soon. Her incapacity has been very frustrating, because she used to be highly active, worked out aerobically and with weights almost every day, and was very involved at school. Through the course of her recovery from surgery, she has come to understand that God often chooses to reveal himself to us in the waiting and the "down time." Though these are hard times, times when we wonder what in the world God is doing or why he has allowed a particular circumstance to happen, it is then that we are called to wait and rely on God. As 2 Corinthians 12:9 says, "My grace is sufficient for you, for my power is made perfect in weakness" (NIV).

TODD works as a graphic designer in Tennessee. He loves the feeling he gets when piloting a snowboard or a motorcycle, watching English Premier League Football, or attending a hockey game when the Nashville Predators are pounding the Detroit Redwings. He also enjoys horsing around with his nieces and nephews. Bible Study Fellowship has increased his knowledge of the Bible and has helped him work through what he believes.

JULIE is a stay-at-home mother of three young children, living in Illinois. She enjoys reading, walking or hiking, fitness and nutrition topics, and spending time with family and friends. She is actively involved in ministry at her church, but lately has been struggling with feeling as if she doesn't know the Lord intimately. Julie's desire is to *know* Jesus in a deeper, more intimate fashion. In other words, she longs to *feel* more for Jesus.

BOB is an ordained minister and seminary teacher. Married for more than thirty years, he and his wife have two sons. Bob assists the pastor and teaches in a Lutheran church near his home. He also tries to encourage young men by coaching high school and American Legion baseball.

JARED lives with his beautiful and patient wife in Boulder, Colorado. As often as they can manage, they enjoy punishing their bodies with multi-state relay runs, triathlons, and eating spicy foods. While adjusting to married life and loving their favorite new band, they help facilitate a small group where they can share and struggle with their friends while digging into God's Word. Jared continues to wrestle with his perspective of the seemingly divisive, denominationally driven, contemporary church, his own personal struggles with pride, and not always being kingdom focused.

TOM is a husband and father and lives in Michigan. He enjoys running, golf, reading, campfires, and watching a good movie. Tom works in sales, and he and his wife, Heidi, homeschool their four children.

About the Author

Matthew Elliott serves as president of Oasis International Ltd., a publisher and distributor of Bibles and Christian books. Oasis makes Christian literature available at affordable prices in English-speaking Africa, Asia, and the Caribbean on a sustainable basis. Matthew's present focus is Africa, where the need and potential for impact is great. The continent of Africa is in the midst of a literature famine. *Experts estimate that more than 200 million African Christians do not have a Bible!* African Christians are hungry to read, hungry to learn, and hungry to explore their faith in ways that only books make possible. A big part of Matthew's mission in leading Oasis is to see this hunger satisfied.

Oasis identifies and empowers African booksellers who understand the crucial role books play in building the church and who have a vision to reach pastors, leaders, and laymen and women of the poor majority. Oasis chooses partners who exhibit business skills, a willingness to learn, and a commitment to operate with sound management principles and financial integrity. Once partners are identified, Oasis offers them books at affordable prices that meet Africa's needs. As their businesses grow, they act as local distributors, giving entrepreneurs the opportunity to grow the local retail book industry. Pastors and leaders are equipped for ministry, and people grow in their faith by reading great books. Moreover, jobs are being created, and economic development is taking place.

You can make a difference! Find out more about the needs of Africa and this transformational approach to book and Bible distribution at www.oasisint.net. Sign up for a prayer update and discover how you might like to be involved.

You can find out more about Matthew Elliott and the ministry of Oasis International at www.faithfulfeelings.com.

Visit www.faithfulfeelings.com to find more resources based on the book *Feel*. There, you can also download a free small group study guide so you can share the experience of this book with your group or church.

The book *Faithful Feelings: Rethinking Emotion in the New Testament* captures Matthew Elliott's research into emotion in the New Testament for pastors, counselors, and students of the Bible. Based on doctoral studies at the University of Aberdeen, *Faithful Feelings* is a readable guide that is accessible to all those who want to dig deeper into the ideas in *Feel*.

Christianity Today, in its review of *Faithful Feelings*, says, "*Faithful Feelings* is a scholarly argument to reorient our thinking about emotion. It presents a sophisticated view of emotion that engages the whole person. . . . *Faithful Feelings* is a great example of faithful engagement with Christian and secular scholarship." (Stanton L. Jones, Provost, Wheaton College in *Christianity Today*, March 2007, 81).

Faithful Feelings is available from Kregel Publications in the United States and IVP (UK) throughout the rest of the world.

WHAT PEOPLE ARE SAYING ABOUT *FAITHFUL FEELINGS*:

"The most thorough study on emotions in the New Testament is now Matthew Elliott's *Faithful Feelings*."

John Piper, in *What Jesus Demands from the World*

"Thank you for producing such a masterful treatment of this important subject. It will be a great resource for people working in my field (the integration of psychology and theology). . . . It is a great piece of work."

James R. Beck, PhD, senior professor of counseling, Denver Seminary

"This is an immensely significant work that breaks new ground, opening a new field of enquiry that those who follow must address."

Craig Keener, professor of New Testament studies, Palmer Seminary, and author of *The IVP Bible Background Commentary: New Testament*

"I have just finished reading *Faithful Feelings* and wanted to write to thank you. It was extremely instructive and even inspiring and will enhance my preaching and pastoral work significantly. You clarified and systematized a lot that I had been instinctively feeling (!)."

Julian Hardyman, senior pastor, Eden Baptist Church, Cambridge, England

"My friend Matt Elliott has opened new windows of thought about a crucial yet often neglected topic. This book will stretch and upgrade your perspectives on your feelings and your faith."

Joseph M. Stowell, former president, Moody Bible Institute

"This book shows originality in its choice of subject, in the application of current research in psychology to ancient texts, in the comprehensiveness of its scope, and to some extent in the interpretation of individual texts. There is no other book that covers the same ground, and the topic is an important one."

I. Howard Marshall, professor emeritus of New Testament exegesis, University of Aberdeen